Disseminating Shakespeare in the Nordic Countries

GLOBAL SHAKESPEARE INVERTED

Global Shakespeare Inverted challenges any tendency to view Global Shakespeare from the perspective of 'centre' versus 'periphery'. Although the series may locate its critical starting point geographically, it calls into question the geographical bias that lurks within the very notion of the 'global'. It provides a timely, constructive criticism of the present state of the field and establishes new and alternative methodologies that invert the relation of Shakespeare to the supposed 'other'.

Series editors
David Schalkwyk, Queen Mary, University of London, UK
Silvia Bigliazzi, University of Verona, Italy
Bi-qi Beatrice Lei, National Taiwan University, Taiwan

Advisory board
Douglas Lanier, University of New Hampshire, USA
Sonia Massai, King's College London, UK
Supriya Chaudhury, Jadavpur University, India
Ian Smith, Lafayette College, USA

Eating Shakespeare: Cultural Anthropophagy as Global Methodology
Edited by Anne Sophie Refskou, Marcel Alvaro de Amorim and Vinicius Mariano de Carvalho

*Shakespeare in the Global South: Stories of Oceans Crossed
in Contemporary Adaptation*
Sandra Young

*Migrating Shakespeare: First European Encounters, Routes
and Networks*
Edited by Janet Clare and Dominique Goy-Blanquet

*Shakespeare's Others in 21st-century European Performance:
The Merchant of Venice and Othello*
Edited by Boika Sokolova and Janice Valls-Russell

Forthcoming Titles
*Reconstructing Shakespeare in the Nordic Countries:
National Revival and Interwar Politics, 1870 – 1940*
Edited by Nely Keinänen and Per Sivefors

Disseminating Shakespeare in the Nordic Countries

Shifting Centres and Peripheries in the Nineteenth Century

Edited by
Nely Keinänen and
Per Sivefors

THE ARDEN SHAKESPEARE
LONDON · NEW YORK · OXFORD · NEW DELHI · SYDNEY

THE ARDEN SHAKESPEARE
Bloomsbury Publishing Plc
50 Bedford Square, London, WC1B 3DP, UK
1385 Broadway, New York, NY 10018, USA
29 Earlsfort Terrace, Dublin 2, Ireland

BLOOMSBURY, THE ARDEN SHAKESPEARE and the Arden Shakespeare logo are trademarks of Bloomsbury Publishing Plc

First published in Great Britain 2022
This paperback edition published in 2023

Copyright © Nely Keinänen, Per Sivefors and contributors, 2022

Nely Keinänen, Per Sivefors and contributors have asserted their right under the Copyright, Designs and Patents Act, 1988, to be identified as the authors of this work.

For legal purposes the Acknowledgements on pp. xvii–xviii constitute an extension of this copyright page.

Cover design by Maria Rajka
Cover image © Slottet Kronborg by Constantin Hansen, 1804–1880

All rights reserved. No part of this publication may be reproduced or transmitted in any form or by any means, electronic or mechanical, including photocopying, recording, or any information storage or retrieval system, without prior permission in writing from the publishers.

Bloomsbury Publishing Plc does not have any control over, or responsibility for, any third-party websites referred to or in this book. All internet addresses given in this book were correct at the time of going to press. The author and publisher regret any inconvenience caused if addresses have changed or sites have ceased to exist, but can accept no responsibility for any such changes.

A catalogue record for this book is available from the British Library.

A catalog record for this book is available from the Library of Congress.

ISBN:	HB:	978-1-3502-0086-9
	PB:	978-1-3502-0101-9
	ePDF:	978-1-3502-0088-3
	eBook:	978-1-3502-0087-6

Series: Global Shakespeare Inverted

Typeset by Integra Software Services Pvt. Ltd.

To find out more about our authors and books visit www.bloomsbury.com and sign up for our newsletters.

To Richard Wilson
Scholar, friend and prime mover of the
Nordic Shakespeare Society

CONTENTS

List of Illustrations	xi
Notes on Contributors	xii
Acknowledgements	xvii

	Introduction	1
1	The first Danish production of *Hamlet* (1813): A theatrical representation of a national crisis Annelis Kuhlmann	31
2	Geijer's *Macbeth* – Page, stage and the seeds of time Kiki Lindell and Kent Hägglund	63
3	Cold maids and dead men: Gender in translation and transition in *Hamlet* Cecilia Lindskog Whiteley	89
4	The poetics of adaptation and politics of domestication: *Macbeth* and J. F. Lagervall's *Ruunulinna* Jyrki Nummi, Eeva-Liisa Bastman and Erika Laamanen	117
5	Søren Kierkegaard's adaptation of *King Lear* James Newlin	157

6 'A blot on Swedish hospitality':
    Ira Aldridge's visit to Stockholm in 1857
    Per Sivefors — 189

7 Shakespeare's legacy and Aleksis Kivi:
    Rethinking Kivi's drama *Karkurit* [The
    Fugitives] *Riitta Pohjola-Skarp* — 211

8 Anne Charlotte Leffler's Shakespeare: The
    perils of stardom and everyday life
    Lynn R. Wilkinson — 247

9 Knut Hamsun's criticism of
    Shakespeare *Martin Humpál* — 269

Afterword: Towards a regional methodology of culture *Alexa Alice Joubin* — 291

Appendix: A timeline of significant Shakespeare-related events in the Nordic countries before 1900 — 297

Index — 317

LIST OF ILLUSTRATIONS

1.1 From Foersom's translation of *Hamlet* (Shakespeare 1807). Photo: Annelis Kuhlmann. Copy held in the Royal Library, Copenhagen. Public Domain. 50

1.2 Production notes relating to the casting of *Hamlet* (Anon. 1722). Photo: Annelis Kuhlmann. Copy held in the Royal Library, Copenhagen. Public Domain. 51

1.3 Cuttings from prompt copy of *Hamlet*, using Foersom's translation (Shakespeare 1887). Photo: Annelis Kuhlmann. Copy held in the Royal Library, Copenhagen. Public Domain. 52

4.1 The frontispiece of *Ruunulinna* (Helsinki, 1834). Photo reproduced with the kind permission of the archives of the Finnish Literature Society (SKS). 126

4.2 Appendix: A structural comparison between *Macbeth* and *Ruunulinna*. 147

NOTES ON CONTRIBUTORS

Eeva-Liisa Bastman holds a PhD in Finnish Literature from the University of Helsinki, Finland. Her main areas of interest are lyric theory and poetry from the early modern period to the Romantic age. She has published on eighteenth-century Pietist hymns, the biblical epic *Ilo-Laulu Jesuxesta* (1690), which is the first written epic poem in Kalevala metre, and the poetry of Aleksis Kivi. Currently, she is working on a project on seventeenth-century occasional poetry at the Finnish Literature Society.

Martin Humpál is Professor of Scandinavian Literature at the Department of Germanic Studies, Charles University, Czechia. In his research he focuses on literature of the nineteenth and twentieth centuries; his areas of specialization include Modernism, narrative theory and Knut Hamsun. He has written two books, one in English and one in Czech: *The Roots of Modernist Narrative: Knut Hamsun's Novels* Hunger, Mysteries, *and* Pan (1998) and *Moderní skandinávské literatury 1870–2000* [Modern Scandinavian Literature 1870–2000] (2006; 2nd edn, 2013), the latter with Helena Kadečková and Viola Parente-Čapková. He has also published numerous articles in scholarly books and journals.

Before retiring, **Kent Hägglund** was Senior Lecturer in Educational Drama at the Institute of Education, Stockholm University. He remains a frequent theatre reviewer and lecturer, as well as co-editing the quarterly journal of the Swedish Shakespeare Society. Publications include *William Shakespeare – En man för alla tider* (2006); he also initiated the 2013 volume *Macbeth 1813,* commemorating the bicentennial of Geijer's translation of Macbeth, and co-edited and wrote much of the material on Shakespeare, *Macbeth*, and Geijer's translation.

Alexa Alice Joubin is Professor of English, Women's, Gender and Sexuality Studies, Theatre, International Affairs and East Asian Languages and Cultures at George Washington University in Washington, DC, where she co-founded and co-directs the Digital Humanities Institute. As research affiliate in literature at the Massachusetts Institute of Technology, she is co-founder and co-director of the open access *Global Shakespeares* digital performance archive. Her recent books include *Shakespeare and East Asia* (2021), *Race* (with Martin Okrin, 2019), *Local and Global Myths in Shakespearean Performance* (co-edited, 2018) and *Shakespeare and the Ethics of Appropriation* (co-edited, 2014).

Nely Keinänen is a Senior Lecturer in the Department of Languages at the University of Helsinki, Finland. She is the editor of a special issue of *Synteesi (Journal of the Finnish Semiotics Society)* on Shakespeare in Finland, and *Shakespeare Suomessa* [Shakespeare in Finland], a collection of essays by translators, directors and actors on doing Shakespeare in Finland. Her essay on the first translation of *Hamlet* into Finnish (1879) recently came out in *Hamlet Translations: Prisms of Cultural Encounters across the Globe*, edited by Márta Minier and Lily Kahn. Keinänen has also translated over thirty contemporary Finnish plays into English. She is on the board of the Nordic Shakespeare Society (NorSS).

Annelis Kuhlmann is Associate Professor in dramaturgy at the School of Culture and Communication at Aarhus University, Denmark. Her research centres on various topics in theatre history and she is currently focusing on theatre historiography as seen through Danish theatre directing. She is also a philologist in Russian language and literature. Her doctoral dissertation, *Constantin Stanislavsky's Theatre Concepts* (1997) is based on Russian sources (Moscow Art Theatre). Her recent chapter on Hamletism, 'Gesture of Love in the dramaturgical appropriation: Shakespeare – Turgenev – Chekhov' (in

Russian) has been included in a book on Ivan Turgenev and his works. She has also published extensively on Odin Teatret.

Erika Laamanen has a PhD in Finnish literature from the University of Helsinki, Finland. In 2018 she defended her thesis dealing with the Finnish Modernist Lauri Viita (1916–1965) and the metalyrical aspects of his poetry. Her publications include articles on modern poetry and metrics.

Kiki Lindell is Senior Lecturer of English Literature, Lund University, Sweden, where she also stages Shakespeare's plays with her students. Recent research contributions: co-editor of a special issue of *Cahiers Shakespeare en Devenir*, entitled *Much Ado About Nothing: A Miscellany of 20th- and 21st-Century Perspectives* (2018); a chapter on the history of *Romeo and Juliet* in Sweden for a volume on *Romeo and Juliet in European Culture* (2018); an article called 'Taking the Ache out of Shakespeare: Teaching Shakespeare's Plays Through Performance' in a special issue on Shakespeare and Education in *Early Modern Culture* (2019).

James Newlin is a lecturer at Case Western Reserve University (USA) in the Department of English, teaching primarily in the Seminar Approach to General Education and Scholarship (SAGES) programme. His research interests focus on Shakespeare's reception in intellectual history, psychoanalysis and film. He has published in *The Journal of Dramatic Theory and Criticism*, *Shakespeare Bulletin*, *SubStance* and elsewhere. He is currently at work on a monograph entitled *Uncanny Fidelity: Recognizing Shakespeare in Twenty-First Century Film and Television*.

Jyrki Nummi is a Professor Emeritus of Finnish literature at the University of Helsinki, Finland. He is the editor-in-chief of the trilingual yearbook of Finnish literary studies *Joutsen – Svanen*. His main interests in literary studies are poetics, most recently historical poetics, nineteenth-century Finnish literature, Finnish Modernism and canon formation. His main publications include monographs on Väinö Linna and Juhani

Aho, and three critical editions of Aleksis Kivi's drama. He is currently working on a two-volume critical edition of Kivi's *Seven Brothers*.

Riitta Pohjola-Skarp is a Docent of Theatre and Drama Research at the University of Tampere, Finland. She defended her dissertation on Georg Büchner at the University of Helsinki in 2004. For many years, she worked as a dramaturg at Nordic Drama Corner (1986–2011) and then taught in the Theatre and Drama Research unit at the University of Tampere. Most recently she has been working on critical editions of Aleksis Kivi's dramas for the Finnish Literary Society, and was editor-in-chief of Kivi's *Karkurit* [The Fugitives] (2017). She has published on Georg Büchner, Heiner Müller, Aleksis Kivi and theories of drama.

Per Sivefors is Associate Professor of English at Linnaeus University, Sweden. His latest book is *Representing Masculinity in Early Modern English Satire, 1590–1603: 'A Kingdom for a Man'* (2020) which will be followed in 2022 by the collection *Changing Satire: Transformations and Continuities in Europe, 1600–1830*, edited with Cecilia Rosengren and Rikard Wingård, for Manchester University Press. He works extensively on the early reception of Shakespeare in the Nordic countries and has recently contributed to the Arden Shakespeare volume *Migrating Shakespeare: First European Encounters, Routes and Networks*, ed. Janet Clare and Dominique Goy-Blanquet. He is chair of the Nordic Shakespeare Society (NorSS).

Cecilia Lindskog Whiteley is a doctoral candidate in English literature at Uppsala University, Sweden. Her thesis focuses on spatiality in early modern drama before Shakespeare. Her writing has previously appeared in *Notes and Queries* and *The Palgrave Handbook of Gothic Origins*.

Lynn R. Wilkinson is Associate Professor of Germanic Studies, Comparative Literature and Women's and Gender Studies at the University of Texas at Austin, USA. She has published *The Dream of an Absolute Language: Emanuel Swedenborg* and French Literary Culture (1996), *Anne Charlotte Leffler and Modernist Drama: True Women and New Women on the Fin-de-Siècle Scandinavian Stage* (2011), and *Laughter and Civility: The Theatre of Emma Gad* (2020), and is currently working on a translation of Anne Charlotte Leffler's writings about London and a study of walking and mobility in the work of George Sand.

ACKNOWLEDGEMENTS

Producing an academic collection is obviously about collaboration, and our first debt is to the scholars, many of them cited in or contributing to this book, who have worked on Nordic Shakespeare. While important work was done in the early twentieth century, we are very happy to see that the field is now revitalizing. We thank our contributors for the hard work they have put into their chapters and for their enthusiasm for this project.

The founding of the Nordic Shakespeare Society (NorSS) in 2015 was a crucial step towards joining scholars in the field and, for this, a further substantial debt is acknowledged in our dedication. Richard Wilson was extremely important in taking the first initiative towards founding the Nordic Shakespeare Society and in organizing the first conference on Nordic Shakespeare at Kingston University in 2015, where many of us met for the first time. Richard's subsequent conferences and other Shakespeare-related events at Kingston have been a continuous source of inspiration for scholars across Europe and beyond. The late Martin Regal served as the first chair of NorSS and his intelligence and wit are still sorely missed. Delilah Bermudez Brataas has been secretary of NorSS from the beginning, doing much of the practical work which keeps the society going.

We wish to acknowledge the European Shakespeare Research Association (ESRA) for providing opportunities to present our work and Alexandra Herlitz for suggesting the cover art. We thank the editors of the Global Shakespeare Inverted series (David Schalkwyk, Silvia Bigliazzi and Bi-qi Beatrice Lei) for accepting this book in the series and Anne Sophie Refskou who offered advice along the way. The team at Bloomsbury Press has been lovely to work with, especially Mark Dudgeon, who has admirably demonstrated the patience and flexibility needed for a book coming together during a global pandemic.

Nely is grateful to the English Studies Master's Programme at the University of Helsinki which provided funds to hire a research assistant, Leena Vahvelainen, who helped put together the timeline. She also thanks her colleagues at the University of Helsinki for listening to her talk about Shakespeare in the Nordic countries, and knowing when to change the subject. Pentti Paavolainen has generously answered innumerable questions about Nordic theatre history. Finally, Nely is deeply grateful to Kimmo Absetz for help with translation, and many other things.

Per wishes to thank Ellinor Broman, for her faith and enthusiasm and for setting the gold standard in translating, editing and producing books. The members of the Early Modern Seminar at the University of Gothenburg have offered consistent support and encouragement, as have his colleagues at the Department of Languages, Linnaeus University. A special thank you is reserved for Janet Clare and Dominique Goy-Blanquet for their invitation to participate in a project on European Shakespeare, resulting in the Arden volume *Migrating Shakespeare*. As current chair of the NorSS, Per also extends his thanks to its members and their work on Nordic Shakespeare in the past and present.

Introduction

Shakespeare in the Nordic countries: Shifting centres and peripheries in the nineteenth century

This collection charts the dissemination of Shakespeare in the Nordic countries from the early nineteenth century up until approximately 1890. Its central premise is that the adoption of Shakespeare entailed a complex negotiation of a series of 'selves' and 'others' that went far beyond the question of influence of Anglophone, German or French cultural 'centres' on a peripheral 'North'. In doing so, it rethinks and challenges notions of centre versus periphery in Shakespeare studies, showing that in the Nordic countries, rather than being concentric, the process of adopting Shakespeare relates to a series of multiple, overlapping and shifting centres and peripheries where England and English culture are just one, and not necessarily the most important, component. In that sense, the book inverts 'global Shakespeare' by rejecting its implications of a single, unitary centre versus an equally unitary periphery, arguing instead the need to see the dissemination of Shakespeare in terms of struggles between several centres of power, located not just outside but also within and between the Nordic countries.

As the book contends, the Nordic countries in the nineteenth century provide a particularly fruitful example for studies of Shakespeare's dissemination, since they provide an accessible view of influence and resistance across the boundaries of the nation-state at a time of historical and cultural upheaval. In the nineteenth century, Shakespeare was beginning to be translated and performed on a larger scale; it was a period when several of the Nordic countries began to define themselves as nation-states, with their own national literatures, often in opposition to other Nordic countries. It was also a century when bonds to other European cultures and languages were in the process of shifting, for example from French classicism towards German Romanticism in the first decades and towards Realism in the latter. The nineteenth century is, moreover, a period when Shakespeare becomes an object of intense personal engagement for many authors, a literary whetstone on which to sharpen one's own authorial identity. In many cases, this was a matter of aligning oneself with broader political or cultural currents. For instance, the Swedish author Anne Charlotte Leffler looks to Juliet as an example of how not to be a woman; the Finnish Aleksis Kivi and Norwegian Bjørnsterne Bjørnson turn to Shakespeare for dramatic models on how to forge a vernacular theatre; while the Norwegian Knut Hamsun's rejection of Shakespeare was arguably part of his general anti-British stance. In other cases, taking on Shakespeare amounted to a profound negotiation of religious dogma, as in the case of Kierkegaard. Altogether, the contributions to the volume, which range from detailed discussion of early translations and productions to analyses of ideologically invested influences on single authors, move beyond the question of influence from the Anglophone cultural sphere to examine a series of relations on both the wider European and the more specific Nordic levels.

The volume significantly contributes to the expansive field of research on Shakespeare's global presence, although it also amounts to a retheorization of several of its assumptions. Speaking of modern transnational productions, Alexa Alice Joubin warns against a reliance on 'polity-driven historiography' leading to 'detailed histories of national Shakespeares' which 'inadvertently create unknowable objects by flattening the artworks against national profiles'.[1] Precisely because the national movements were strong in the Nordic countries, the present collection seeks to avoid an alignment with narrowly defined national Shakespeares and instead hopes to shed light on exchanges and parallels between the countries – and between them and other spheres of influence outside Britain. Importantly, the concept of 'global Shakespeare' has been questioned for its Eurocentric or Anglocentric implications and the term 'rhizomatics' (adapting Deleuze and Guattari's concept) has been proposed as a more accurate tool for capturing the diversity of the process by which Shakespeare was disseminated.[2] Terms like 'glocal' have also been used frequently in the context of international Shakespeare studies.[3] While such concepts have been valuable in dismantling hierarchical modes of thinking in Shakespeare criticism, the present volume suggests that they are insufficient to understand the complexities of Nordic Shakespeare. An important assumption behind the collection is that concepts like 'centre' and 'periphery' still have a certain validity, provided that one also emphasizes their inescapable plurality and the fact that they interlock in crucial ways. Due to their largely shared history and culture it makes sense to treat the Nordic countries in relation to each other, but it is also imperative to recognize the differences between them and the diversity of their 'selves' and 'others'. This is an implication to which terms like 'rhizomatics' are insufficiently attuned.

It has frequently been observed that Shakespeare was mediated through French and, later, German culture in the eighteenth and nineteenth centuries; however, the volume challenges the notion that this process was merely one of Nordic periphery versus western European centre. Indeed, as some of the contributions to the volume show, early translations and performances bear the mark of complex negotiations of German, French and English influences, with varying results. In the case of Denmark, re-appropriating *Hamlet* in a time of political upheaval during the Napoleonic wars meant wresting the play out of the hands of a political enemy. In other cases, the appropriation of Shakespeare involved combining European influences with local folk traditions. The class restructurings of Europe and the rise of the middle class throughout the century also meant that Shakespeare became a significant element in bourgeois education, a fact that is also reflected in several contributions to the book. Shakespeare was becoming an ideal (or sometimes, an object of aversion) for authors and readers across the Nordic countries, part of a shared European rather than strictly English cultural heritage. What is more, in some cases, such processes entailed an emerging identification of the Nordic countries as part of an emerging global North: the African-American actor Ira Aldridge, who starred as Othello and Shylock in Stockholm in 1857, could be pinpointed in the press as a passionate 'Southerner' who was a fundamental 'other' to the mentality of people from the North. In short, influences from the English cultural sphere were only one factor, and often not even the most important one, in the spread of Shakespeare in the Nordic countries.

Methodologically, the volume considers the dissemination of Shakespeare in terms that avoid privileging text over performance. Landmark productions, for example, are considered as significant events that align themselves with the political dynamics of their time (Kuhlmann; Sivefors). Moreover, the book explores the ways in which translators do not simply transfer the text to another language but are active creators of meaning (Lindell and Hägglund; Lindskog Whiteley). It also discusses the ways in which Shakespeare serves as a foil for authors working in other media than the theatrical (Humpál; Newlin; Wilkinson), or, conversely, for authors who strive to forge a distinctly vernacular theatrical tradition (Nummi, Bastman and Laamanen; Pohjola-Skarp).

In terms of coverage, while the volume does not purport to be an exhaustive 'history of Shakespeare in the Nordic countries in the nineteenth century', it does include contributions on four of the five present-day Nordic states (Denmark, Finland, Norway and Sweden).[4] This is in line with the ambition to chart the complexity of power relations as described above, the goal to move beyond an Anglocentric conception of Shakespeare's dissemination and an emphasis on shared history and processes of self-definition. Moreover, the volume is predominantly concerned with Shakespearean drama – a focus that is consistent with the ambitions of translators and performers in the period. As for chronology, the volume stops on the threshold of a period when Shakespeare became part and parcel of more specifically defined projects of national self-definition in countries such as Norway (independent in 1905), Finland (independent in 1917) and Iceland (independent in 1944). A second volume in the series will chart this development in more detail.

Previous work on Nordic Shakespeares

If the various movements of national self-definition became strong in the nineteenth and early twentieth centuries, it is significant, perhaps, that much of the ground-breaking academic research on Shakespeare in the Nordic countries was carried out during or shortly after these political processes. Works by, for example, Mikko V. Erich (1916) and Yrjö Hirn (1916) on Finland, Martin Ruud (1917 and 1920) on Denmark and Norway, Nils Molin on Sweden (1931) and Stefán Einarsson (1940) on Iceland were not followed up by extensive research and, despite a long and varied history of Shakespearean translation and performance in all Nordic countries up until the present day, the small body of academic work is in sore need of updating and expansion. Existing studies tend to be local and focus on particular individuals or institutions rather than addressing the general history of Shakespeare in the Nordic countries.[5] What is missing from these national accounts of national Shakespeare is a broader understanding of how all the countries shared influences yet also competed and how not only Britain but also the rest of Europe and beyond served as continuous sources of ideals and antipathies. This is not 'national' Shakespeare, but neither is it 'global' Shakespeare in the sense often understood by recent scholarship.

Political, linguistic and educational background in the Nordic countries

At the beginning of the period covered in this volume, there were only two independent kingdoms in Northern Europe (Denmark and Sweden), whereas towards the end of it independence movements had been firmly established in what are today Finland, Iceland and Norway. The late eighteenth and early nineteenth centuries had, as in much of the rest of Europe, been a period of political upheaval with considerable impact on later political and cultural developments. In the words of H. Arnold Barton, 'in all areas of Scandinavian life ... essential lines of development can be traced to ideals formulated and in large part realized in government and society between the Seven Years' War and the end of the Napoleonic conflict'.[6]

Early in the revolutionary period, Denmark and Sweden managed mainly to stay out of the military conflicts riling Europe, but were heavily involved in the war effort due to their status as neutral merchant shippers. Denmark had a long history of British alliances and, in the decades before the period covered here, Britain had provided English princesses for Danish kings (e.g., Christian VII married Caroline Mathilde, the sister of George III).[7] Through its German-speaking provinces, Denmark also had close ties with the vast German-speaking areas of Europe. For Sweden, Britain was an important trading partner (e.g., Scottish merchants were active in Gothenburg).[8]

Historically and culturally, Sweden also had close links with France. Gustav III (r. 1771–1792) had visited the French court and designed his own to emulate it. However, his own evident taste for French culture did not rule out attempts to harness the links between an emerging Swedish bourgeoisie and German and, to some extent, British, culture.

Between Denmark and Sweden there were more local rivalries with the status of Norway having been a particular source of tension. From 1397 to 1523, the three kingdoms of Denmark, Sweden and Norway (which included what is now Iceland and Finland) were joined in the Kalmar Union and, when Sweden broke away in 1523, Norway remained aligned with Denmark. In the 1770s, the Swedish king Gustav III began eyeing Norway, but Norway remained loyal to the Danish king. By the early nineteenth century, the geopolitical map had been substantially redrawn. In 1809, Sweden's Finnish territories were ceded to Russia in the wake of the Finnish War, and Finland was made an autonomous Grand Duchy within the Russian Empire, becoming self-governing for the first time in its history. In 1814, Norway was annexed by Sweden owing to Denmark's siding with Napoleonic France, a move organized by Sweden's crown prince Jean-Baptiste (Karl Johan) Bernadotte, a former field marshal in Napoleon's army. Like Finland, Norway achieved greater self-rule under the new alliance and the Norwegian constitution adopted in 1814 was one of the most democratic in Europe, with some 45.5 per cent of men above the age of 25 granted the right to vote (compare the 1832 British reform bill, which granted suffrage to 10 per cent).[9] Only Denmark remained an absolutist monarchy, although it, too, got a constitution when Frederik VII acceded to the throne in 1849.

As political allegiances shifted, so did linguistic and cultural ones. At the beginning of the nineteenth century, the linguistic situation in the Nordic countries was complex. In Denmark-Norway, the prestige language (and the language of the court, military and administration) was High German, followed by Danish, spoken by most of the people in Denmark, followed by Norwegian, itself divided into more and less prestigious variants,

Riksmål (closer to Danish) and Landsmål (closer to Old Norse). In Sweden-Finland, the language of administration was Swedish and, to an extent, French, especially in the first decades of the century. Swedish was spoken in Sweden and some of the coastal villages of Finland, while the bulk of the population in Finland spoke Finnish. Throughout the Nordic region, the educated classes spoke German and French in addition to their local vernacular, while in Finland, Swedish was used extensively in administration, commerce and education, even after its annexation by Russia in 1809. To some extent Danish, Norwegian and Swedish are mutually intelligible, especially in written form, but Finnish, which is not an Indo-European language, was virtually unknown outside its home country. During the nineteenth century, efforts were made in Norway and Finland to raise the status of these languages, including by translating Shakespeare, but it should also be noted that in the late eighteenth and early nineteenth centuries, even Danish and Swedish were considered unsuitable theatrical languages by an educated élite who were used to seeing plays performed in French or German.

Advances in education, which were among the most progressive in Europe, may also have helped to spread knowledge of Shakespeare. The first comprehensive systems of primary education in the North were introduced in this period and, while Shakespeare did not become part of the primary school curriculum until late in the nineteenth century, his works entered the university world considerably earlier. For example, the Romantic coteries at Uppsala in the early nineteenth century were keen on reading Shakespeare even if they did not necessarily do so in English. Instead, the cult was obviously indebted to German Romanticism, but beyond such trends, Shakespeare was more systematically introduced in university courses. Indeed, the translator of the first complete set of Shakespeare's plays into Swedish, Carl August Hagberg (1810–1864), was a professor of aesthetics and modern languages who regularly lectured on Shakespeare at Lund University beginning in the 1840s and, towards the end of his life, August Strindberg would recall how he and his fellow students at Uppsala University in the 1860s and 1870s had deemed the protagonist of *Julius Caesar* 'badly drawn'.[10] In 1859 and again in 1864, Fredrik Cygnaeus (1807–1881) dedicated a lecture series in Helsinki to drama, covering G.E Lessing and Friedrich Schiller in addition to Shakespeare; Aleksis Kivi attended both sets of lectures.[11]

Outside the institutions of learning, works by Shakespeare in English had circulated since the eighteenth century, not least in provincial cities with no local access to higher education. Once translations began to appear, they gradually spread well outside the educated élites; indeed, for the publisher Gleerup, Hagberg's Swedish translations (1847–1851) were a considerable economic success and were frequently re-issued well into the twentieth century.[12] Towards the mid-century, it is clear that Shakespeare had become an obvious point of reference for authors and intellectuals: as James Newlin suggests in the present volume, Kierkegaard's engagement with Shakespeare as a reader and spectator was significant enough for him to imitate the plot of *King Lear* in his works. In a different vein, for an early feminist writer like Anne Charlotte Leffler, Juliet would serve as a problematic model of romantic love (see Wilkinson's chapter). As the century progressed and aesthetic ideals were shifting, Shakespeare would even be rejected as insufficient and irrelevant in understanding the complexities of contemporary life: this proto-Modernist view was articulated by the Norwegian Knut Hamsun towards the end of the 1800s (see Humpál's chapter). Clearly, such wholesale dismissal can only be understood in light of the canonical status that Shakespeare had now attained.

Shakespeare translations

The spread of Shakespeare in translation in the Nordic countries was, to some extent, structured by relations between the countries themselves. With Denmark and Sweden being the two independent states in Northern Europe at the beginning of the nineteenth century, it was Danish and Swedish translations that were chronologically first, whereas the budding attempts at Finnish, Icelandic and Norwegian Shakespeares came later, partly in reaction to the use of Danish and Swedish on the stage. In terms of repertoire, the earliest Nordic translators focused especially on tragedy, with *Hamlet, Macbeth* or *Romeo and Juliet* often chosen as the first play; translators seem to have been variously influenced by German and French versions though, in some cases, also claimed to be working directly from English.[13]

The first translation into Danish appeared in 1777: *Hamlet*, by Johannes Boye. As far as is known, this was also the first published translation of a full play by Shakespeare into any Nordic language. Later, in the 1790s, Nils Rosenfeldt translated several other plays into prose, including *Macbeth*, *Othello*, *All's Well That Ends Well*, *King Lear* and *The Merchant of Venice,* claiming that Shakespeare's poetry was 'detrimental to the freedom and clarity of expression'.[14] The most significant early translations into Danish were made by Peter Foersom (1777–1817), starting with *Julius Caesar* and mainly including the tragedies popular in the Romantic period.[15] In 1813, his *Hamlet* was produced, with Foersom playing the title role (see Kuhlmann's chapter). Foersom seems to have translated from English, using editions by George Steevens and Edmond Malone.[16] Sille Beyer (1803–1861) adapted several of Shakespeare's comedies into Danish in the manner of Scribe's comédies-vaudevilles, which were popular in Danish and Norwegian theatres in the 1850s–1870s. It was, however, the complete version by Edvard Lembcke, published in 1861–1873, that became to Denmark what Hagberg's translation was already becoming to Swedish culture. Lembcke, who modestly claimed his first volume of translations was a revised version of Foersom's, thought that his own work had been made possible by the 'return to a simpler and more natural form of expression'[17] in the Danish language. Specifically, he found the Germanisms of Foersom's translations problematic although he politely described them as children of their time.[18] Like Hagberg's, Lembcke's Shakespeare was an assertion of the importance of vernacular culture and language and would continue be re-issued and read well into the twentieth century.

In Norway, linguistic tensions paralleled political tensions with Denmark, and these influenced the translation of Shakespeare into Norwegian.[19] Early performances of Shakespeare used Danish translations virtually by default, although there had been attempts to translate fragments of plays into Norwegian as early as 1782.[20] In 1844, the first production of a Shakespeare play in Norway, *Macbeth*, used Foersom's Danish translation, with Danish actors. The Norwegian Nils Hauge translated *Macbeth* in 1855 into Dano-Norwegian, while Ivar Aasen, trying to develop Landsmål into a literary language, translated fragments of *Romeo and Juliet* in 1853; around the same time, he translated Hamlet's 'To be or not to be' speech, though it was not published until 1911.[21] The first translation into modern Norwegian was not until 1881, when Hartvig Lassen (1824–1897) translated *The Merchant of Venice* in an edition to be used in schools, influenced by Hagberg's Swedish translation and Schlegel's German.

In Sweden, early translators also focused on tragedy, apparently sometimes relying on Ducis' French adaptations and, perhaps also, German versions.[22] Interestingly, for performances in the 1780s and 1790s of *Hamlet* in Gothenburg – a town noted for its connections with Britain – the play is said to have been translated directly from English, although the translations themselves have been lost.[23] It was not until 1813 that a Swedish translation of Shakespeare was published. This was *Macbeth* by Erik Gustaf Geijer, who knew English and had spent a year in England, but who was also influenced by Schiller, among others (see Lindell and Hägglund's chapter). We know even more about the influences on the previously mentioned Hagberg in his work on the first complete Swedish edition. He used George Steevens' and Samuel Johnson's edition, probably in Isaac Reed's revised version of 1824, as well as Edmond Malone's and James

Boswell's edition from 1821 with Steevens' notes (the 3rd Variorum). Apparently, he also had access to Warburton's older edition and he was familiar with Schiller's, Schlegel's and Tieck's German editions and may have read Foersom's Danish translations from 1807–1816.[24] What this shows is just how wide and varied the web of influences was and, even if there was a very clear trend towards emphasizing the need for philologically correct translations from English, attention was paid to continental norms and standards and to the translations into other Nordic languages. At the same time, the philological ideals could clash with convenience or moral standards when the translations were put on stage. When, for example, Hagberg's translation of *Hamlet* was used for numerous performances at the Royal Theatre in Stockholm in the 1850s and 1860s, it was drastically edited, removing the roles of Fortinbras and Guildenstern.[25]

In Finland, too, early translators focused on *Macbeth*.[26] Jacob Fredrik Lagervall's *Ruunulinna* (1834) is a free adaptation of *Macbeth*, set in Finland, and utilizing the Kalevala metre which was at the time being resurrected as part of the national awakening (see the chapter by Nummi, Bastman and Laamanen). However, its reception was mixed and the adaptation was never performed. It was not until 30 years later, in anticipation of the 1864 Shakespeare tercentenary celebrations, that a new translation was undertaken by Kaarlo A. Slöör (Finnicized pen name Santala) (1833–1905). This more faithful translation also received mixed reviews, demonstrating the linguistic anxieties which slowed the adoption of Shakespeare in Finland. August Ahlqvist (1826–1889), a professor of Finnish, proclaimed that the language was not yet up to the rigours of translating Shakespeare:

> In our opinion, it is still too early to begin translating Shakespeare into Finnish. Our language lacks the vocabulary to discuss the exalted things the poet describes; it is still too unstable and formless; it still wobbles clumsily and staggers awkwardly in its new poetic clothes. And I doubt we will ever

get Shakespeare's works to sound in Finnish like they sound in Swedish for example. The Finnish language is simply too far removed from the Germanic languages.[27]

Nevertheless, Finns looked to the translation of classic texts, not just Shakespeare but also Schiller, Hugo and many other writers, as a way for these small vernacular languages to prove their worthiness on the European cultural stage. In 1864, to this end, a celebration of Shakespeare's tercentenary was held in Helsinki, attended by around 700 people. The elaborate decorations included a plaster cast of the poet made by Carl Eneas Sjöstrand. There were readings from *Julius Caesar* as well as the new *Macbeth*. Fredrik Cygnaeus gave a patriotic address, dismissing the linguistic and cultural anxieties raised by the likes of Ahlqvist and celebrating Finnish folk traditions as already being at the level of Shakespearean tragedy:

> But above all else, what gives us the right to read Shakespeare as a kindred soul is the fact that in places our *Kalevala* displays the spirit, the world view, which approaches that of Shakespearean tragedy. I'm thinking in particular of the tragic conflict at the heart of the Kullervo story, which makes us think of similar phenomena in the tragedies of the British poet.[28]

This example demonstrates just how complex centres and peripheries could be: on the one hand, Shakespeare represents the heights of British (German and French) drama, a goal to aspire to, but, at the same time, local traditions represent an equally important centre, speaking to others on their own terms, as equals. The musical numbers rounding out the Helsinki tercentenary celebration also nod to wide-ranging European influences and included the German Felix Mendelssohn's music from *A Midsummer Night's Dream* and 'Rule Britannia'. As we will examine more closely in our next volume, translating Shakespeare became an important part of these nationalist movements at the end of the nineteenth century.

Shakespeare in early Nordic theatre

For the most part, translation efforts were responding to theatrical needs. Both Denmark and Sweden had a performance history of Shakespeare that antedates the time period covered in this volume, with early translations and performances sometimes inspired by early Romanticism.[29] In Sweden, provincial theatres had picked up Shakespeare long before his plays were first performed in the capital. Gothenburg, Norrköping and Karlskrona, even as far afield as Turku and Oulu in Finland, all saw early productions from the 1770s onward. For example, Swedish players led by Carl Gottfried Seuerling (1727–1795) performed *Romeo and Juliet* as well as Molière, Racine and Voltaire. It seems likely that this *Romeo and Juliet* was based on Christian Felix Weissen's German adaptation, though Ducis's French version is also a possibility.[30] The provinces, in many cases, lacked permanent theatre buildings and were visited by travelling companies. In Sweden, however, the local theatre in Gothenburg had its own company in the 1780s and 1790s and the theatre building would later serve various travelling companies. The lack of permanency for this institution is significant: it would take several decades into the nineteenth century until the provinces had a substantial enough middle class to make permanent theatres and companies commercially viable.

Despite this history of provincial Shakespeare, *Hamlet* was not staged at the Royal Theatre in Stockholm until 1819. Several factors may explain this; for example, the rise of a provincial bourgeoisie, often with close ties to Britain and the fact that the cultural élite in Stockholm, including the members of the Swedish Academy, which was founded in 1786, tended to be strongly influenced by French classicism.[31] While these influences were notably in decline by the 1810s, the royal monopoly on theatre and opera in the capital (1798–1842) meant that new productions of Shakespearean plays were relatively few. Significantly, therefore, the 1850s were, in many ways, a turning point, with premieres of a number of Shakespearean plays both at privately run venues and at the Royal Theatre. Also, for the first time, the whole canon of Shakespeare's plays became available in Swedish in Hagberg's previously mentioned translation. Both reading and theatre-going were now firmly established as essential pastimes among the educated bourgeoisie although, in the theatres themselves, classicist conventions lingered on to some extent.[32] Reviews of Shakespearean performances sometimes called for a new, fresh approach, although when such approaches were introduced, they could also spark controversy, as demonstrated by the visit of Ira Aldridge in 1857, which resulted in a major newspaper debate that exemplified how aesthetics and politics could intertwine (see Sivefors's chapter). What is more, many Shakespearean plays – *Richard II* or *King Lear*, for example – were considered unsuitable fare for the royal stage due to their depiction of weak or even mad kings.[33] It was instead the privately run smaller theatres who not only performed Shakespeare more frequently, but were also more successful in catering to the taste of the theatre-going middle class. However, while productions in the latter part of the century signal a gradual movement towards realism and naturalism, the interest in Shakespeare in the latter part of the century faded compared to the early days of Romanticism and the mid-century, although there were exceptions.[34]

The Swedish Shakespeare tercentenary of 1864 arguably reflected these problems and the ways in which they were handled by the royal institution. In Britain, the 1864 celebrations were fraught with contradictions in terms of class allegiances; as Anthony Taylor suggests, for reformers and radicals in the period they provided 'the most lasting opportunity to reclaim Shakespeare for popular culture'.[35] In Sweden, however, the celebrations can be said to cement class divisions rather than attempting to overcome them: the grand jubilee at the Royal Theatre was split between its two venues, with the Stora Teatern (the Great Theatre) solemnly taking on *Hamlet* and the smaller Dramatiska Teatern running comedy fare in the form of *Twelfth Night*. As Fridén argues, the implication was not only that of different areas of competence among the actors, but of distinct target groups: presumably, comedy would have been less appealing to the members of the nobility and court. At the same time, Shakespeare seems to have become identified very much as a prerogative for the connoisseurs of the artistic and learned world.[36] If anything, such a development hints at the ease with which Shakespeare could now serve as a point of reference, a source of imitation and even antipathy among writers and thinkers in the Nordic countries. It has been said about the British tercentenary celebrations that 'Shakespeare had never been celebrated on such a scale before'[37] and, while this is largely true also of the much more modest Swedish jubilee, the ideological impetus behind the celebrations was, understandably, different in many respects, just as the Swedish celebration was different from the Finnish which, due to its own political situation, emphasized class and cultural unity.

The performance history of Shakespeare in Denmark initially trailed behind Sweden: as noted previously, a not particularly successful production *of Hamlet* was first performed in 1813, with the translator, Peter Foersom, in the starring role. This production, which has been called a 'gothic *Hamlet*',[38] may have owed something to the new trend of Romanticism introduced especially by Adam Oehlenschläger (1779–1850), whose Nordic tragedies were influenced by Shakespeare. But the rise of literary Romanticism, with all its associated bardolatry, did not entail a consistent performance tradition of Shakespeare; indeed, the first production of *King Lear*, in 1816, was cancelled after only three performances. Like in Sweden, the years around 1850 in many ways constituted a pivotal point; the first private playhouses in Copenhagen were founded in 1848 and 1857. New acting ideals, with a greater insistence on realism and verisimilitude, were reflected in various Shakespearean performances by actors such as Johanne Luise Heiberg and Frederik Høedt.[39] Heiberg's 1847 performance of Juliet (at the age of 35) is celebrated by Kierkegaard in *Crisis in the Life of an Actress*, as a rebuttal to those who believe that an older actress cannot capture the depth of Juliet's character. Heiberg also achieved great success in Sille Beyer's adaptations of Shakespearean comedy, for example, *Twelfth Night* (1847), *As You Like It* (1849), *All's Well That Ends Well* (1850) and *Love's Labour's Lost* (1853), though her most significant Shakespearean role was said to be Lady Macbeth, which she took over from Anna Nielsen in 1860. Whereas Nielsen had played Lady Macbeth as 'an older and consciously evil figure', Heiberg's Lady 'defied tradition as a younger, attractive, fiery creature, recently married and ecstatic with ambition from the outset of the play'.[40]

At the beginning of the nineteenth century, Norwegian theatre was largely dominated by Danish, although resentment about this state of affairs was rising and efforts were made to translate and then perform Shakespeare in Norwegian vernaculars. Early performances of Shakespeare in Norway used Danish translations such as Foersom's of *Hamlet*, *Romeo and Juliet* and *Macbeth*. The latter, staged in 1844, was the first performance of a complete play by Shakespeare. Here, too, the mid-century constituted a significant turning point: in Christiania (present-day Oslo) during 1840–1870 there were stagings of a substantial part of the canon (*Othello*, *Romeo and Juliet*, *As You Like It*, *All's Well That Ends Well*, *The Taming of the Shrew*, *Much Ado about Nothing*, *Twelfth Night*, *The Merchant of Venice*, *Winter's Tale*, *A Midsummer Night's Dream*). The theatre in the second-biggest city, Bergen, also saw productions of *As You Like It* and *Twelfth Night* (the latter adapted from German).

Bjørnstjerne Bjørnson's *A Midsummer Night's Dream* (1865) at the Christiania Theatre (Oslo) provides further insight into some of the linguistic tensions between Danish and Norwegian. The text used was an earlier translation by Oehlenschläger, with music by Mendelssohn. The translation was based on Tieck's version originally done for the court theatre at Potsdam, from which it made its way to Stockholm and then to Christiania.[41] In terms of pronunciation, by 1865, the Christiania Theatre was mainly employing Norwegian actors speaking with Norwegian pronunciation, but less than a decade earlier, Bjørnson had organized a 'whistle concert' protesting the hiring of the Danish actor Ferdinand Schmidts, as he thought the Danish style of acting conveyed 'the decorous' but not 'the genuine and true'.[42] In terms of language, then, Bjørnson insisted on using Norwegian pronunciation and viewed classics like Shakespeare 'as a means of measuring the growing abilities of the actors', still an issue in mid-century Norway.[43]

A separate controversy demonstrating the shift from Romantic to more realistic staging played out in the press over Bjørnson's stage machinery, specifically the elaborate spectacle then dominating the Victorian stage in England and elsewhere in Europe, but which was beyond the technical and financial means of the theatre. Bjørnson wanted to move away from the elaborate stage design and effects typical of Romanticism. One reviewer provides a good description of this aesthetic, by objecting that: 'Large, established theatre companies convey the full imaginative power of the play by using an elaborate wardrobe, multicolored lights, a well-choreographed ballet, and sensational backdrops and sound effects.'[44] Bjørnson responded that Norwegians are 'a healthy nature loving people with unending forest impressions behind us' and thus only need 'a gentle reminder' of what a forest looks like. Indeed, he criticizes what he considers to be overly elaborate sets: 'I appeal to those Norwegians who have been abroad and know how wretched indeed it is to see waterfalls cascading over a backdrop or ships manoeuvring on rollers.'[45] Demonstrating the interconnectedness of the European theatre scene, in these debates specific reference is made both to England and Germany, as Ruud summarizes:

> Englishmen often stage Shakespeare's romantic plays more elaborately. They even show us a ship at sea in *The Tempest*. But Shakespeare has fled England; they are left with their properties, out of which the spirit of Shakespeare will not rise. It is significant that the most distinguished dramaturg

of Germany, Dingelstedt, planned a few years before to go to London with some of the best actors in Germany to teach Englishmen how to play Shakespeare once more.[46]

We can thus see how Shakespeare was claimed both by Romanticists but also later by realists who explicitly rejected Romantic aesthetics, for example, the Swedish translator Hagberg (see Lindskog Whiteley's chapter) and also in the push and pull of Romanticism and realism in the Shakespeare-influenced play by Aleksis Kivi (see Pohjola-Skarp's chapter).

Centres and peripheries in the Nordic countries: A small case study

The above discussion already gives an idea of the complex and varied links between theatres in the Nordic countries and Europe, and we turn now to a more specific look at how these might have been realized at an individual level, as seen in the career of the Swedish actor Hedvig Charlotte Raa-Winterhjelm (née Forsman) (1838–1907). During her career, Raa-Winterhjelm performed in four of the Nordic countries, in three languages and in many of the genres typical of nineteenth-century European theatre, from melodrama to high Romanticism (both German and French) and later in the realistic and naturalist traditions, represented most significantly by Henrik Ibsen.

Touring companies were an important component of theatrical exchange across the Nordic countries and early in her career, Raa-Winterhjelm was mainly employed by them, travelling all over Sweden and Finland, later adding Norway and Denmark to the mix. Having finished her studies at the Royal Dramatic Theatre, at the age of 21 Raa-Winterhjelm joined the travelling company of Oskar Andersson, which was heading to Helsinki for the third winter in a row. She later joined Edvard Stjernström's company in Stockholm, where she acted with Ulrik Torsslow who, in 1819, had made his debut at the Royal Dramatic Theatre playing Hamlet. Later, together with her first husband Frithiof Raa, she joined the Åhman-Pousette company, which had agreed to go to Helsinki to help establish a permanent Swedish-speaking company there and which also toured extensively around the Swedish provinces. In the 1870s, now married to the Norwegian journalist Kristian Winterhjelm, Raa performed more exclusively in Sweden. In 1883 she teamed up with the Swedish actor August Lindberg in the first European production of Henrik Ibsen's *Ghosts*, playing Mrs Alving; that production travelled around Sweden, Norway and Denmark.[47] Much of this travel would have been done by sea and coach, as railways came rather late to the Nordic countries.

Not only were actors travelling around the Nordic countries to perform but they, along with their audiences, also went to other places in Europe to study or simply to see what the large European theatres had on offer. Raa-Winterhjelm came to Paris in the early 1860s to study acting and, again in the early 1870s, took time off to travel in Europe, where she saw productions at the Burgtheater in Vienna. The Finnish theatre director Kaarlo Bergbom often travelled to Germany and France while up-and-coming actors sought to study with famous teachers such as Marie Niemann-Seebach in Dresden, as did the young Finn Ida Aalberg in 1878 and 1880. Earlier in the century, Frans Michael Franzén (1772–1847), a Swedish poet of Finnish descent, had seen one of the earliest performances of *Romeo and Juliet* at the age of eight or nine; he later visited France, Germany and England, where he saw Kemble playing a number of Shakespearian roles.[48]

Nordic reviewers also displayed knowledge of the continental theatre scene. For example, Raa-Winterhjelm was compared favourably to European actresses. As a young actress in the late 1850s and early 1860s, she was compared to such continental greats as Friederike Gossmann (Vienna) and Augusta Formes (Berlin).[49] Commenting that he had seen the best that Europe had to offer, the Finnish intellectual Fredrik Cygnaeus (1807–1881) said that he could only compare Charlotte's Lady Macbeth to Adelaide Ristori's, the Italian actress who toured with great success in Europe and the United States.[50] Such comments reinforce the interconnectedness of European theatre, showing both that the Nordics looked to Europe for models, but also felt that their home-grown efforts were fully on a par with them.

The roles of Charlotte Raa-Winterhjelm provide insight into the typical repertoire of mid-century Nordic theatre and the significance of Shakespeare within it. In the early nineteenth century, the Nordic countries embraced German and French Romanticism, and Raa-Winterhjelm played roles in such works as Schiller's *Mary Stuart*, *Don Carlos* and *The Maid of Orleans*, Victor Hugo's *Mary Tudor* and *Lucrezia Borgia*, and Alexandre Dumas's *Queen Margot*. The melodramas, so popular in nineteenth-century European theatre, were also performed, for example, Charlotte Birch-Pfeiffer's *Jane Eyre*, with Charlotte Raa starring in her first travelling season in 1859–1860 to great acclaim. New works by Nordic writers were also included, such as those by Cygnaeus, whose lectures on Shakespeare inspired the Finnish writer Aleksis Kivi (see Pohjola-Skarp's chapter). Shakespeare's plays were a small but significant part of this repertoire and, for many theatre companies, Shakespeare became a test by which they judged their skills and accomplishments. In 1866, Charlotte played Ophelia (with her husband Frithiof as Laertes), then in subsequent years Goneril (Frithiof as Albany), Desdemona (Frithiof as Iago), Beatrice to Frithiof's Benedick, and in 1870 what became her signature Shakespearean role, Lady Macbeth.[51] In addition to performing these roles in Swedish, in 1873 Raa became the first professional actor to perform Shakespeare in Finnish – Ophelia's and Lady Macbeth's mad scenes – which she also performed (in Swedish) as set pieces in Sweden and Norway. In Finland, these first Shakespearean performances had a lasting impact, breaking a barrier which not many years earlier had felt impenetrable.

A shift from Romantic to more realistic acting styles can also be seen over the course of Raa-Winterhjelm's career, reflecting similar changes across Europe. About her Lady Macbeth, one reviewer remarked that 'Mrs Winterhjelm's acting style is a little different from what we are used to. Hers, I would say is more classical, whereas ours is more realistic'.[52] While in the minds of some, Raa-Winterhjelm was on the old-fashioned side of this divide, towards the end of her career she, too, began to work towards more naturalistic acting. One of her set pieces had long been Ophelia's mad scenes, which she performed in 1874 in Christiania (now Oslo). She had apparently researched the role in an insane asylum; a Norwegian doctor working in the field commented how realistic the portrayal was. According to a reviewer, her performance was 'impressive for its artistic moderation, without the slightest hint of exaggeration, which in this scene it would be easy to fall into'.[53]

While Raa-Winterhjelm might be an exceptional case, her multilingualism is nevertheless typical of the educated classes in the Nordic countries, which made it relatively easy for them to keep up with developments elsewhere in Europe. In addition to her native Swedish, Raa-Winterhjelm spoke fluent German, French and English. She also knew a little Italian and later learned Finnish and passable Norwegian. It was said that she could read Latin by the age of nine.[54] In addition to performing in Swedish and Finnish, Raa-Winterhjelm also occasionally performed in Norwegian. For example, in 1877, Charlotte toured Norway with the Swedish singer Signe Hebbe, thrilling audiences with her performance of Ibsen's poem '*Terje Vigen*', which she recited in 'with astonishing skill in Norwegian'.[55] Nordic audiences were also familiar with bilingual or multilingual Shakespeare, as seen in Ira Aldridge's visit to Stockholm in 1857 (see Sivefors's chapter).

The linguistic tensions noted above can also gradually be seen in the reception of Raa-Winterhjelm's performances. As nationalist movements expanded in Norway and Finland, audiences became less interested in hearing accented Norwegian or Finnish, however much they had earlier applauded Raa-

Winterhjelm's efforts to promote Finnish-language theatre. In 1894, 25 years after starring in Aleksis Kivi's *Lea*, the first Finnish-language play performed by a professional theatre and 21 years after her first triumphant Finnish-language performances of Shakespeare, Raa-Winterhjelm was invited back to Finland, where she performed Lady Macbeth in Finnish, receiving less than stellar reviews, with one reviewer commenting on her pronunciation:

> It is admirable how well an actress speaking a foreign language can capture the nuances of what she is saying. Her pronunciation is relatively good, only sometimes she stretches out a consonant too long or accents end rhymes as is done in Swedish, her mother tongue.[56]

Comments like these show that the vernacular languages were themselves growing in prestige among the educated classes and during the next decades, enormous efforts would be made to translate Shakespeare into these languages and establish national theatres to perform them.

The structure of the book

The volume is organized chronologically. The first three chapters examine the earliest translations and performances of Shakespearean tragedy in Denmark and Sweden coinciding with political struggles between the countries, in terms of influences from the broader European arena. While translation directly from English became increasingly common, the intellectual and political contexts suggest a much more complex set of dependencies. Appropriately, the first chapters focus on Shakespeare's Danish play which was, unsurprisingly, a source of both attraction and controversy, and also on *Macbeth* which features prominently in early translations. Annelis Kuhlmann analyses the earliest translations of *Hamlet* into Danish, focusing on the one by Peter Foersom in 1813, which the author claims was an attempt by the Danish crown and the Royal Theatre of Copenhagen to reassert power at a time of political defeat by re-appropriating a story from Danish history. The same year saw the first translation of *Macbeth* into Swedish by Erik Gustaf Geijer. Kiki Lindell and Kent Hägglund examine this translation as an attempted break from dependence on French or German Shakespeare, in this case Schiller's German version, in favour of translation directly from English. The authors situate the translation in its turbulent historical context and question why it was never staged. In her chapter, Cecilia Lindskog Whiteley analyses differences in the treatment of Ophelia in the three earliest published translations of *Hamlet* into Swedish: Granberg (1819), Bjurbäck (1820) and Hagberg (1847), looking firstly at how Shakespeare gained cultural eminence in Sweden, as well as at shifting cultural constructions of gender at a time of struggle for women's rights.

The remaining chapters consider Shakespeare and the production of literary and national identity. As noted above, by the mid-nineteenth century, Shakespeare had become a significant influence on writers, dramatists and philosophers as they sought to reinforce their own national voices in vernacular languages. Jyrki Nummi, Eeva-Liisa Bastman and Erika Laamanen examine the first adaptation of *Macbeth* into Finnish, J. F. Lagervall's *Ruunulinna* [The Castle of the Crown] (1834), which illustrates the ways early Finnish authors worked to develop a vernacular literature both by linking their works to major European traditions as well as by using the resources of local folk traditions. While Lagervall's text is explicitly linked to nationalistic concerns, by the 1840s Shakespeare could serve as a whetting stone and source of imitation in sometimes unexpected places. James Newlin shows how, for Søren Kierkegaard, *King Lear* was a source of intense personal engagement but also of re-enactment at the character and plot level, revealing Kierkegaard's complicated debt to Romanticism. Taking up more theatrical concerns,

Per Sivefors discusses the reception of the African-American actor Ira Aldridge's performances in Stockholm as Othello and Shylock and traces how the racial stereotyping of comments in the press is aligned with changing ideals of acting and aesthetics in the mid-nineteenth century as seen, for example, in the case of Charlotte Raa-Winterhjelm.

A related theatrical theme is explored by Riitta Pohjola-Skarp in her chapter on the Finnish Aleksis Kivi's *Karkurit* [The Fugitives], Kivi's most Shakespearean play, which Pohjola-Skarp studies in the context of the competing pull of German Romanticism and realism, both as represented by Shakespeare, a struggle which determined the direction drama took in Finland. Returning to ideas about Shakespeare and gender, Lynn R. Wilkinson examines the ways *Romeo and Juliet,* among other Shakespearean works, influenced the great Swedish feminist writer Anne Charlotte Leffler and her idea of woman, providing an illuminating parallel to the Victorian focus on Shakespeare's female characters.[57] Just as Shakespeare figured in the shift between Romanticism and realism, as seen in Aleksis Kivi, Shakespeare figures in the shift in Norway between realism and early modernism, as seen in Knut Hamsun's critique of Shakespearean characters, whom he dismisses because they are incapable of reflecting the 'nerve' of contemporary urbanized life, as discussed by Martin Humpál. By the 1880s, Shakespeare had become well-enough established in the intellectual mindset to merit wholesale rejection by an author like Hamsun; while his anti-Shakespearean tirades have been read as part of his overall anti-British stance in politics, his very rejection arguably testifies to the grip that Shakespeare had come to have.

What comes next in the history of Shakespeare in the Nordic countries is a more thorough and politicized appropriation of Shakespeare in emerging national projects. To some extent, the present volume deals with budding movements in Finland and Norway, but the next collection will pay more systematic attention to these processes, including in Iceland. The present volume therefore has a cut-off date just before the time when these processes were coming into their own.

Notes

1. Joubin, 'Global Shakespeare Criticism', 432.
2. For example, Lanier, 'Shakespearean Rhizomatics'.
3. See, for example, Orkin, 'Local, Global, and "Glocal"'.
4. As Shakespeare did not have a significant impact on Icelandic culture until later in the nineteenth century, Iceland will be discussed in more detail in a subsequent volume that covers the period approximately 1890–1940.
5. For studies that do attempt a more comprehensive perspective see, for example, Sorelius, ed., *Shakespeare and Scandinavia* which is more a collection by Nordic scholars than a focused study on Nordic Shakespeare, and the brief overview of early translations in Smidt, 'The Discovery'. Occasional discussion of Shakespeare can be found in general surveys such as Marker and Marker, *A History*, e.g. 104–5 and 270–5.
6. Barton, *Scandinavia*, 383.
7. There was also a certain Shakespearean flavour to these Anglo-Danish links: Christian VII saw Garrick perform *Richard III* in London in 1768 (Langen, *Den afmægtige*, 262–3), and Caroline Mathilde would later be dethroned and imprisoned at the real-life Kronborg following the Danish *coup d'état* of 1784.
8. Sivefors, 'Trade Routes', 195.
9. Barton, *Scandinavia*, 344–5.
10. Strindberg, '*Julius Caesar*', 19. The translator responsible for the first complete version of the Sonnets (1871) was also a university professor of aesthetics at Uppsala, Carl Rupert Nyblom.
11. Pohjola-Skarp, 'Karkurit', 55.
12. Monié, *Ord som himlen når*, 262–3.
13. As Hans Östman suggests, the amount of literary material reaching Sweden directly in English rather than through French or German translation may have been underestimated (*English Fiction*, 19).
14. Smidt, 'The Discovery', 95.
15. Smidt, 'The Discovery', 96.

16 Smidt, 'The Discovery', 96.
17 Lembcke, 'Forord', v; our translation.
18 Lembcke, 'Forord', iv.
19 For the nationalist implications of Norwegian language politics, see Hoel, *Nasjonalisme*.
20 Ruud, *Shakespeare in Norway*, 1–10.
21 Ruud, *Shakespeare in Norway*, 105.
22 Molin, *Shakespeare och Sverige*, 13.
23 Sivefors, 'Trade Routes', 191.
24 Monié, *Ord som himlen når*, 241–2.
25 Monié, *Ord som himlen når*, 261.
26 It is impossible to say why *Macbeth* figures so prominently in early Nordic translation of Shakespeare. The Nordic peoples historically had close ties to Scotland, and Macbeth is, in many ways, the quintessential Romantic tragic hero, offering plenty of opportunity for emotional display. At least in Finland, in the 1870s there was a fascination with madwomen, and Ophelia's and Lady Macbeth's mad scenes were popular Shakespearean set pieces. For further discussion of *Macbeth* in connection with the earliest Swedish translation, see Lindell and Hägglund's chapter.
27 Quoted in Hellemann, *Suomen Kirjallisuus*, 471–2.
28 Rein, 'Muuan Shakespeare-juhla', 1.
29 For the earliest performance history in Sweden, see the recent Sivefors, 'Trade Routes'.
30 Aaltonen, 'La Perruque', 109.
31 Sivefors, 'Trade Routes', 199–200.
32 Fridén, '"Att vara"', 104–6.
33 Fridén, '"Att vara"', 106.
34 For example, the 1884 *Hamlet* at the Royal Theatre has been considered a landmark production in its emphasis on historical accuracy and artistic coherence. See Lagerroth, 'Den djärve traditionsbrytaren', 265–9.
35 Taylor, 'Shakespeare and Radicalism', 373.
36 Fridén, '"Att vara"', 109.

37 Foulkes, *Shakespeare Tercentenary*, 51.
38 Marker and Marker, *A History*, 105.
39 Marker and Marker, *A History*, 199–22; Ruud, *Shakespeare in Denmark*, 86–90; also, Sivefors' chapter in the present volume.
40 Marker and Marker, *A History*, 120–1.
41 Ruud, *Shakespeare in Norway*, 155.
42 Schmiesing, 'Bjørnson', 466, 473.
43 Schmiesing, 'Bjørnson', 466.
44 Quoted in Schmiesing, 'Bjørnson', 468.
45 Quoted in Schmiesing, 'Bjørnson', 473.
46 Ruud, *Shakespeare in Norway*, 155–6.
47 Krohn, *Lea*, 349, 360.
48 Molin, *Shakespeare och Sverige*, 72.
49 Krohn, *Lea*, 31.
50 Krohn, *Lea*, 234.
51 Krohn, *Lea*, 78–9.
52 Krohn, *Lea*, 405–6.
53 Quoted in Krohn, *Lea*, 247.
54 Krohn, *Lea*, 101, 19.
55 Krohn, *Lea*, 283.
56 Krohn, *Lea*, 406.
57 Poole, *Shakespeare*, 92–7.

Works cited

Aaltonen, Sirkku, 'La Perruque in a Rented Apartment: Rewriting Shakespeare in Finland', *Ilha do Desterro: A Journal of Language and Literature* 36 (1999), 141–59.

Barton, H. Arnold, *Scandinavia in the Revolutionary Era, 1760–1815* (Minneapolis, 1986).

Bosman, Anston, 'Shakespeare and Globalization', in Margreta De Grazia and Stanley Wells, eds, *The New Cambridge Companion to Shakespeare* (Cambridge, 2010), 285–300.

Bulman, James C., ed., *The Oxford Handbook of Shakespeare and Performance* (Oxford, 2017).
Delabastita, Dirk, Jozef De Vos and Paul Franssen, eds, *Shakespeare and European Politics* (Newark, 2008).
Delabastita, Dirk and Lieven D'hulst, eds, *European Shakespeares: Translating Shakespeare in the Romantic Age* (Amsterdam, 1992).
Einarsson, Stefán, 'Shakespeare in Iceland: A Historical Survey', *ELH*, 7/4 (1940), 272–85.
Erich, Mikko V., *William Shakespeare ja hänen runoutensa* (Helsinki, 1916).
Foulkes, Richard, *The Shakespeare Tercentenary of 1864* (London, 1984).
Fridén, Ann, '"Att vara eller inte vara": Shakespeare på kunglig scen i 1800-talets Stockholm', in Claes Rosenqvist, ed., *Den svenska nationalscenen: Tradition och reformer på Dramaten under 200 år* (Stockholm, 1988), 102–23.
Hellemann, Jarl, *Suomen Kirjallisuus VIII*, ed. J. Tarkka (Helsinki, 1970).
Hirn, Yrjö, 'Shakespeare i Finland', *Finsk Tidskrift*, 4 (1916), 245–70.
Hoel, Ole Løkensgard, *Nasjonalisme i norsk målstrid 1848–1865* (Oslo, 1996).
Joubin, Alexa Alice, 'Global Shakespeare Criticism Beyond the Nation State', in James C. Bulman, ed., *The Oxford Handbook of Shakespeare and Performance* (Oxford, 2017), 423–40.
Krohn, Helmi, *Lea: Hedvig Charlotte Winterhjelm Ihmisenä ja Taiteilijana* (Helsinki, 1922).
Lagerroth, Ulla-Britta, 'Den djärve traditionsbrytaren', in Ulla-Britta Lagerroth and Ingeborg Nordin Hemmel, eds, *Ny svensk teaterhistoria*, ii: *1800-talets teater* (Gidlunds, 2007), 261–76.
Langen, Ulrik, *Den afmægtige: En biografi om Christian 7* (Copenhagen, 2008).
Lanier, Douglas, 'Shakespearean Rhizomatics: Adaptation, Ethics, Value', in Alexa Joubin and Elizabeth Rivlin, eds, *Shakespeare and the Ethics of Appropriation* (Basingstoke, 2014), 21–40.
Lembcke, Edvard, 'Forord', in *William Shakspeare's Dramatiske værker*, i (Copenhagen, 1861), iii–vi.
Marker, Frederick J. and Lise-Lone Marker, *A History of Scandinavian Theatre* (Cambridge, 1996).

Molin, Nils, *Shakespeare och Sverige intill 1800 – talets mitt: En översikt av hans inflytande* (Gothenburg, 1931).

Monié, Karin, *Ord som himlen når: Carl August Hagberg – en levnadsteckning* (Stockholm, 2008).

Orkin, Martin, 'Local, Global, and "Glocal"', in Bruce R. Smith and Katherine Rowe, eds, *The Cambridge Guide to the Worlds of Shakespeare* (New York, 2016), 1070–77.

Östman, Hans, *English Fiction, Poetry and Drama in Eighteenth Century Sweden, 1765–1799: A Preliminary Study* (Stockholm, 1983).

Pohjola-Skarp, Riitta, 'Karkurit – viisinäytöksinen murhenäytelmä' in Aleksis Kivi, *Karkurit*, ed. Riitta Pohjola-Skarp et al. (Helsinki, 2017), 53–97.

Poole, Adrian, *Shakespeare and the Victorians* (London, 2004).

Rein, Th[iodolf], 'Muuan Shakespeare-juhla 52 vuotta sitten', *Sunnuntai* 15–16 (1916), 1–2.

Ruud, Martin, *An Essay Toward a History of Shakespeare in Norway* (Minneapolis, 1917).

Ruud, Martin, *An Essay Toward a History of Shakespeare in Denmark* (Minneapolis, 1920).

Schmiesing, Ann, 'Bjørnson and the Inner Plot of *A Midsummer Night's Dream*', *Scandinavian Studies*, 74/4 (2002), 465–82.

Sivefors, Per, 'Trade Routes, Politics and Culture: Shakespeare in Sweden', in Janet Clare and Dominique Goy-Blanquet, eds, *Migrating Shakespeare: First European Encounters, Routes and Networks* (London, 2021), 189–207.

Smidt, Kristian, 'The Discovery of Shakespeare in Scandinavia', in Dirk Delabastita and Lieven D'hulst, eds, *European Shakespeares: Translating Shakespeare in the Romantic Age* (Amsterdam, 1992), 91–103.

Sorelius, Gunnar, ed., *Shakespeare and Scandinavia* (Newark, 2002).

Strindberg, August, '*Julius Caesar*: Shakespeare's Historical Drama', in Sorelius, ed. *Shakespeare and Scandinavia*, 19–30.

Taylor, Anthony, 'Shakespeare and Radicalism: The Uses and Abuses of Shakespeare in Nineteenth-Century Popular Politics', *The Historical Journal*, 45/2 (2002), 357–79.

1

The first Danish production of *Hamlet* (1813): A theatrical representation of a national crisis

Annelis Kuhlmann

William Shakespeare's *Hamlet* is solidly connected to the history of Denmark. This is primarily due to the location of Elsinore, north of Copenhagen, and to the connection with the medieval Scandinavian legend about Amleth, transcribed by Saxo Grammaticus in *Gesta Danorum*. This chapter, however, charts the theatrical history of the first production of *Hamlet* in Danish on 12 May 1813, analysing the interpretational choices made for this particular production at the Royal Danish Theatre in Copenhagen at a time of crisis in Danish history.

In the first years of the nineteenth century, Denmark and Sweden found themselves on opposite sides in the Napoleonic Wars and historical alliances were fracturing. In this situation of geopolitical conflict, the translator, Peter Thun Foersom (1777–1817), who also played Hamlet, and the director, Frederik Schwarz (1753–1838) chose essentially to de-politicize Shakespeare's play, turning it more into a patriotic Danish family drama. In what can be seen as self-censorship, references to countries outside Denmark–Norway were removed, e.g., Laertes is sent to Norway; the younger male characters are advised not to travel abroad (Paris, Wittenberg etc.) so as not to end up in a war; and the entire Fortinbras plot has been eliminated.

Behind the present dramaturgical decoding of *Hamlet* is an understanding of theatre and drama as embedded practices of acting techniques and staging in a contextual frame. This context includes royal interest in *Hamlet*, the production's roots in late German Enlightenment and early Danish Romanticism and the material conditions of the Royal Danish Theatre, where sets recycled from previous nationalistic plays set the tone for *Hamlet*. Finally, I discuss the long-lasting effects this production had on Danish directorial traditions, where Foersom's and Schwarz's dramaturgical solutions held sway until late in the century.

Royal interest in *Hamlet*

The selection of *Hamlet* for the first Danish-language production of Shakespeare can perhaps be traced to the interest of King Christian VII (1749–1808) in Shakespeare's works. During a visit to London in 1768, the 19-year-old King went to Drury Lane and met with the famous actor, David Garrick.[1] Christian VII had a printed version of *Hamlet* from the JEJ Boydell Shakespeare Gallery, published 29 September 1796, which I found in the library of Her Majesty the Queen,

Margrethe II. Significantly, this version is complete and has no cuts or alterations whatsoever. The preface, by George Steevens whose research was an inspiration to Foersom in his translations, is from 1791.[2]

In thinking of the first Danish production of *Hamlet*, we must remember that there was no democracy in the country at that time: The Royal Danish Theatre was literally the king's own theatre, where the king's handling of Danish affairs was reflected in the dramaturgical solutions and actions taking place on the stage. Until 1849, when Denmark moved to a constitutional monarchy, the theatre followed the same autocratic/absolute model as the monarchy. The 1813 production of *Hamlet*, situated at the heart of the country's political power, can thus be seen as 'playing a role': to calm audiences, prevent them from seeing potential governmental problems and discouraging political conflict. Time really was out of joint, due to the profound economic, political and warfare crisis within the state of Denmark.[3]

German *Hamlet* in Odense, Denmark

Another important context of the first Danish-language production of *Hamlet* is German-language productions performed in Odense.[4] In 1791, supported by local noblemen from castles on Fyn and smaller islands with German family bonds, Carl Heinrich Friebach (1739–96) was invited to establish a theatre, with a group of forty members, which could perform in German, understood by the educated elite. Friebach's theatre group was well known in Denmark among aristocratic theatre lovers and had performed in Altona, a wealthy city under the Danish monarchy. On 7 March 1792, in the banquet hall of the town hall in Odense, Friebach's group performed Friedrich Schröder's German translation of *Hamlet*.[5] Schröder's translation had been used previously in Hamburg with Schröder himself playing Hamlet.[6] In the local

Odense newspaper, an anonymous reviewer commented that this *Hamlet* was much better than one he had seen some years earlier in Germany. He had also conferred with other people, who knew about tragedies (*sørgespil*), and everyone agreed that this performance was very successful.[7]

A decade passed before the influence of this German performance was seen, in the first Danish production in Copenhagen at the Royal Danish Theatre. When Friebach's group performed the German *Hamlet* in Odense, Frederik Schwarz saw the performance, as he was in Odense to build a theatre school there. Schwarz would go on to direct the first Danish *Hamlet* in Copenhagen. However, Schwarz had other contacts with *Hamlet* as well. In 1793, he saw David Garrick performing Shakespeare at Drury Lane in London and it seems likely that Garrick inspired him to continue planning to stage *Hamlet* at the Royal Danish Theatre. In his journal, Schwarz wrote a small poem, dated Copenhagen 22 March 1793: 'Be tiny in yourself! Be large to Danish honour! / So you can be more to Denmark than Garrick to England'.[8]

Borders and limits for *Hamlet* at the Royal Danish Theatre

In 1777, a prose translation of *Hamlet* had been published in Danish by Johannes Boye, at the time a 21-year-old student (Shakespeare 1777), but it had not been performed on stage. Foersom's context was different; he was translating for performance and, indeed, was planning on playing Hamlet himself.[9] Examination of the prompt copy reveals how the translator and director moulded the tragedy into a play suitable for the Danish monarchy during a time of radical political difficulties, showing the extent of artistic censorship in the historical and political context.[10] The earliest Danish performance of *Hamlet* thus reflected not only theatrical tendencies but also the historical changes taking place around Denmark's borders. To date, most previous research on this production has focused on the linguistic and stylistic aspects of the translated text.[11] For example, Paul Erik Høy has investigated the stylistic choices of a number of Hamlet translations into Danish, concluding that the Danish language in Foersom's translation is unnecessarily archaic and highly poetic, with Christian vocabulary relating to the notion of the consciousness and questions of doubt in the soliloquies changed from pagan doubt to ethical godliness.[12] Little work, however, has been carried out on the socio-political and cultural milieu in which Foersom's translation was performed. The present chapter therefore seeks to show how this production becomes a truly Danish *Hamlet* not just at the Royal Danish Theatre, but also in the history of Danish theatre in the early nineteenth century.

Shakespeare's text already contextualizes political issues relating to the heir to the throne and the continuity of the monarchy, underlined by the death of Hamlet's father, the old king and the passing of the crown to the dead king's brother, Claudius, who marries the newly widowed Gertrude. Prince Hamlet's suspicions about his father's death are mirrored in the play-within-the-play, *The Mousetrap*, performed – under Hamlet's guidance and after providing the actors with his preferred artistic direction – in front of the newly married royal couple. On one level, Prince Hamlet hopes to glimpse the newlyweds' reaction and so gain confirmation of his suspicions. On another level, however, this theatrical mirror offers insight into the limits of power, both within geopolitical and artistic contexts.[13] In the political realities of Danish society in 1813, the narrative of *Hamlet* might similarly have been seen as having a potentially destabilizing effect on the audience, since Hamlet's instructions to the players were cut. It seems that the performance, in a sense, risked becoming a double mousetrap for the spectators, who were all-too-aware of political instability and questions of succession.

Europe had just witnessed a decade of political turmoil following the French Revolution. During the Napoleonic wars, Denmark had backed Napoleon, while Sweden sided with the British. This split left Denmark with the British nation as an enemy, as seen in the Battle of Copenhagen in 1801, followed by the bombardment by the British fleet in 1807, resulting in the loss of a large portion of the Danish fleet. The bombardment resulted in severe fires, tremendous destruction and human loss. When Foersom published his translation of *Hamlet* in 1807, the country was in dire financial straits, and divided between conservative and liberal forces. The political situation continued to evolve between the translation's publication and the first performance in 1813. Christian VII died in 1808, succeeded as king of Denmark and Norway by his son Frederik VI (1768–1839). Frederik VI wished to find a peaceful solution to the problem of Norway, which the Swedish king was hoping to annex, and which itself was torn between remaining loyal to Denmark or declaring its independence and electing its own king. Both Frederik VI and his Norwegian-born minister of foreign affairs, Niels Rosenkrantz (!), thought of Denmark as a Scandinavian state.[14] Then, at the beginning of 1814, under the terms of the Treaty of Kiel, Denmark had to accept the loss of Norway, which was forced into an alliance with Sweden. Suddenly, geographical borders had been redrawn and these new boundaries had an impact on the arts in general and theatre more specifically.

Of course, as Cay Dollerup has pointed out, in its day, Shakespeare's *Hamlet* was itself responding to political events connected to English succession: 'When the tragedy was first produced in London in 1601/2, on the eve of the end of Queen Elizabeth I's long and important reign, it was obvious that James VI of Scotland would succeed her on the English throne, and James' wife was a Dane, Queen Anna'.[15] Several scholars have suggested that, historically speaking, Shakespeare must have been aware of the Danish monarchy and the realities surrounding Elsinore.[16] At the same time, with Shakespeare's tradition of doubling spaces, using both oxymoron and distancing techniques, this information is not only to be perceived on the concrete level of geopolitics but also as a poetic expression at the symbolic visual level, such as when Hamlet claims that 'Denmark's a prison',[17] followed by his comment to Rosencrantz:

ROSENCRANTZ
Then is the world one.

HAMLET
A goodly one, in which there are many confines, wards, and dungeons – Denmark being one o'th' worst.

ROSENCRANTZ
We think not so, my lord.

HAMLET
Why, then 'tis none to you; for there is nothing either good or bad, but thinking makes it so. To me it is a prison. (*Ham* 2.2.243–50)

This comment on topicality is at the same time both innocent and polemic, subtly suggesting the opposite of a unified world. Later, this is emphasized by Hamlet's comments on the world as theatre. In *Hamlet*, the displacement of topicality onto a theatricalized setting becomes the tool Hamlet uses to question Claudius' guilt. In the Danish context, the play also has another kind of topicality, of Denmark as a cross-cultural and transnational place of encounter. On the narrative level, a number of countries and monarchies are mentioned, for example France (Laertes' return to Paris), Germany (Hamlet and Horatio were studying in Wittenberg), Norway (Prince Fortinbras), Poland (the late king Hamlet and the prince of Norway) and England (the ambassadors). All these names and places can be seen as dualities since, on one level, they refer to people in and from real geographical locations while, on another, the people and places are simply words in the fictive narrative. In the version used for the theatre production of *Hamlet* in 1813 at the Royal Danish Theatre, by contrast, all situations concerning foreign affairs were cut, so that they would not call attention to the spectators' international mind set or even imagination. The play ended up being a local Danish play, adapted to political realities.

Danish cultural ownership of *Hamlet* before the Danish constitution

Foersom's translation of *Hamlet* was extremely influential in creating a Danish understanding of Shakespeare's play that lasted until 1864, when Edvard Lembcke (1815–1897) published his translation of *Hamlet,* largely based on Foersom's translation. In important ways, *Hamlet* was turned into a kind of Danish national narrative.[18] Peter Foersom had entered The Royal Danish Theatre in Copenhagen as an actor in 1798 and the following year became a member of the theatre's permanent artistic staff. As an actor, Foersom would have primarily performed in the early romantic repertoire which was fashionable at the time. In doing so, he came across Danish playwrights like Johannes Ewald (1743–1781) and Adam Oehlenschläger (1779–1850), both of whom often had their poetry associated with Shakespeare's; Oehlenschläger also translated *A Midsummer Night's Dream* (1816).[19] The biographer Nicolai Bøgh (1843–1905), who nearly a century later wrote a biographical sketch about Peter Foersom in *En levnedsskildring* (1895), commented on the actor's decision to create a *Hamlet* for Danish audiences in the following manner:

> One ended then up with *Hamlet*, because the assumption was that a play, taken from Saxo and set in Denmark, should be of some interest to contemporary audiences; it was also the perception, that it would succeed even if only the principal character was well performed, and it was expected that Foersom was the man for that job; he did not have any higher artistic wish than to play this role, 'even if it was only this one time'.[20]

In this quotation it is apparent that, even at the end of the nineteenth century, the connection of historical *Hamlet* to the history of Denmark was still assumed to be why it was chosen to be performed in the early years of the century. This assumption also says something about the understanding of artistic reality and the notion of mimesis. *Hamlet* was announced then, as a *new* (according to the newspaper advertisement), *contemporary play*, contextualizing contemporary matters of territorial loss and disarmament.[21]

Peter Foersom's translation of *Hamlet*[22]

In terms of genre, the translation of *Hamlet* was not called a tragedy, but *Sørgespil* – a direct translation of the German notion of *Trauerspiel* – well-known from Lessing's notion of bourgeois tragic genre, used for works like *Miss Sara Sampson* (1755) and *Emilia Galotti* (1772), the latter still actively performed in Danish at The Royal Danish Theatre in the 1810s. One of the reasons why this genre notion is relevant here has to do with the dominant understanding in Denmark that tragedies could not be justified in classical forms. On the one hand, the German classicist tradition used the Trauerspiel notion, which reached Danish theatres, and this genre had a huge impact on Ewald, who adapted it to his own style. On the other hand, pure tragedy was no longer being taken seriously. In 1772 the Copenhagen-based Norwegian poet, Johan Herman Wessel (1742–85) had written *Love without Stockings (Kjærlighed uden Strømper)*, a generic parody of French classicist tragedy, which made it difficult in Denmark to perceive French classicist tragedy as a serious genre. The French *drame bourgeois*, however, had some affinity in Copenhagen circles around the Royal Court Theatre, due to earlier performances of a few of Denis Diderot's plays.

In a letter to Knud Lyne Rahbek (1760–1830), the director of the Royal Danish Theatre, Foersom acknowledges some of the difficulties which he had faced with the translation:[23]

> Dear Professor Rahbek! – or even better, as you have allowed me – dear Rahbek! Here comes Hamlet and I hope he commends himself to you. Some *errors calami* may have escaped my attention, which I ask that you excuse. I have used Steevens' text, since I did not have any better; however, I often left him where scenes from *Hamlet* have been set or written in a way which I liked more. There are a couple of gaps as I still await some information from Malone's edition, which I look out for on a daily basis.
>
> Concerning the verse in my translation, you will now and then notice some irregularities, and perhaps at certain places even notice that I have ignored the rules. In that regard, I ought to say that where rules are missing in my version, there is also a lack of rules in the original. I have also permitted myself some little mistakes with the meter, where the correct meter would remove vigour and power from the poet. The audience should not be aware of such changes; likewise they will not be noticed by those who only read and do not scan the piece. It seems to me that it is so easy to get used to being indulgent with such things, and finally one may begin to love them like a couple of freckles which the burning summer sun has left on the face of a person you love. With regards the larger changes in the translation, I ask for indulgence, as it was not written in a scientific manner, and by an *ex professor* who left science at a time when he should have begun to worship it. Thus, Hamlet and I commend ourselves to your indulgence and friendship.
>
> Yours truly,
29 Sept 1805. P. Foersom.[24]

Once on the staff of the Royal Danish Theatre, Foersom explored different artistic avenues, including translation for the stage. In 1803 he delivered his first, a translation of Shakespeare's *Julius Caesar,* and it is known that he had also begun working on *Hamlet.*[25] The theatre did not dare stage *Julius Caesar,* as it was considered too political. This reaction provides some background to the choices Foersom made when translating *Hamlet,* especially in terms of the omissions in the staged production.

Beginning in the 1770s, dramas in the repertoire of the Royal Danish Theatre were published prior to appearing on stage. This practice gave the audience and censors the occasion to read, interpret and express their critique before the play was produced. Foersom first published his translation of *Hamlet* in 1807, six years prior to the stage production.[26] In 1811, a revised edition of Foersom's translation of *Hamlet* came out.[27] While, as we saw above, Foersom speaks of translating directly from English, scholars have noted influences from German Shakespeare as well. Rubow, for example, says that 'undoubtedly it seems that he has used the still unaccomplished Schlegelian translation as his guide for the whole and the details'.[28] Schlegel's German translation of *Hamlet* became available to readers in 1798 and Foersom is likely to have heard about it from Rahbek, who was well-informed about German theatre, especially the Nationaltheater in Hamburg. The two had been discussing *Hamlet* since the late 1790s. Øyvind Anker also draws our attention to the influence of Schröder's translation, which was used for the earlier productions at Hamburg Nationaltheater, 1777–1778.[29] Rahbek was not satisfied with Schröder's solution to Act 5, which he had turned into a happy ending, so that neither Hamlet nor Laertes die.[30] Rahbek was convinced that not even in England, Germany or France would there be fewer changes to the text than he had made together with Foersom.

The volume that includes Peter Foersom's translations of both *Julius Caesar* and *Hamlet,* dated on the frontispiece 1806, but published the following year, begins with a preface listing sources used during the translations as well as some of the considerations from the translation process.[31] Additionally, both plays are followed by further comments from Foersom. In the case of *Hamlet* these read:

> Each reader, who, impartial and without prejudice, stands in front of this masterpiece, will be moved and penetrated by its perfection, without having Johnson, Steevens etc. at hand: – and this person will see the inner structure of the work, he opens the shrine with the magic key, which Germany's Shakspear has handed him in his Wilhelm Meister.
>
> (Foersom, trans., *Tragiske værker*, 236).

Fascinatingly enough, Foersom expects his audience to have reading knowledge of both English and German. On the front page of his translation of *Hamlet*, Foersom used a quotation from the Berliner romanticist, Novalis (1772–1801), saying: 'O! einsam steht und tiefbeträbt, / wer heiß und fromm die Vorzeit liebt!'. In the 1790s, Novalis was greatly inspired by Shakespeare's poetry, especially in Schlegel's new translations, which were described as having similarities with Goethe's poetry in *Wilhelm Meisters Lehrjahre* (1795–1796), in which *Hamlet* is discussed at length.[32] These representatives of the German ideals of poetry certainly also inspired Foersom, who was aware of translations and stagings of *Hamlet* in France, Italy and Germany by Wieland, Eschenburg and Schlegel, respectively. The latter published several versions, some of which Schröder staged in Hamburg. Interestingly, according to announcements in newspapers, extracts from those stagings were performed in Danish at the Royal Court Theatre in Copenhagen in February 1813, a few months before the opening night of Foersom's *Hamlet*.[33] Due to the historically close relationship between Germany and Denmark, the theatre-going elites of contemporary Copenhagen often attended performances shown in Hamburg, which also makes it highly likely that Schlegel's translations of *Hamlet*, performed in 1778 and 1782 at the Hamburg Nationaltheater, were a reference point for early Danish translations. One noticeable influence seems to be Schlegel's decision to cut out the character of Fortinbras, so that he does not ascend to the Danish throne. Schlegel also replaced the characters' names with more German-sounding names. According to Rubow, there is no doubt that Foersom had used Schlegel's, at that time unfinished, translation as a guideline for the whole and for some details of the play.[34]

Some of these German translations and performances were taking place while Foersom was working on his own translation of *Hamlet*, and which made him comment on Hamlet's multiple layers of understandings, both inside and outside the theatre. Concerning the compositional order, it gives interesting comments about the dramaturgical consequences of adapting Shakespeare's play for contemporary Danish reality.

> I mean the characters' outer relations, by which they are brought from one place to another, or one way or another are connected by certain random events, to be too insignificant, and only tangentially to be mentioned, or simply eliminated them. Probably these threads are only thin and loose, but they pass through the whole play, and they hold together what otherwise would fall apart, and also really do fall apart, when you cut them off, and think that you have done more than enough, when you let the endings remain.
> (Foersom, trans., *Tragiske værker*, 247)

Foersom was apparently eager to remove the majority of details referring to the characters having relationships with foreign countries:

> To those outer relations I count the riots in Norway, the war with the young Fortinbras, the legation to the old uncle, the settled dispute, the young Fortinbras' expedition to Poland, and his return by the end. Likewise, Horatio's

return from Wittenberg, Hamlet's wish to go there, Laertes' trip to France, his return, Hamlet being sent to England, his imprisonment by the pirates, the death of both the officers at the court after the Uriah letter: all these are circumstances and events, which could make a novel wide and broad; however, the unity in this play, in which furthermore, the hero has no plan, is harmful and highly full of errors.

However, those errors are like decorative pillars on a building, which you do not dare to remove, without having first built a firm wall underneath. My suggestion is thus not at all to touch upon those bigger situations; but as a whole, and in singularities, to spare them as much as possible, to throw away all those outer, single, spread out and distractive motives at once, and replace one single alternative in their place, which is also in the play, and that is the riots in Norway. Here is the plan.

After Old Hamlet's death, the newly conquered men of Norway become unruly. ... Horatio knows the old King; since he has been part of his last battlefield and considered of note; as such the first ghost-scene will not lose anything as a result of this change. The new King now gives audience to Horatio, and sends Laertes to Norway with the news, that the navy soon will land; meanwhile Horatio will fight back with its equipment: meanwhile, the Mother will not allow Hamlet to go to sea with Laertes.
(Foersom, trans., *Tragiske værker*, 247–9)

In the afterword, Foersom legitimizes his reducing of outer political circumstances by pointing out that, in most editions of the play, the character of Fortinbras is cut out, and this seems to be the approach he took with regard to Schwarz's first staging of the play in Denmark. As John A. Mills has demonstrated, there are several examples of *Hamlets* where Fortinbras has been removed, including those by Barrymore,

Betterton and Macready. Foersom himself mentions that he knew about Betterton's version.[35]

The first Danish production of *Hamlet*

When Shakespeare's *Hamlet* was first produced at the Royal Danish Theatre on 12 May 1813, Frederik Schwarz directed; in his prompt copy, he signed the volume as 'Hr. Instructeur'.[36] Schwarz, 16 May 1813'. He received this copy as a present after the opening night of *Hamlet*. The position of 'stage director' was not yet frequently used; however, Schwarz had formally held this title since the end of the eighteenth century, since he was founder of the Dramatic Society, where he taught those at an early stage in their acting careers.[37] Those who carried out the work of *instructeur* were often actors themselves. In this section, I analyse how stage design, as well as the cuts mentioned above, can be seen as responding to the historical moment.

The first Danish *Hamlet* has been characterized as belonging to *Guldalderen* [The Golden Age]. This 'definition' can, especially in retrospect, illuminate some of the dramaturgical choices of the 'stage design' of *Hamlet*, as Torben Krogh states:

> There were a number of choices made for the *Hamlet* that was performed for the first time on 12 May 1813, and which was introduced by a prologue by Oehlenschläger, spoken by Foersom, who also played the role of Hamlet. There was not much money spent on the mise en scène. A few new costumes were acquired, 'a skull', some 'bones made out of twigs' and a few wings were painted, five of which represented tumuli. The inventory shows that otherwise, only older settings were used, like the hall from *Herman von Unna*, the lord lieutenant and the queen's room from *Dyveke*, and a room from *Niels Ebbesen* ... That Foersom was dissatisfied with the rehearsal facilities becomes

evident from a letter, in which he says, that 'our theatre is probably the only one, in which a play like *Hamlet* would be performed after 2 or 2½ rehearsals'.[38]

It is interesting that the notion of 'mise en scène' appears here, as this performance took place in the very early stages of professionalized stage directing. The term is normally dated to 1820 and primarily connects to the French tradition, referring to the Parisian boulevard theatres in the early days of industrialization. This perhaps demonstrates that even though leftovers from other performances were reused as set decoration for *Hamlet*, there seems to have been an aesthetic and perhaps even subtle idea in the mise en scène. The staging, designed by Schwarz, aimed to help the actors remember where to place themselves in the arrangement on stage, especially as they had a very short time to rehearse the whole arrangement.

These recycled stage settings, however, are also significant in the ways they evoked a heroic Danish past, in part by being connected to earlier celebrations of Danish royalty. For example, the *Hamlet* production recycled stage settings previously used for celebrating Christian VII's birthday, 29 January. It was not uncommon to reuse settings from production to production, and this can also be seen as a sign of the theatre's limited budget.[39] Significantly, there were absolutely clear visual references to national pride, as the settings were known from particular kinds of plays all going back one way or another to celebratory performances given around the king's birthday.[40] Images in these settings referred to Danish mythology and history; in particular they evoked recent heroic characters. The technical stage facilities at the Royal Danish Theatre were quite humble, but sets from three earlier performances helped to establish a nationalist tone for the production.

One of these was A. F. Skjöldebrand's *Herman von Unna*, a contemporary German libretto, published in 1800 and set to opera music by Georg Joseph Vogler (1749–1814) and dance by Vincenzo Galeotti (1733–1816). *Herman von Unna*, performed at the king's birthday celebration, contained a series of adventures set in the fifteenth century in which the proceedings of a secret tribunal, under the emperors Winceslaus and Sigismond, was revealed. The symbol of such narrative reference speaks to the audience of not only royal celebrations, but also double narratives of the history of power and defeat.

Other settings came from Ole Johann Samsøe's contemporary play *Dyveke* (1795), named for Christian II's mistress (1490–1517) who died after eating a poisoned cherry. Dyveke inspired many composers and Samsøe's version was performed at the king's birthday celebration on 30 January 1796. Some members of the audience at the early performances of Foersom's *Hamlet* must have remembered the image of the Queen's room where Dyveke experienced such a tragic death. The scenic artist Thomas Bruun created the decorations, which have been identified as some of the first 'gothic' indoor decorations in Denmark, although his outdoor sceneries referenced more romantic landscapes. Bruun had taken over from Peter Cramer (1726–82), whose name has been linked to this particular decoration, known as 'Cramer's Hall' or the more intimate term, 'Capinet'.[41]

Finally, settings were recycled from Christian Levin Sander's *Niels Ebbesen af Nørreriis eller Danmarks Befrielse* (1797), about the Danish nobleman, Niels Ebbesen (1308–40) who in a conflict killed Gerhard III, count of Holstein, the ruler of Jutland between 1332–1340 when there was no Danish monarch. This narrative was yet another symbolic national reference to the conflict inside *Hamlet,* as if pointing to a latent threat in the actual political situation in the spring of 1813. The late eighteenth-century version of *Niels Ebbesen* became very popular, presumably because the nationalistic slant seemed relevant during the culmination of the Napoleonic war. Both *Dyveke* and *Niels Ebbesen* are today considered as almost national mythological material and were revived on the eve of the Second World War to celebrate national resistance.

At the beginning of the nineteenth century, it was quite common to re-use the same stage settings for several theatre productions.[42] These images referencing other repertory (including patriotic national) celebrations can be seen as having a certain kind of double imaginative force, expressing symbolic meanings in *Hamlet*. When most of the critical-reflective passages from Shakespeare's text were cut, and thus not spoken on stage, the visual settings would speak the unspoken words, referring to crime, such as murder and poisoning, but also to national identity and patriotism. The intention of the set design for the first performance of *Hamlet* was to emphasize the similarity to late-medieval warfare. This had become part of the Danish national narrative and, in retrospect, can be seen as the beginning of a national stage canon.

In addition to the ways settings were used to highlight Danish power, the cuts by Foersom and Schwarz to the text work to depoliticize the play, drawing the audience's attention away from the current political crisis. By cutting out Fortinbras, the entire Norwegian subplot in the play was reduced to a minimum.[43] In the Dramatis Personae, some of the characters have been crossed out by hand: namely Voltemand and Cornelius, the Danish ambassadors, as well as Fortinbras, Prince of Norway. As Øyvind Anker points out, this was a consequence of various scenes and parts of scenes involving these characters having disappeared from the translation. For example, in Act 4, the entire fourth scene has been deleted, a logical consequence of having deliberately cut out Fortinbras. Therefore, Fortinbras never returns from Norway with an army to fight the Poles for a patch of ground. By eliminating themes of foreign affairs and borders, *Hamlet* is turned into a domestic play about Danish royalty, rendering it politically suitable for the times.

References to the state of Denmark were also cut. According to Karen Krogh, the exchange beginning with Marcellus' line 'Something is rotten in the state of Denmark' and Horatio's answer, 'Heaven will direct it' (*Ham* 1.4.90–1) was deleted in the performance version of the play's manuscript.[44] In addition, the 'Krigsmarsch' in the final act was also cut, meaning there are no references to war in the state of Denmark. These cuts have the effect of turning what is partly a political tragedy into a family one, as if also deciding that 'war is a concern in foreign countries, not Denmark', leaving readers/spectators with only an illusory image and memory of theatre as reflecting the world. While such cuts were commonplace at the time, for example the German version by Schröder includes the march, from that point of view the omission was not common practice in the most influential contemporary theatre translations and productions. Cuts connected to Norway removed the potential for subliminal references to the existing political situation when the play was first staged. This is not only a matter of cutting out lines, but it is also cutting out cultural memories of events affecting the Danish Crown. However, this case also shows that silence speaks louder than words, as these omissions trace their own trajectory of silence in the theatre.

There were other cuts as well, connected to different sorts of concerns. For example, Schwarz removed Hamlet's advice to the players (*Ham* 2.2). This is a radical solution of an explicitly theatrical quality, as the play hereby loses its rehearsal theme as an artistic subplot, indicating that theatre as an art form could affect society. This cut impacts the play's complexity, on an artistic level creating a kind of 'double moral' regarding the position of a bourgeois citizen and the Royal Danish Theatre itself. In addition, the dialogue between Osric and Hamlet, as well as the duel between Hamlet and Laertes was also cut, the latter significantly reducing images of violence in the play.

The legacy of Foersom's *Hamlet*

The notion of borders works in both time and space. This is why it is also useful to look at Foersom's *Hamlet* from a diachronic perspective.

There are other handwritten notes in another copy of Foersom's translation of *Hamlet*, held in the Royal Danish Theatre's library. These begin with a list of names of the persons, who, over time, were in charge of the 'regie' (placing actors and

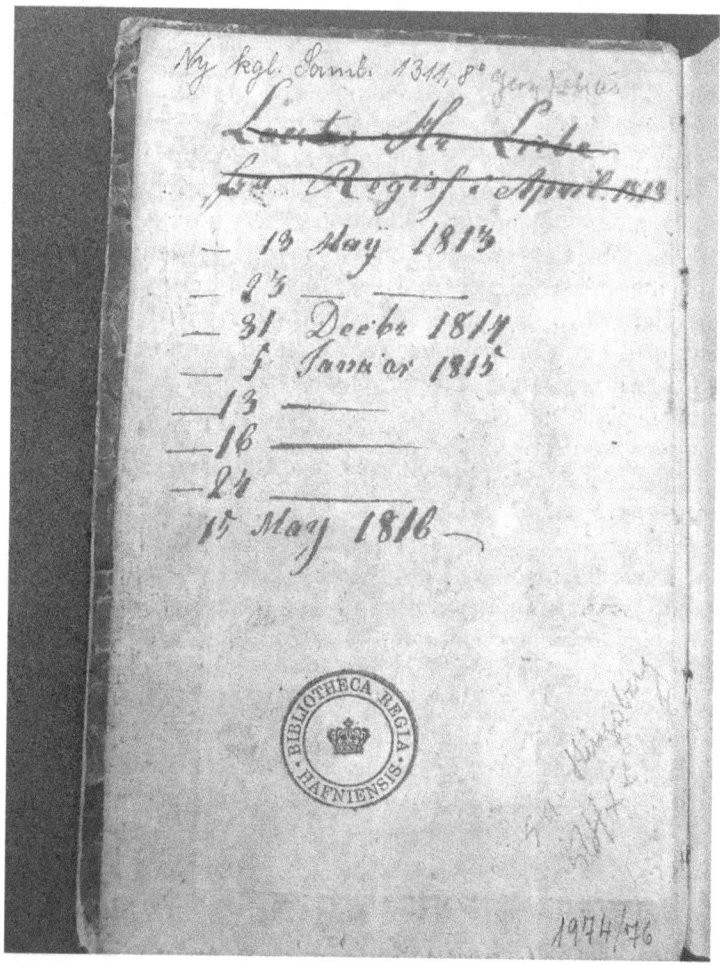

FIGURE 1.1 *From Foersom's translation of* Hamlet, *submitted for publication 1806.*

props on stage) starting in April 1813 and progressing through the nineteenth century. These notes also provide details of names of actors at the theatre, for instance, on 18 May 1872, Hr Holst, Seeman (Laertes), Hr Nyrop (Marcellus). The notes suggest that different actors in various revivals used this text and that Foersom's 1813 *Hamlet* did not disappear from the Danish theatre repertoire for several decades. Many sources also mention that Foersom's translation influenced the later translation by Edvard Lembcke.[45] The fact that this copy apparently served generations of actors through a large part of the nineteenth century speaks to the importance of Foersom's translation for performance practice over a very long period of time, surviving other versions, for example the announcement of Hans Christian Wosemose's translations of Shakespeare's complete dramatic works.[46]

In the book on repertory and roles from The Royal Theatre, 1722–1896, it becomes clear that Fortinbras was absent from many productions of Hamlet in Denmark throughout the nineteenth century.[47]

While eliminating the Norwegian subplot was also done in other countries, in the Danish context it seems to have

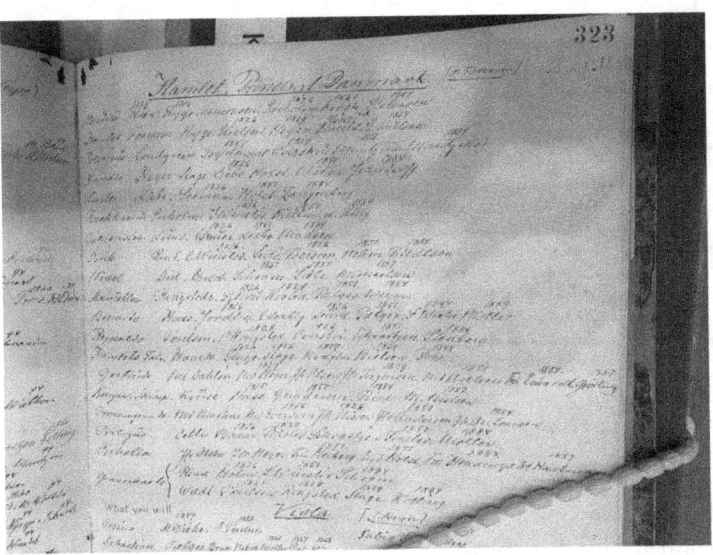

FIGURE 1.2 *Production notes relating to the casting of* Hamlet.

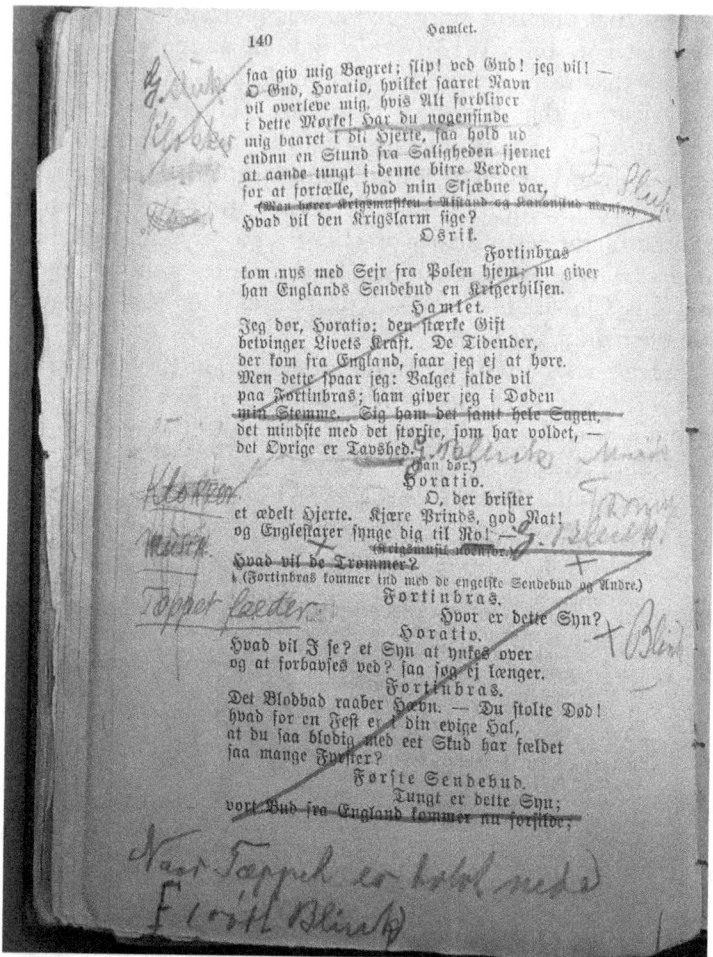

FIGURE 1.3 *Cuttings from prompt copy of* Hamlet, *using Foersom's translation. This version was used for decades during the nineteenth century.*

begun as a political solution responding to the crisis of the Danish kingdom at the beginning of the nineteenth century. These efforts may be read as a deliberate effort to manipulate the audience into forgetting the economic and political crisis of the monarchy and to deny what was rotten in the state of Denmark. A political meta-level has thus been cut out of the history of Danish representations of Shakespeare's *Hamlet*, and the absence resonates in its own way.

The consequences of this omission are numerous. Presumably, relatively few spectators had read the original play or the translation. This meant that not all spectators were able to make their own interpretations of Shakespeare's take in *Hamlet* on the Danish crown's relations with Norway. They were also unable to understand the consequences of the edited dramaturgy of *Hamlet*, as a way to make invisible the possible perspectives on the contemporary political riots in Norway that occurred in 1813–1814. Few sources contain any documentation of spectators who witnessed this production of *Hamlet*. One exception is Christian Molbech, for whom the production became a revelation of Shakespeare's world. In an intense correspondence (more than 200 letters), which Molbech had with Rahbek's wife, Kamma, from 22 March 1813 to 17 December 1814, one letter in particular mentions his enthusiasm about *Hamlet*. The Royal Danish Theatre archive also includes a heavily edited copy of the third edition of Edvard Lembcke's translation of *Hamlet*, which is based on Foersom's (1887). This was used as a prompt copy[48] as late as 1910 at the Royal Danish Theatre, providing evidence that the same editing occurred for about a century. This must have had a significant impact on how *Hamlet* was interpreted in the Royal Danish Theatre.

Although a cut version of *Hamlet* continued to be played on the Danish stage, it is also important to note that the play was hardly performed during the entire nineteenth century. This avoidance of *Hamlet* became even more amplified in the decades following the first performance, when J. L. Heiberg became director of the Royal Danish Theatre. Heiberg's own folklore musical play, *Elverhøj* [Elves' Hill] from 1828, with music written by Friedrich Kuhlau, includes the character of Christian IV, directly referring to the king as a real person.[49]

This production was commissioned by Frederik VI for the wedding of his daughter and became the new national play referring to Danish royalty. It was performed often, whereas *Hamlet* seems to have been marginalized. In a sense, *Elverhøj* simply took over the function of the emblematic *Hamlet*, which for a long time was perceived as a sentimental drama. In the early nineteenth century, drama seemed to turn away from political topics towards more uncritical entertainment: a repertoire of well-made plays, many by Eugène Scribe and other French contemporary playwrights, were turned into vaudeville performances. These had a more entertaining sentimental function rather than appealing to a critical response from an audience.[50]

Conclusions

This chapter has shown that, in the early nineteenth century, Danish audiences received *Hamlet* in an ideologically edited version of the original play, which had been re-written to become a truly Danish play. In hindsight, we can see that it offered what would probably best be called a patriotic and nationalist interpretation of this Shakespearean classic. Whereas Shakespeare's *Hamlet* dramaturgically shows its theatre machinery, this was hidden in the first Danish version; Hamlet's instructions to the players were cut and set decorations recalled earlier celebrations of the king (who had died five years before). In addition, the first Danish *Hamlet* set out not to trigger memories of recent political problems: references to Fortinbras and Norway, war and the bankrupt state of the nation were cut. The Danish *Hamlet* in a way confuses theatre and history and thus eventually eliminates some of the artistic paradoxes contained in Shakespeare's *Hamlet*.

The Danish *Hamlet* seems to have been used as political propaganda at a time when there was a risk of political rebellion in the country. The line 'something is rotten in the state of Denmark' could definitely have sounded like a critique of the ruling classes at the start of the nineteenth century and had to be cut. The play was edited so that potentially provocative ideas that might have resonated with the audience's contemporary experiences and perceptions were eliminated or muted, presenting a sanitized vision of the country's history, or at least of the trauma of the state of Denmark. The *Hamlet* available at the Royal Danish Theatre was plain and non-critical; the Norwegian subject matter – so pertinent to the recent national loss – was not presented at the Royal Danish Theatre until the late nineteenth century. In Foersom's *Hamlet*, these cuts have the effect of eliminating what is today referred to as symbolic 'subtext'. Shakespeare's text is stripped of its complexity. Critique is killed *from* the stage. From a dramaturgical perspective, this editing becomes more significant if it is viewed as a way of hiding Denmark's colonialist past. The Ghost does not trouble 'the conscience of the king' in the Danish *Hamlet*. Indeed, it could be argued that this lack of conscience seems to be where 'rotten' begins.

Notes

1   Langen, *Den afmægtige*, 262–3.
2   The research for this chapter is based on findings in the Royal Library, the archive of the Royal Danish Theatre, located in the National Archive, and from the archives of Her Majesty the Queen, Margrethe II's library, located at the Royal Palace Amalienborg. The archives mentioned are in Copenhagen and the translations from Danish are all mine.
3   In March 1813, two months prior to the opening night of *Hamlet* at the Royal Danish Theatre, the conflict between Denmark and Sweden escalated due to pressure from Russia and Great Britain in the Napoleonic war. Negotiations broke down; it became clear that a growing crisis in the kingdom was inevitable (Barton, *Scandinavia*, 322–4).

4   According to Stig Albrechtsen's register, three foreign productions of *Hamlet* visited the town hall in Odense before the first Danish production at the Royal Danish Theatre in Copenhagen. Two productions, by Carl H. Friebach, who played Laertes (7 March 1792) and Franz Heusser (1 April 1796), used Friedrich Schröder's translation. Friebach collaborated with Henrik Berggreen on the stage design. The third production was Johann H. Gørbing Frank's society (20 November 1812), though further information is not available (Albrectsen, *Shakespeareopførelser*, 5). See also Dyrbye, *I kunsten*, 16–21.

5   See also Marker and Marker, *Scandinavian Theatre*, 109–10.

6   Shakespeare, Schröder, and Brockmann, *Hamlet*. In the same year (1777), Johannes Boye's first translation of *Hamlet* from English into Danish was published. The translation in prose was never produced for the stage (Boye, trans., *Hamlet*).

7   H, review in *Fabers Fyenske Avertissments-Tidende*, 9 March 1792, 3. One may assume that the reporter refers to Johann Georg Sulzer, *Allgemeine Theorie der schönen Wissenschaften und Künste*, i–iv (1771–1774), which was quite popular and much discussed in Denmark. Lessing's *Hamburgische Dramaturgie* was never translated into Danish. Only German-reading audiences would be familiar with this famous diary, which was not even published in English until 1890.

8   Schwarz, *Stambog*.

9   Boye, trans., *Hamlet*.

10 Kallenbach and Kuhlmann, 'Towards a Spectatorial Approach', 24.

11 Major examples are in the work of Martin Ruud, Paul V. Rubow, and Alf Henriques (see Works cited). The most recent *Dansk teaterhistorie*, i, very briefly mentions this *Hamlet* production (Kvam, Risum and Wiingaard, *Dansk teaterhistorie*, 204).

12 Høy, *Oversættelsesproblematikken*, 46.

13 Rubow, *Shakespeare og hans samtidige*.

14 Glenthøj, *Skilsmissen*, 82.

15 Dollerup, *Denmark*, 61.

16 Bergsøe, *The Real Hamlet*; Berry, 'Shakespeare's Elsinore'; Hohnen, 'Hamlet's Castle'; Refskou, 'Whose Castle'.

17 Cited from Shakespeare, *Hamlet*, Arden ed., 2.2.242.

18 A basic link was based on geography. In the present chapter it is not important if Elsinore in Shakespeare's play *is* the same place, called Elsinore, situated in the north of Zealand (Sjælland). Nor is it important if Shakespeare's text refers to a location in Jutland as described in the chronicles of Saxo Grammaticus, published by Danish theologian, poet and politician, N. F. S. Grundtvig, in 1815, shortly after the first Danish *Hamlet* production. Having said this, I am aware that some studies would emphasize a comparison of the historical Elsinore and Shakespeare's use of Elsinore, see Bergsøe, *The Real Hamlet*; Berry, 'Shakespeare's Elsinore'; Hohnen, *Hamlet's Castle*; Lupić, 'The Mobile Queen'.

19 This poetic context could explain some of the impact of the Danish romantic aesthetics on Foersom's language in his translation of *Hamlet*. Foersom also frequently visited Knud Lyne Rahbek – of whom more below – and his wife, Kamma, who at Bakkehuset, in Frederiksberg, had salons for poetry by the most recognized poets, such as the national romanticist, Adam Oehlenschläger and the writer of fairy tales and stories, Hans Christian Andersen.

20 Bøgh, *Peter Foersom*, 50.

21 Advertisements in the local newspapers, not only from Copenhagen, but also from different towns in Denmark, show that both Boye's and Foersom's translations were available on subscription in bookstores. So, a certain readership around *Hamlet* must have existed.

22 According to a handwritten note, placed with Frederik Schwarz's copy of the manuscript in The Royal Library in Copenhagen and written by the much later Danish politician Viggo Starcke on 5 December 1966, Peter Foersom wrote his translation at Egegården, a mansion in Ørholm (information from theatre historian, Ida Neiiendam). He apparently worked in a glasshouse in the garden that is no longer on the estate.

23 Professor Knud Lyne Rahbek was quite influential at the turn of the nineteenth century. He was a university professor, translator, rector of Copenhagen University and director of the Royal Danish Theatre in Copenhagen – altogether quite a powerful persona in cultural and intellectual life. Rahbek had extensive knowledge of French Enlightenment theatre theories as well as

dramaturgical practices in Hamburg. Rahbek translated several of Diderot's works (Diderot, *Herren af Diderots theatralske Verker*). A few years later, Rahbek published his own thoughts on the art of acting (Rahbek, *Breve*).

24 Bøgh, *Peter Foersom*, 45. Unfortunately, Foersom does not explain what he is referring to.
25 Rubow, *Hamlet i original*, 5.
26 Foersom, trans., *Tragiske Værker*; Shakespeare 1807.
27 Rubow, *Shakespeare paa dansk*, 22.
28 Rubow, *Shakespeare paa dansk*, 23.
29 Anker, 'Den første Shakespeare-forestilling'.
30 Anker, 'Den første Shakespeare-forestilling', 88.
31 Foersom, trans., *Tragiske Værker*.
32 See Goethe, *Wilhelm Meister*, book 4, chapter 13.
33 '17 February 1813', it says in the newspaper, *Den til Forsendelse med de Kongelige Rideposter privilegerede Danske Statstidende* 'is performed a theatrical performance in five acts, consisting of scenes from Shakespear-Schröder's *Hamlet, Prinds af Danmark*' (8 and 12 February 1813). Friedrich Ludwig Schröder's *Hamlet* interpretation became famous in 1776, when he performed it at the Nationaltheater in Hamburg, where he was the theatre director. The advertisement states that *a Danish audience already knew Hamlet, influenced by German theatre*. In addition, performances of *Hamlet* at the Théâtre Français in Paris with Talma were reported in Danish newspapers. Altogether, it means that there was some knowledge about the play, three months before it was presented at the Royal Danish Theatre.
34 Rubow, *Shakespeare paa dansk*, 23.
35 Foersom, *Tragiske Værker*, 236.
36 'Instructeur' in Danish old theatre language corresponded to the notion of stage director, coming from the French theatre vocabulary of the early nineteenth century, eventually becoming 'metteur en place' and later 'metteur en scène'. The latter version of the term had become frequent by the time of Henrik Ibsen, and was especially connected to his practice.
37 Jørgensen, *Frederik Schwarz*, 172–80; Shakespeare 1813.

38 Quoted in Henriques, *Teatret*, 69.
39 Marker and Marker, *Scandinavian Theatre*, 105–10.
40 Anker, 'Den første Shakespeare-forestilling', 102.
41 Jørgensen, 'Teatermalerne'.
42 Heiner, Oehlenschlägertidens sceneregi', 97–105.
43 The first Swedish production of *Hamlet*, in 1819, had similarly cut Fortinbras out. Marker and Marker note that it had become a tradition to shorten the play, 'generally follow[ing] the lead of traditional English stage versions' (Marker and Marker, *Scandinavian Theatre*, 110).
44 Anker, 'Den første Shakespeare-forestilling', 99; Krogh, 'Hamlet', 106.
45 See, e.g., Henriques, 'Shakespeare og Danmark'.
46 Wosemose, trans., *Hamlet*; Anon., 'Fædrelandet', 2. It is striking that Hans Christian Wosemose never had his translations of Shakespeare's works performed. However, Wosemose seemed to have been interested in that. He gave a special memorial talk at Foersom's funeral, honouring him as the Danish Garrick (Anon, 'Wosemose',).
47 *Repertoire- og rollefortegnelse*.
48 By prompt copy, I refer to a copy of the play in which 'keys' for lifting a curtain, changing a set, etc. are marked.
49 Müller-Wille, 'Ghostly Monarchies', 74.
50 Aschengreen, *Engang*, 1969.

Works cited

Albrectsen, Stig, *Shakespeareopførelser i Danmark, 1792–1987: en registrant over danske &udenlandske Shakespeareopførelser opført på danske teatre, i radio og i TV*. (Copenhagen, 1988).

Anker, Øyvind, 'Den første Shakespeare-forestilling på dansk. "Hamlet" på Det Kongelige Teater 1813. Et fund og litt forskning', *Fund og Forskning* 18 (1971), 83–110.

Anon., 'Wosemose til Foersoms Ære', in *Kiøbenhavns Kongelig Alene Priviligerede Adresse Contoirs Efterretninger* (28 January 1817).

Anon., 'Fædrelandet (om Wosemoses planer om at udgive sin oversættelse af Shakespeares samtlige dramatiske værker)', in *Aalborg Stiftstidende og Adresse-Avis* (22 January 1834).

Aschengreen, Erik, *Engang den mest spillede: Studier i Eugène Scribes teater i Frankrig og Danmark* (Copenhagen, 1969).

Barton, H. Arnold. *Scandinavia in the Revolutionary Era, 1760–1815* (Minneapolis, 1986).

Bergsøe, Paul. 1950. *The Real Hamlet, Shakespeare and Elsinore* (Copenhagen, 1950).

Berry, Ralph, 'Shakespeare's Elsinore', *The Contemporary Review*, 273 (1998), 310.

Bøgh, Nicolaj, *Peter Foersom: en Levnedsskildring* (Copenhagen, 1895).

Boye, Johanes, trans., *Hamlet. Prinz af Dannemark* (Copenhagen, 1777).

Diderot, Denis. *Herren af Diderots theatralske Verker, tillige med en Samtale over den dramatiske Digtekunst*, trans. Knud Lyne Rahbek, Peter Christian Zeuthen and Johan Rudolph Thiele, 2 vols (Copenhagen, 1779).

Dollerup, Cay, *Denmark, Hamlet, and Shakespeare: A Study of Englishmen's Knowledge of Denmark towards the End of the Sixteenth Century, with Special Reference to Hamlet* (Salzburg, 1975).

Dyrbye, Holger, *I kunsten kan livet kendes: Odense Teater i 200 år*, ed. Jørgen Thomsen and Johnny Wøllekær (Odense, 1996).

Foersom, Peter, trans., *Tragiske Værker* (Copenhagen, 1807).

Glenthøj, Rasmus, *Skilsmissen: Dansk og norsk identitet før og efter 1814*, University of Southern Denmark Studies in History and Social Sciences, 443 (Odense, 2012).

H., [untitled], *Fabers Fyenske Avertissements-Tidende eller de til Forsendelse med Posten Kongelig allene privilegerede Fyens Stifts almindelige Adresse-Contoirs Efterretninger* (9 March 1792).

Heiner, Jørgen, 'Oehlenschlägertidens sceneregi', in Svend Christiansen and Povl Ingerslev-Jensen, eds, *Til Adam Oehlenschläger 1779–1979: Otte afhandlinger* (Copenhagen, 1979), 97–105.

Henriques, Alf, *Shakespeare og Danmark indtil 1840: Vurdering, Opførelse, Oversættelse, Efterligning* (Copenhagen, 1941).

Henriques, Alf, *Teatret paa Kongens Nytorv* (Copenhagen, 1948).

Henriques, Alf, 'Shakespeare and Denmark: 1900–1949', *Shakespeare Survey*, 3 (1950), 107–15.

Hohnen, David, *Hamlet's Castle and Shakespeare's Elsinore* (Copenhagen, 2010).

Høy, Paul Erik, *Oversættelsesproblematikken fra Johannes Boye til Ole Sarvig: Studier i centrale danske Hamlet-oversættelser* (np, 1971).

Jørgensen, Lisbet, *Frederik Schwarz: Den tænkende kunstner* (Copenhagen, 1997).

Jørgensen, Niels Peder, 'Teatermalerne Peter Cramer og Thomas Bruun og Det Kongelige Teaters stuedekoration fra 1785', in Per Lykke, ed., *Applaus!* (Copenhagen, 2011), 127–58.

Kallenbach, Ulla, and Annelis Kuhlmann, 'Towards a Spectatorial Approach to Drama Analysis', *Nordic Theatre Studies*, 30/2 (2018), 22–39.

Krogh, Karen, 'Hamlet', in *Shakespeare i TV* (Stockholm, 1964), 100–155.

Kvam, Kela, Janne Risum, and Jytte Wiingaard, *Dansk teaterhistorie* (Copenhagen, 1992).

Langen, Ulrik, *Den afmægtige: En biografi om Christian 7* (Copenhagen, 2008).

Lupić, Ivan, 'The Mobile Queen: Observing Hecuba in Renaissance Europe', *Renaissance Drama*, 46/1 (2018), 25–56.

Marker, Frederick J., and Lise-Lone Marker, *The Scandinavian Theatre: A Short History* (Oxford, 1975).

Müller-Wille, Klaus, 'Ghostly Monarchies – Paradoxical Constitutions of the Political in Johan Ludvig Heiberg's Royal Dramas', in Jon Stewart, ed., *The Heibergs and the Theater: Between Vaudeville, Romantic Comedy and National Drama* (Copenhagen, 2012), 67–94.

Rahbek, Knud Lyne, *Breve fra en gammel Skuespiller til hans Søn* (Copenhagen, 1782).

Repertoire- og rollefortegnelse for Det kgl. Teater 1722–1896. M. nogle indklæbede skuespillerautografer. Manuscript quarto, archive of the Royal Danish Theatre.

Refskou, Anne Sophie, 'Whose Castle is it Anyway?: Local/Global Negotiations of a Shakespearean Location', *Multicultural Shakespeare: Translation, Appropriation, and Performance*, 15/1 (2017), 121–32.

Rubow, Paul V, *Shakespeare paa dansk: Et Udsnit af den litterære Smags Historie* (Copenhagen, 1932).
Rubow, Paul V, *To Kroniker om Hamlet* (Copenhagen, 1939).
Rubow, Paul V, *Shakespeare i Nutidsbelysning* (Copenhagen, 1948).
Rubow, Paul V, *Shakespeare og hans samtidige: en Række kritiske Studier* (Copenhagen, 1948).
Rubow, Paul V, *Shakespeares Hamlet, Kritiske og historiske Bidrag* (Copenhagen, 1951).
Rubow, Paul V, 'Shakespeare-Overleveringen', *Berlingske aftenavis* (Copenhagen, 1955).
Rubow, Paul V, *Hamlet i original og oversættelse: Festskrift udg. af Københavns Universitet* (Copenhagen, 1961).
Ruud, Martin B, *An Essay Toward a History of Shakespeare in Denmark* (Minneapolis, 1920).
Schwarz, Frederik, *Stambog* (1793). Manuscript, Royal Library, Copenhagen.
Shakespeare, William, *Hamlet, Prinds af Danmark; Om Sørgespillet Hamlet Prinds af Danmark* (np, 1813).
Shakespeare, William, Friedrich Ludwig Schröder, and Johann Franz Hieronymus Brockmann, *Hamlet, Prinz von Dännemark; Ein Trauerspiel in 6 Aufzügen* (np, 1777).
Wosemose, H. C., trans., *Hamlet, Prince af Danmark: Sørgespil* (Copenhagen, 1834).

2

Geijer's *Macbeth* – Page, stage and the seeds of time

Kiki Lindell and Kent Hägglund

Introduction

When the Swedish poet, historian and philosopher Erik Gustaf Geijer (1783–1847) published his translation of Shakespeare's *Macbeth* in 1813, this was not only the first published Swedish translation of any Shakespeare play, but also, as far as can be proved,[1] the first translation of a complete Shakespeare play to be made directly from the English language, rather than by way of a French or German translation.

Despite holding multiple official positions, keeping him very much in the public eye (History Professor, MP and member of the Swedish Academy, to mention just a few), among his contemporaries the 30-year-old Geijer was chiefly renowned and celebrated as a poet; hence, it would be natural for a twenty-first-century reader to imagine that a Shakespeare translation by Geijer's hand would be met with considerable interest in Swedish theatres. Yet none of the subsequent Swedish productions of *Macbeth* made use of Geijer's translation. Instead, the 1830s saw no less than two new translations, each specially commissioned for a particular production: a planned 1831 production at the Royal Dramatic Theatre in Stockholm was cancelled, but a translation had already been commissioned by Johan Henrik Thomander (1798–1865); the 1838 staging at Djurgårdsteatern, Stockholm, utilized a new translation done after Schiller's German version from 1800. The first Royal Dramatic Theatre production (in 1858) used the translation by Carl August Hagberg (1810–1864) whose complete translation of Shakespeare's plays (1847–1851) has become established as the Schlegel-Tieck of Sweden – though the production team actually added a small sprinkling of Geijer's text to the ingredients in their cauldron. This is as close as Geijer's translation came to being used for performance in the nineteenth century. In fact, despite its obvious literary qualities, Geijer's version has *never* been staged in its entirety. In this chapter, we aim to investigate why this is so and provide some possible answers to the question, in the process 'unseaming' and examining Geijer's translation in the various lights of stage text and closet drama.

Beginning with a contextualizing overview of the changing literary and linguistic landscape around the turn of the century, we aim to trace Geijer's way to Shakespeare within it and people that landscape with some of those who wandered there with him – fellow Romantics, disapproving Classicists, friend and foe, innocent flower and serpent beneath. The chapter will conclude with a brief look at the later fate of the Scottish play in the hands of Geijer's successors.

English, Shakespeare and Sweden: Setting the scene

If this lack of nobility and decency continues on our stages, I would not be surprised if one day at the Opera we were to see Jove getting drunk, Mars in a fist-fight in the marketplace, and Venus doing something even worse. (Christoffer Bogislaus Zibet, head of the Royal Swedish Opera, after seeing *Macbeth* performed in Paris, 1784)[2]

Shakespeare, so idolized by the English, had a particular knack for making a mish-mash of the strongest, most sublime thoughts, the most ingenious and astonishing imagination: barbarity, superstition, the lowest of thoughts and expressions, unevenness in style, etcetera'. (The tutor Peter Moberg, after seeing *Macbeth* performed in Edinburgh, 1785)[3]

The story of Shakespeare's arrival in Sweden has much in common with many other European countries: here as elsewhere, Shakespeare's plays became part of the battleground between the French Classicist style and taste (represented by the testimonies given above) that had dominated the stage for so long and burgeoning German Romanticism. It is also, as stated in the introduction to this volume, the story of centre versus periphery, of city versus provincial small-town culture. Shakespeare's plays were performed by touring companies in the provinces long before they were ever admitted to the Classicist-dominated royal stages of the capital: between the first performance in 1776 of *Romeo and Juliet* by a touring company in the small town of Norrköping and the first Shakespeare production ever to grace a royal stage in Stockholm (*Hamlet*, in 1819) there is an astounding 43-year gap.[4] And in spite of this (tolerably successful[5]) *Hamlet*, the capital persisted in its prejudice, both against Shakespeare and against provincial theatre; so, for instance, seven years later, Geijer's friend the German author and salon hostess Amalia von Helvig (1776–1831) wrote in a letter from Berlin that 'Shakespeare's genius has appeared on our stage with *Hamlet*. It is such a shame that this branch of the fine arts shows no signs of taking off in Stockholm'.[6] Still in 1841, the theatre critic O. P. Sturzen-Becker (nom de plume Orvar Odd) could make snide remarks about provincial touring companies in a

Stockholm-based Sunday newspaper, asking: 'Why leave the snug domestic provincial stages ... to offer yourself up as victims to a spoiled, fastidious and difficult-to-please urban audience which demands genuine talent rather than well-intentioned mediocrity?'.[7]

At the time, English cultural influence was anything but strong;[8] as was the case with most other (Northern) European countries, Shakespeare was mostly imported by way of Germany and France where the main interest lay – not so much for his own sake but as a dramatist whose work interested the French and the Germans. Paris was the place where plays were seen and judged (thus, Paris is where Zibet, scouting for new plays for King Gustav III's theatre, happened to see *Macbeth*; see above). The literary élite went to Dresden and Berlin to hear Tieck read his own and Schlegel's Shakespeare translations; there is a wealth of testimonies by Swedish literati of Tieck's inspiring Shakespeare recitations – not least by Geijer himself, as well as by his circle; more of this later.[9]

In view of this French and German hegemony, it is hardly surprising to find that French and German were still the main foreign tongues learned, read, spoken and heard from the stage by Swedes at this time. Thus, those early readers-cum-theatregoers who were at all familiar with Shakespeare would mostly be so through, for instance, La Page's (1746) or Le Tourneur's (1776) French translations or Ducis's acting versions. King Gustav III was among those early readers of Shakespeare in French.[10] He borrowed freely from Shakespeare's *Richard III* for a pivotal scene in the libretto for the 1786 opera *Gustav Wasa*;[11] and, despite Zibet's poor assessment of *Macbeth* in Paris in 1784 (above), the king's own French troupe played *Le Macbeth* (in Ducis's version) in 1791. Before Geijer's *Macbeth* broke new ground, the Romantics seemed equally happy to enjoy their Shakespeare second-hand, with what Gierow calls 'a German visa'; as Inga-Stina Ewbank has pointed out, '[t]hough the Swedish Romantic poets often used a notional Shakespeare as a stick to beat their French-classical predecessors with, they did not translate him'.[12]

Nevertheless, English, long treated like the ugly duckling among the modern languages in that it was neither 'necessary' like German nor 'useful' like French,[13] was creeping in this petty pace from day to day towards recognition as useful (if not yet necessary), literally hand-in-hand with a growing interest in Shakespeare, since the study of English was often conducted simply by working one's way through a piece of poetry, prose or drama, dictionary in hand. Esaias Tegnér (1782–1846), Geijer's contemporary and fellow poet, learned English this way, beginning with *The Poems of Ossian*, from thence moving on to *Hamlet*.[14] As for dictionaries to use in this (or any other) way, these were also becoming more readily available as demand grew: in the entire eighteenth century there had only been four new Swedish/English dictionaries, but now there had been four in just the first two decades of the nineteenth century.[15] For those who did not dare to tackle entire literary masterpieces, there were also anthologies, handbooks, textbooks, primers and readers. In 1792, Brutus's speech on the death of Caesar was the first Shakespeare excerpt to be anthologized, though not identified as the work of Shakespeare; however, nine years later (in 1801), an ambitious primer written by none other than the very Peter Moberg who had seen and described *Macbeth* in Edinburgh in 1785 (quoted above) contained Hamlet's famous monologue – but also, in addition, foregrounding Shakespeare and his position in English Literature in a short text.[16]

Speaking of Peter Moberg, another way of learning modern languages was, of course, undertaking a species of educational Grand Tour around Europe, picking up languages through immersion. For rich young men, travelling in this manner in the company of a tutor had become quite the thing; for young(ish) men with more erudition and brains than family and fortune, the option was to *be* that tutor, accompanying wealthy young scions of the aristocracy and bourgeoisie abroad. This was Moberg's mission when he saw *Macbeth* in Edinburgh in 1785; and this, too, was what caused Erik Gustaf Geijer to spend almost a year in England in 1809–1810,[17] in the process encountering the magic of Shakespeare (and John Philip Kemble) on stage. Moberg was a linguist rather than a man of letters, but his reaction to *Macbeth* (quoted above) is similar to Zibet's, in that it is fairly typical of the received opinion among French Classicists, of Shakespeare as a bizarre barbarian. Ten years later, the poet Frans Michael Franzén (1772–1847), on the same tutorial errand, was already an ardent reader and admirer of Shakespeare's plays; he saw Kemble's *Hamlet* and *Macbeth*, but was disappointed by Kemble and Mrs Siddons as Macbeth and Lady Macbeth, as well as by the witches: 'I wanted them light, *hovering* as they themselves call it ... I wanted to feel the magic, the supernatural; but instead, the witches were played by three men, one of whom took it upon himself to be comical, thereby ruining and disrupting all the horror that this scene ought to invoke'.[18]

Geijer and Shakespeare

The last of the three travelling temporary tutors whose encounters with Shakespeare on stage are described in this chapter, Erik Gustaf Geijer, arrived in London ten or 15 years after Franzén; he did not see John Philip Kemble's *Macbeth* (though Donner claims that he may have seen a pantomime version of the play[19]), but he, like Franzén before him, saw Kemble as *Hamlet*. However, by now, the times were different: where, in the mid-1780s, Zibet and Moberg had seen the work of a barbarian and in the mid-1790s Franzén had been disappointed in the crudeness of Shakespeare's witches, a decade-and-a-half later, Geijer too saw the barbarian, the crude sense of humour, but found it infinitely exciting: 'How excellent is the use of the low and ridiculous in [Shakespeare's] dramatic plays!'.[20] Taking the Gravedigger in *Hamlet* as an example, Geijer claims that 'he dwells among things rank and gross in nature; yet he is contented, professing a crude and happy philosophy of life among the decaying bones'.[21]

As suggested by the casual CV provided in the introduction to this chapter, Erik Gustaf Geijer was something of a Renaissance man; he himself likened his interests to the fingers of one hand (the five fingers being philosophy, history, rhetoric, poetry and music) and refused to give up a single one: 'if I am denied variation in my daily occupation, I am done for', he claimed, proving the truth of this statement by seemingly perpetually undertaking new things.[22] In March 1812, less than two years after his English adventure, he had found a new outlet for his restless energy: in a letter to Esaias Tegnér, Geijer wrote that '[i]n my spare time, I amuse myself with trying to translate *Macbeth*; but Shakespeare is proving unruly and difficult to play with'.[23]

Why, then, did Geijer choose this difficult play? This is a question which may have more than one answer – the most pragmatic alternative being that it is the shortest of the tragedies and thus a comparatively short piece of work into which to sink one's teeth. Another plausible reason would be to relate it to Geijer's admiration for Friedrich von Schiller;[24] *Macbeth* is the only Shakespeare play translated by Schiller and what would be more natural than for Geijer to choose a play where it would be possible to walk in the footsteps of, and refer to, his great predecessor throughout the work? That said, it should be pointed out that although Geijer seems to have embarked on his great task working from Schiller's German version, once the training-wheels were off he forged ahead working straight from the English original, claiming Shakespeare's play, not just for the Swedish language, but also perhaps partly for a Swedish context: Molin suggests that Geijer not only found Shakespeare's witches reminiscent of those of Nordic folklore, but also strengthened that similarity further in his own translation.[25] Thus, Geijer's translation of *Macbeth* – originating in his love of Shakespeare in English, undertaken as a project mediated through Schiller's German, subsequently skipping (or at least lessening the influence of) the middle-man – became a part of a shared European rather than strictly English cultural heritage.

At this point, it is tempting to indulge in a piece of speculation, suggesting that in addition to the previous good, solid reasons, there might a third, more fanciful motivation behind choosing the Scottish play: the politically interested Geijer might have heard echoes of recent Swedish – and European – history in the plot of *Macbeth*. In 1809, merely four years earlier, Sweden had been the scene of a *coup d'état*, followed by a change of dynasty. The Swedish king, Gustav III, had been assassinated at a masked ball in 1792 – an assassination which may have been partly plotted by (and was almost certainly condoned by) his brother Duke Carl, who took over the regency during the minority of Gustav III's heir Gustav Adolf (only 13 at the time of his father's murder); Gustav IV Adolf was, in turn, ousted and ultimately replaced by a competent officer from the Napoleonic wars, Jean-Baptiste Bernadotte. For Gustav III, read King Duncan, for Gustav Adolf, Malcolm, for Duke Carl, Macbeth; read Bernadotte's descendants for Banquo's and there is the plot of *Macbeth* bounded in a nutshell.[26]

Despite the difficulties in wrangling *Macbeth*, Geijer seems to have carried out the work in just a few months. In late November of the same year as his letter to Tegnér, he wrote to his fiancée that the translation was nearly in printable condition; in February 1813 he wrote that the publishers were pestering him for the preface and in early March he promised the translation to her, finished and published, by the next post.[27] The translation was extensively reviewed (on the whole favourably) in *Swensk Literatur-Tidning* in July the same year.[28]

Macbeth: Geijer's translation choices

In the above-mentioned preface to the translation, Geijer states that he has tried to follow the original as closely as possible. In making this pre-emptive defence, he seems aware that he may be laying himself open to criticism on two counts: first, by adhering too closely to Shakespeare's text (whereas the preference of readers possessing 'the good fortune of having been born in an enlightened age' might be for the translator to 'give the old Briton a few lessons in good taste'). The second point on which Geijer anticipated criticism was not that his translation adhered too closely to some of Schiller's changes – but that it *did not adhere closely enough.*

Ewbank has likened the work of the translator to that of a New Critic, claiming that in some senses, 'no one, not even an editor, knows the workings of the language in a play so well as a translator who has had to confront every word in a peculiarly intense way and in its relation to every other sign in the verbal texture of the play'.[29] If we apply Ewbank's simile to the two translators, Geijer is certainly more of a New Critic in his approach to the text than Schiller, whose work is as much an adaptation as it is a translation, coming as it did with an agenda: in bringing the play into agreement with contemporary taste and style, he made it acceptable for the stage of the Weimar Theatre.[30] In order to achieve this, Schiller extensively bowdlerized the play (among other things removing taste-offending references to urine samples, laxatives and lax morals), and also made some major structural changes – the three most radical being the removal of Act 4.2 (the murder of Macduff's family), the reworking of the Porter's speech (Act 2.3), changing it from the topical prose ravings of a grotesquely comical drunkard to a blank-verse 'morning hymn, praising the beauty of the dawning day'[31] and adding moral motivation to the witches, extending their part and making them dignified and godlike.

As previously stated, Geijer retains Shakespeare's witches, warts, beards and all; he does follow Schiller in removing Act 4.2,[32] but his Porter is restored to his Shakespearean (prose-speaking) role – restored, that is, except for the short conversation with Macduff and Lenox, which Geijer too has bowdlerized (or 'Schillerized' – Hammarsköld's mischievous term[33]), 'for reasons that those who know the original will easily understand' as Geijer says in his preface. One guesses that the Porter's references to what drink provokes and unprovokes (namely nose-painting, sleep, urine and lechery) may have something to do with this decision.

Thus, Geijer is mostly true to the aim of the preface, staying as close to the original as possible – but when he *does* depart from it, it is generally to follow Schiller.[34] Whether this is a good or a bad thing seems to be a question of personal taste among those scholars who have discussed the matter: for instance, while Borelius claims that Geijer's relative freedom from Schiller makes him more successful in retaining some of Shakespeare's boldest imagery and expressions, Donner maintains that when Geijer is left to fend for himself without Schiller's help, he is often at sea: 'Frequently, we see Geijer faltering or mistranslating passages which have been left out or rewritten by Schiller'.[35] Donner provides the reader with a curious example of this, in the shape of the word 'limbeck' (*Mac* 1.7.68), which occurs in a line not included by Schiller and which Geijer seems to have misunderstood as 'limbo', in that his line describes 'the receipt of reason' as a deserted wilderness rather than as an alembic, heated with evaporating wine.[36] However, as Donner also points out,[37] Schiller was dependent on the earlier prose translations into German by Wieland and Eschenburg – and when those fail, Schiller is, in fact, the one actually leading Geijer astray: for instance, Wieland's original mistaking 'baboon' (*Mac* 4.1.37) for 'baby' gradually developed into an amusing disaster in four generations when the mistake was perpetuated first by Eschenburg and then Schiller, with Geijer bringing up the rear.[38]

Even for Geijer, for whom the English language was not an obstruction per se, there are stumbling blocks and barriers in the text – some of which turned out to be insurmountable, for one reason or another. Some of these barriers resulted in what look like conscious circumlocutions and avoidance strategies: for instance, the word 'equivocator' (*Mac* 2.3.8), is given as *advokat* (lawyer) – thus avoiding the difficulty of translating the sentence in a way that would make the topical references to the trials following the Gunpowder Plot comprehensible to a Swedish audience.[39]

Another difficulty is presented by the subtle usage of 'thou' and 'you' in the play, especially between Macbeth and Lady Macbeth. Mostly, Geijer's translation simply follows the original in this too, but the few deviations that it makes seem to indicate that Geijer may not be taking the difference between the two modes of address into active account in his work. The problem is twofold for a Swedish translator: on the one hand, both words do exist in Swedish – *du* (thou) and *ni* (you) – but whereas the English 'thou' is obsolete, the Swedish *du* is not, thus making the Swedish choice between *du* and *ni* a much more pragmatic, much less nuanced affair. As the actual words *du/ni* are there to choose from, a choice *must* be made between them – but in the words of Clas Zilliacus the Swedish usage, straightforward and uncomplicated, hampers the translator dealing with the type of usage seen in Shakespeare's plays, with you/thou as 'deictic markers that alter the dynamics of the discourse'; according to him, '[t]he characters enter into relations with each other which are unstable; their status may be revoked, altered, up- or downgraded'.[40] However, Zilliacus also states, resignedly, that '[a] great deal of printer's ink has been spilled on the difference between *you* and *thou* in Elizabethan English. Most of it has been spilled in English, which goes to show that the feeling for this extinct distinction has gone numb'.[41] For modern and future translators, Zilliacus seems to be hinting that cutting one's losses and going for the uniform adoption of *du* might be a viable and pragmatic solution – but for a nineteenth-century translation such as Geijer's, this was not an option and the niggle (a small one, but still a niggle) remains.

As regards prosody, Geijer the poet is on safe ground. In the preface, he states that 'Shakespeare's iambs flow unconstrained, and cling to the subject, like rich drapery to a sumptuous body'[42] and that he has done his utmost to be faithful to these. Generally speaking, he has been successful in this ambition; in fact, the reader may feel that the easy flow of Geijer's verse, clinging 'like rich drapery' to Shakespeare's own, is the strongest feature of his translation – an impression corroborated by Kristian Smidt, who claims that 'both his diction and his blank verse reflect the fluency and freedom of Shakespeare's language'.[43] Being proficient in blank verse seems an achievement in itself, in a periphery modelled on French and German centrality and in a culture more at home with the alexandrine.[44]

Zilliacus also draws attention to a built-in difference between the two languages that often complicates Swedish–English metrical translation – namely the fact that Swedish prosody tends to favour the trochee. Partly, this is a result of the Swedish wealth of trochaic verbs and verb forms, but it is also due to the fact that, in Swedish, the definite article is suffixed to the noun.[45] Perhaps we may even go so far as to claim that the Swedish language is trochaic in its very nature; Geijer himself certainly seems to corroborate this bold statement when, left to his own devices and in his own tongue, he more or less consistently renders 'iambic' names as trochees in the play: the trochaic *MAC*-beth is used no less than 27 times (compared to only a single iambic Mac-*BETH,* plus a few inconclusive cases); likewise, the trochaic *MAC*-duff occurs 13 times (against only one Mac-*DUFF*). As a point of reference, there is no variation of stress on already trochaic names (Banquo, Malcolm, Siward). This trochaic bias often results in hypermetrical syllables and feminine endings – a phenomenon not unusual in translations of course (since a feminine ending adds another syllable to expand into for the ever-cramped translator), but Geijer carries this device to the limit at times. Thus, for instance, in Macbeth's 'dagger' soliloquy in 2.1, Geijer has more than twice as many feminine endings as Shakespeare's original; whereas, in the 25 lines of Macbeth's soliloquy on his fear of Banquo (3.1), Shakespeare has 18 masculine endings and only seven feminine ones, Geijer (who has added one line to the soliloquy) has reversed the numbers, with 18 feminine endings and only eight masculine ones.

The general trochaic bias has, however, not rescued the witches' trochaic tetrameter from being tampered with metrically: in their first two scenes (1.1 and 1.3), Geijer's witches are found going rogue, in that the doggerel incantations of the original are interwoven with (or broken up by) frequent anapaests and dactyls, gaining more syllables but losing the effect of those regular, almost hypnotic, trochees. In 4.1, however, the regular trochaic tetrameter of the original is back, no galloping anapaests disrupting the supernatural stomping around the cauldron.

Returning to the praise due on the blank verse level, Geijer's use of stichomythia and enjambment follows Shakespeare's very closely and with great sensitivity. The latter is especially noticeable in the second half of Macbeth's soliloquy in 3.1,[46] mentioned above; here, in the driving, feverish realization of the consequences of the murder of Duncan ('For Banquo's issue have I filed my mind'), the translator's propensity for feminine endings matters less. In fact, the enjambed lines, feverishly stumbling forwards, in rage and indignation, to the inevitable conclusion that paradise is lost and eternal peace surrendered for the benefit of somebody else, gain rather than lose from the feminine endings, the argument tumbling forward irresistibly.

As suggested above, not everything is brilliant about Geijer's *Macbeth*; yet is certainly good enough for us to ask: why was it never used in the theatre? Again, as with Geijer's choice of play, no definite answer can be given – but there is the strong possibility that Geijer never intended his translation to be anything other than a closet play, to be perused in silence.[47] Like Schiller, he may have realized that a playable version required adaptation – however, *unlike* Schiller, actively choosing to prioritize faithfulness to the original over playability. Or perhaps he made no conscious choice but simply envisaged a closet drama all along; this type of translation, often 'poetry-centred, page-oriented rather than stage-oriented',[48] was not unusual at the time, and Geijer himself was certainly not averse to the concept. During a visit to Germany in 1825, he spent an evening in Tieck's Dresden home, listening to Tieck reading *Henry IV* in Schlegel's translation. In his *Memoirs*, Geijer describes it as 'a presentation of such overall truthfulness and refinement in the small details that in comparison a stage performance seems rough and crude'.[49] The fact that Geijer had seen this very play, *Henry IV* part 1, performed on stage (with Kemble as Hotspur) during his year in England did not prevent him from claiming that, as far as he could recall, the impression that the London performance made was in no way comparable to that made upon him by Tieck's reading.[50]

Whatever Geijer's own ambitions for his translation may have been, a footnote regarding topical events should perhaps be added here. For the first Swedish *Macbeth* (the 1838 production mentioned in the introduction) a new translation was commissioned, as previously stated. We do not know if Geijer's translation was ever under consideration for this production – Geijer had no contacts within the theatre world, so it is perhaps unlikely – but, if it was, Time itself anticipated that exploit: as Fridén points out, '[e]arly in 1838, Geijer had painfully left his conservative beliefs to join the opposition, losing his old friends without gaining any new'.[51] It is surely not too fanciful to imagine that a translation by the hand of an apostate might be considered an unwise choice; it would certainly not have done the production any favours with Sweden's recently established theatre censorship.

Playability is to do with much more than the to-be-or-not-to-be of bowdlerizing and political censorship, of course; both those concerns put aside, was Geijer's *Macbeth* otherwise playable, and would it be considered playable now? To a twenty-first-century reader, it is difficult to determine what, in Geijer's translation, is the twin effect of Anglicisms and cumbersome grammar and what is merely early-nineteenth-century poetic diction, but one thing remains clear: the language is very far from the Romantic ideal of 'the real language of men'. However, in spite of this, Geijer's translation certainly was not unread, unused or even unspoken. Geijer's friend the writer and salon hostess Malla Silfverstolpe (1782–1861) reports in her *Memoirs* that, in April 1816, Geijer himself read *Macbeth* to Amalia von Helvig, as part of the effort to comfort and distract her in her sorrow after the sudden death of her little son from scarlet fever (one cannot help feeling that *Macbeth* is an unfortunate choice of reading matter for a recently bereaved parent – at least until one remembers that Geijer had followed Schiller in removing the scene where Macduff's wife and little ones are murdered).[52] A few years later, in 1821, Silfverstolpe's *Memoirs* tell of a stage reading of *Macbeth*, requiring that everyone had their own copy of the play; Malla humorously relates how the sudden demand for Geijer's *Macbeth* flummoxed the local bookseller, who complained that he had not sold five copies a year since the translation was published and consequently had packed it away in storage – and now, 20 people, one-by-one, had come asking for it in a single day.[53]

Perhaps a stage reading like that in 1821 would still be a possibility today, precisely 200 years later – thus treating the translation as a closet drama of the Romantic era rather than a playable tragedy by Shakespeare. Apart from this, it is difficult to see how Geijer's *Macbeth* could be given stage life without substantial revisions. Today's Swedish audiences are usually well versed in English; the play might still get away with the occasional Anglicism, but the trochaic names (MACbeth etcetera) would pose a problem, as would the occasional obsolete grammar and vocabulary, such as *fal* (an archaic word for venal), *förvägna* ('overbold' in the original), and *underpant*. This last, obsolete word means 'token, sign, pledge', but to the average Swede, more anglophile than archaically orientated, the line 'Hvi gaf den då en underpant af lycka' (corresponding to 'Why hath it given me earnest of success' in *Mac* 1.3.134) would certainly give associations to strangely talismanic undergarments rather than to archaic tokens.

Geijer's *Macbeth*: Afterlife and Epilogue

In November 1849, the Shakespeare translator Carl August Hagberg was apparently busy translating *Macbeth*, in the process consulting the work of his predecessor; in a letter to his brother, he describes 'the Old Man's' (Geijer's) translation as 'very uneven, now verbatim, now rambling off on its own'.[54] Nevertheless, Hagberg adopted Geijer's witch scenes virtually verbatim in his translation, acknowledging his indebtedness to Geijer in several footnotes (where he also explains restoring the correct iambic pronunciation of the names Macbeth and Macduff). This freely acknowledged obligation makes Geijer's work seem particularly important to Hagberg, given two other cases where Hagberg defaults on acknowledging his possible indebtedness to other translators: strong (though not conclusive) external evidence suggests that Hagberg had been given Johan Henrik Thomander's unpublished translation for the cancelled 1831 *Macbeth* production.[55] Hagberg's silence on this point may simply indicate that he decided not to use any of Thomander's material; however, the additional fact that Hagberg actually adopted (or slightly adapted) some 20 lines from the anonymous *Swensk Literatur-Tidning* reviewer's translation of Act 4.2 (the murder of Macduff's family – see note 31) without acknowledgment may leave the reader's confidence in Hagberg's generosity a little dented.[56] Be that as it may – as stated, in the case of Geijer at least, Hagberg's indebtedness is openly acknowledged.

Subsequent nineteenth-century *Macbeth* productions were usually based on Hagberg's translation; however, the 1858 staging saw Hagberg's text doctored by the literary advisor F. A. Dahlgren, who also drew on Geijer's translation.[57] And nearly a century later, even the director Ingmar Bergman's 1948 *Macbeth* production in Gothenburg had a sprinkling of Geijer in it – although how much or little remains debatable.[58]

The year after *Macbeth*, Geijer published a poem called 'Shakespeare' – subsequently revising and re-publishing it in 1835.[59] A few lines from it:

> Hast seen a play of puppets on the stage?
> A quaint and ceremonious procession;
> They walk, and stand, and act, and thus they show us
> A small and tidy slice of human life.
> (...)

> But lo, behind the stage – the puppeteer
> Controls the reins of great affairs of state,
> Holding the fates of many in his hands;
> Himself a Fate, unseen, who, if he chooses,
> To wield his pow'r against his own creation
> May pull to pieces tiny wooden bodies
> And break the strings of human puppets' hearts.
> (...)
> All falls apart. That life was an illusion,
> And so is ours – the insight overwhelms us
> That life is futile, signifying nothing.[60]

Perhaps this poem tells us something of how Geijer saw Shakespeare – a Prospero, an all-powerful puppeteer, wielding his magic – but the wording also carries echoes of Macbeth's 'Tomorrow and tomorrow' soliloquy, with its resigned, even cynical, view of our inability to be more than walking shadows or the main characters even in our own little lives.

Although Geijer did not return to Shakespeare in his own artistic production, it seems likely that the love of Shakespeare, conceived in his youth, blossoming during his year in England, developed, matured and coming to fruition through the work on *Macbeth*, stayed with him throughout the remainder of the seven ages of man. In 1845, ten years after the reworked 'Shakespeare' poem, Geijer gave a series of lectures on European culture and history. In two of these, he makes the claim that in English post-reformation literature, art has married truth – stating, with a Jonson-esque flourish, that the truest visionary of all is Shakespeare:

> The visionary eye of the poet is not merely concerned with the airy images of the invention; it pierces through to the innermost centre of the human soul, finding in its tapestry the divine golden thread uniting us all. Of all the poets in the world, none has possessed this visionary eye to a greater extent than Shakespeare. ... His are immortal tales, at once telling us of a certain era, and of the human condition in general.[61]

Less than two years later, Geijer was no more. The date of his death – 23 April – befits an ardent admirer of Shakespeare. He died in 1847, the year in which Carl August Hagberg published the first volume of his Shakespeare translations; versions that would eclipse all other Shakespeare in Swedish and under whose translating Genius, Geijer's is rebuked. This, however, actually chimes with Geijer's own hopes for the future: in the preface to his *Macbeth*, Geijer generously states that his warmest wish is to be a mere trailblazer for better translations in years to come. Though Hagberg may be the greatest Swedish translator, Geijer will forever remain the first, blazing a trail not just for future Shakespeare translators, but also for the mutability of the bonds to other European cultures and languages, as well as for the movement towards a specific Nordic literary identity.

Notes

1. When in 1787, 26 years before Geijer's *Macbeth*, *Hamlet* was first performed in Sweden, in Gothenburg, the advertisements claimed that the play was 'translated from the English, written by the famous Shakesear [*sic*]'; however, substantiating this claim is impossible since, '[u]nfortunately, but not surprisingly, it is lost and the identity of the translator remains unknown' (Sivefors, 'Trade Routes', 189–91).

2. Lindell, 'Star-crossed lovers', 160. The translation of this letter, originally written in French from Zibet to King Gustav III, is taken from a Swedish translation (published in Personne, *Svenska teatern*, ii, 147). Unless otherwise stated, all translations from Swedish into English, prose or poetry, in this chapter are made by Kiki Lindell. Shakespeare's name, given variously as Shakspere, Shakspeare and Shakespere in the original texts, has been changed into Shakespeare for reasons of consistency.

3. Hägglund, *William Shakespeare*, 173.

4   Hillberg, ed., *Teater*, 555.

5   The stage production itself was well received (Molin, *Shakespeare och Sverige*, 101); even a bulwark of French Classicism like Carl Gustaf af Leopold (1756–1829) reluctantly admitted that Shakespeare's 'old wives' tale' looked better than expected (Personne, *Svenska Teatern*, iv, 19). However, Per Adolf Granberg's (1770–1841) translation (in prose, except *The Mousetrap*, which was given partly in alexandrines) was extensively criticized (Avén, 'Hamlet', 161–85, Monié, *Ord som himlen når*, 262). In a letter to a literary colleague, the writer Lorenzo Hammarsköld (1785–1827) indignantly maintains that Granberg seems to have taken a perverse pleasure in manhandling and mangling the text (Personne, *Svenska teatern*, iv, 19).

6   Stiernstedt, ed., *Amalia von Helvigs brev*, 464.

7   Nordmark, 'Vägfarande komedianter', 114.

8   A Swedish exception was provided by the internationally orientated Gothenburg on the West Coast for which Britain was a crucial trade partner where 'trade and culture literally went hand in hand' (Sivefors, 'Trade Routes', 196).

9   Molin, *Shakespeare och Sverige*, 106–8.

10 Vingedal (*Shakespeares ordmagi*, 6) claims that King Gustav read La Place's translation, whereas Personne (*Svenska teatern*, iv, 146–7) maintains that he read Le Tourneur's version.

11 Skuncke, 'Gustaviansk teater', 201–2. In a double dream sequence, Gustav Wasa and the Danish King Christian are both visited by spirits; Gustav by a guardian angel, Christian by the ghosts of murdered Swedish noblemen (thus, predictably, the future King Gustav Wasa is cast as Richmond rather than Richard III in this royal scenario).

Incidentally, the king was not the only playwright influenced by Shakespeare at the time. In the (never performed) opera *Jorund* – written by the very same Granberg whose translation of *Hamlet* was so heavily criticized (see note 5) – there is a scene with 1,000 trees marching as part of a prophecy (clearly derivative of the Scottish play); there is also the gratuitous gouging out of a character's eyes, plus a woman dressing up as a man and going in search of her beloved (suggesting that the author had also drunk deep from *King Lear* and *Two Gentlemen of Verona*). In *Swensk Literatur-Tidning* – the same publication where Geijer's *Macbeth* was reviewed (see note 32) – *Jorund* was given a vastly entertaining slating (quite possibly by the same anonymous reviewer who had undertaken *Macbeth*), for its plagiarism as well as for its abysmal quality in general. However, the opera was given a prize by the Swedish Academy in 1812 (this was arguably neither the first nor the last time that the Swedish Academy would show what some might consider inferior judgement).

12 Gierow, *Johan Henrik Thomander*, 236; Ewbank and Lindell, 'Scandinavia', 479–80.
13 Bratt, *Engelskundervisningens framväxt*, 29.
14 Bratt, *Engelskundervisningens framväxt*, 52.
15 Bratt, *Engelskundervisningens framväxt*, 174–6. One of these new dictionaries (first published in 1807) was developed by none other than the ubiquitous Granberg, ridiculed writer of *Jorund* and reviled translator of *Hamlet* (see notes 5 and 11). As a lexicographer he was more successful; his dictionary went into a second edition as late as in 1832 (Bratt, *Engelskundervisningens framväxt*, 271).
16 Bratt, *Engelskundervisningens framväxt*, 98–9 and 269–70; Molin, *Shakespeare och Sverige*, 8.
17 In Geijer's case, linguistic immersion proved so effective that even into his old age, his wife described how when under strain he would walk around muttering, in English, 'Damn! Damn!' under his breath (Burman, 'Vem var Erik Gustaf Geijer', 43).
18 Quoted in Molin, *Shakespeare och Sverige*, 89.
19 Donner, *Svenska översättningar*, 5.
20 Flemberg and Hägglund, 'Geijer om Shakespeare', 239.
21 Landquist, *Geijer*, 58–9; Donner, *Svenska översättningar*, 11.
22 Burman, 'Vem var Erik Gustaf Geijer', 11–12.
23 Flemberg and Hägglund, 'Geijer om Shakespeare', 242. The word Geijer uses is *hårdlekt* – a dialectal word from his native Värmland province, denoting something that is unwieldy, resisting any effort to play with, shape or mould it. Incidentally,

C. A. Hagberg corroborated Geijer's opinion more than 30 years later, calling Macbeth 'the most difficult of all Shakespeare's tragedies' (Donner, *Svenska översättningar*, 3).

24 Landquist, *Geijer*, 70–1.

25 Molin, *Shakespeare och Sverige*, 141. Molin claims that this sense of familiarity may have been part of what drew Geijer to *Macbeth*. Thus, paradoxically, one of Geijer's points of departure from Schiller's translation of *Macbeth* may signal a rival (or at least additional) motive for choosing that very play.

26 It may be added that, unlike Macbeth, Duke Carl had already known how to play-act in his days as an also-ran; in the amateur theatricals at Gustav III's court, he had been praised as an excellent actor – even though the courtier Axel von Fersen criticized his diction and his 'puny stature' (Levertin, *Teater*, 66); here was another 'dwarfish thief' in the making, apparently.

27 Flemberg and Hägglund, 'Geijer om Shakespeare', 242–3.

28 The anonymous reviewer was probably Lorenzo Hammarsköld, who criticized Granberg's *Hamlet* translation and may have reviewed Granberg's *Jorund* as well (see notes 5, 11 and 15). He certainly liked Shakespeare and disliked Granberg enough to qualify as the main suspect in both cases and he had a history of highly impertinent reviews: Esaias Tegnér was so incensed by a damaging review that he wrote a satirical poem called 'Lorenzo Hammarspik' (twisting the offender's martial and aristocratic family name of *Hammer-shield* into the more plebeian *Hammer-nail*, savouring of rude mechanicals), ridiculing Hammarsköld's lack of talent and learning, and his inflated opinion of his own abilities. A few particularly scathing lines:

> Your flair for tongues is quite unique,
> Though readers cry in anguish:
> Don't write in Swedish, Hammarspik,
> Nor any other language.

29 Ewbank, 'Shakespeare Translation', 5.

30 Donner, *Svenska översättningar*, 145; Ranke, 'Shakespeare Translations', 167. Schiller's translation proved very successful on stage and was used, in Weimar and elsewhere, until at least 1855.

31 Donner, *Svenska översättningar*, 11.
32 For this, he is roundly criticized in *Swensk Literatur-Tidning*; the anonymous reviewer even takes it upon himself to translate the missing scene, publishing it together with the review.
33 Hammarsköld, in a letter about Geijer's *Macbeth*, qtd in Ljunggren, *Svenska vitterhetens häfder*, 563).
34 Donner, *Svenska översättningar*, 19–20.
35 Borelius, 'Geijer och Schiller', 87; Donner, *Svenska översättningar*, 55.
36 Donner, *Svenska översättningar*, 58.
37 Donner, *Svenska översättningar*, 107.
38 Donner (*Svenska översättningar*, 126–7) also draws attention to one point where Geijer has fortunately withstood the siren call of Schiller, namely the scene showing Banquo's murder (*Mac* 3.3). Where Shakespeare spends a mere two-and-a-half lines on setting the scene ('The west yet glimmers with some streaks of day' etc.), Schiller's murderers wax lyrical, speaking four-and-a-half lines of what sounds like an extract from Goethe's *Erlkönig* or Schubert/Müller's *Winterreise*:
    Am Abendlichen Himmel
   Verglimmt der letzte bleiche Tagesschein.
   Der Wandrer, der sich auf dem Weg verspätet,
   Strengt seiner Schritte letzte Kraft noch an,
   Die Nachtherberge zeitig zu erreichen.
39 The reviewer in *Swensk Literatur-Tidning* criticizes Geijer's choice and maintains that he has misunderstood the word, either by accident or on purpose, citing Warburton's 1747 gloss of 'the inventors of the execrable doctrine of equivocation', the members of the Jesuit order.
40 Zilliacus, 'Notes', 146, 145.
41 Zilliacus, 'Notes', 145.
42 Geijer, 'Macbeth', 54.
43 Smidt, 'Discovery', 102.
44 Zilliacus, 'Notes', 143. The difference between the two, at least in Swedish usage, is appositely expressed by Karl Ragnar Gierow, who claims that the alexandrine is not a meter but a

mindset and blank verse is not an idiom but a living, breathing skin (*Johan Henrik Thomander*, 238).

45   Zilliacus, 'Notes', 143.
46   Donner (*Svenska översättningar*, 137–8), though generally preferring Schiller to Geijer, also praises this particular speech.
47   Ann Fridén (Macbeth, 37) claims that 'Geijer translated for readers, not for the theatre' although it is perhaps only natural that in the preface to the *Macbeth* translation, Geijer should address an imaginary *reader* rather than *spectator*, since a preface would be a thing for the reader regardless of whether the play-text itself was meant for the page or the stage.
48   Habicht, 'Romanticism', 49.
49   Quoted in Molin, *Shakespeare och Sverige*, 107.
50   Incidentally, similar thoughts are voiced by the above-mentioned Frans Michael Franzén; in the journal he kept in England, he reflects on the curiously disappointing nature of drama on stage: 'How rare it is to find an actor entirely convincing; how seldom he fills the room you made for him in your imagination when you read the part' (Hägglund, 'Shakespeare', 200).
51   Fridén, Macbeth, 37.
52   Grandison, ed., *Malla Silfverstolpes memoarer*, ii, 267.
53   Grandison, ed., *Malla Silfverstolpes memoarer*, iii, 41–2.
54   Donner, *Svenska översättningar*, 58–9; Vingedal, *Shakespeares ordmagi*, 17.
55   Gierow, *Johan Henrik Thomander*, 240–2.
56   Our warm thanks to Fredrik Tersmeden for alerting us to Hagberg's indebtedness to the anonymous translator.
57   Fridén, Macbeth, 44.
58   Fridén, Macbeth, 186–7.
59   Landquist, *Geijer*, 59; Flemberg and Hägglund, 'Geijer om Shakespeare', 251.
60   First published in *Poetisk Kalender* (1814), later revised and re-published in *Skaldestycken* (1835).
61   Geijer, 'Den Ny-Europeiska odlingens hufvudskiften', 341.

Works cited

Anon., review of 'Macbeth. Tragedie af Shakespeare', in *Swensk Literatur-Tidning*, 26 (3 July 1813), columns 401–12.

Anon., review of 'Macbeth. Tragedie af Shakspeare', in *Swensk Literatur-Tidning*, 29 (24 July 1813), columns 445–55.

Anon., review of 'Skaldestycken af P. A. Granberg', in *Swensk Literatur-Tidning*, 21 (28 May 1814), columns 317–27.

Avén, Göran, 'Hamlet på Kungl. Teatern 1819', *Nya Teaterhistoriska Studier*, 12 (1957), 161–85.

Borelius, Hilma, 'Geijer och Schiller', *Samlaren*, 26 (1905), 61–91.

Bratt, Ingar, *Engelskundervisningens framväxt i Sverige: Tiden före 1850* (Stockholm, 1977).

Burman, Carina, 'Vem var Erik Gustaf Geijer?', in *Macbeth 1813: E. G. Geijer översätter Shakespeare* (Stockholm, 2013), 11–43.

Delabastita, Dirk, and Lieven D'hulst, eds, *European Shakespeares: Translating Shakespeare in the Romantic Age* (Amsterdam, 1993).

Donner, Heinrich Wolfgang, *Svenska översättningar av Shakespeares Macbeth: Schillers inflytande på Geijers översättning* (Åbo, 1950).

Ewbank, Inga-Stina, 'Shakespeare Translation as Cultural Exchange', *Shakespeare Survey*, 48 (1996), 1–12.

Ewbank, Inga-Stina and Kiki Lindell, 'Scandinavia', in Michael Dobson et al., eds, *The Oxford Companion to Shakespeare* (2nd edn, Oxford, 2015), 479–80.

Flemberg, Henrik, and Kent Hägglund, 'Geijer om Shakespeare', in *Macbeth 1813: E.G. Geijer översätter Shakespeare* (Stockholm, 2013), 235–59.

Fridén, Ann, *Macbeth in the Swedish Theatre 1838–1986* (Malmö, 2013).

Geijer, Erik Gustaf, 'Shakespeare', in *Skaldestycken* (Upsala, 1835).

Geijer, Erik Gustaf, trans. *Macbeth*, in *Macbeth 1813: E. G. Geijer översätter Shakespeare* (Stockholm, 2013).

Geijer, Erik Gustaf, 'Den Ny-Europeiska odlingens hufvudskiften med särskildt afseende på de akademiska studierna. Föreläsningar höstterminen 1845', in *Samlade Skrifter*, i (Stockholm, 1849), 179–349.

Gierow, Karl Ragnar, *Johan Henrik Thomander. Fysionomi i tre belysningar* (Stockholm, 1975).

Grandison, Malla, ed., *Malla Montgomery Silfverstolpes Memoarer*, ii: *1804–1819* (Stockholm, 1909).
Grandison, Malla, ed., *Malla Montgomery Silfverstolpes Memoarer*, iii: *1819–1825* (Stockholm, 1910).
Habicht, Werner, 'The Romanticism of the Schlegel-Tieck Shakespeare and the History of Nineteenth-Century German Shakespeare Translation', in Delabastita and D'hulst, eds, *European Shakespeares*, 45–54.
Hagberg, Carl August, trans., *Shakespeares dramatiska arbeten*, ix (Lund, 1850).
Hägglund, Kent, *William Shakespeare. En man för alla tider* (Stockholm, 2006).
Hägglund, Kent, 'Shakespeare på Erik Gustaf Geijers tid', in *Macbeth 1813: E.G. Geijer översätter Shakespeare* (Stockholm, 2013), 190–234.
Hägglund, Kent, 'August Strindberg and William Shakespeare', *Strindbergiana*, 29 (2014), 21–36.
Hillberg, Olof, ed., *Teater i Sverige utanför huvudstaden* (Stockholm, 1948).
Landquist, John, *Geijer: En levnadsteckning* (Stockholm, 1954).
Levertin, Oscar, *Teater och drama under Gustaf III: litteraturhistorisk studie* (Stockholm, 1889).
Lindell, Kiki, 'Star-crossed lovers in Sweden', in Juan F. Cerdá, Dirk Delabastita and Keith Gregor, eds, *Romeo and Juliet in European Culture* (Amsterdam, 2017), 159–75.
Ljunggren, Gustaf, *Svenska vitterhetens häfder efter Gustaf III: sdöd*, iv (Lund, 1890).
Monié, Karin, *Ord som himlen når: Carl August Hagberg – en levnadsteckning* (Stockholm, 2008).
Molin, Nils, *Shakespeare och Sverige intill 1800-talets mitt: En översikt av hans inflytande* (Gothenburg, 1931).
Nordmark, Dag, 'Vägfarande komedianter', in Ulla-Britta Lagerroth and Ingeborg Nordin Hennel, eds, *Ny svensk teaterhistoria*, ii: *1800-talets teater* (Hedemora, 2007), 99–125.
Personne, Nils, *Svenska teatern: några anteckningar*, ii: *Från Gustaf III: sdöd till Karl XIV Johans ankomst till Sverige: 1792–1810* (Stockholm, 1914)
Personne, Nils, *Svenska teatern: några anteckningar*, iv: *Under Karl Johanstiden 1818–1827* (Stockholm, 1916).

Ranke, Wolfgang, 'Shakespeare Translations for Eighteenth-Century Stage Productions in Germany: Different Versions of *Macbeth*', in Delabastita and D'hulst, eds, *European Shakespeares*, 163–82.

Shakespeare, William, *Macbeth*, ed. Sandra Clark and Pamela Mason, The Arden Shakespeare (London, 2015).

Sivefors, Per, 'Trade Routes, Politics and Culture: Shakespeare in Sweden', in Janet Clare and Dominique Goy-Blanquet, eds, *Migrating Shakespeare: First European Encounters, Routes and Networks* (London, 2021), 189–208.

Skuncke, Marie-Christine, 'Gustaviansk teater', in Sven-Åke Heed, ed., *Ny svensk teaterhistoria*, i: *Teater före 1800* (Hedemora, 2007), 188–217.

Smidt, Kristian, 'The Discovery of Shakespeare in Scandinavia', in Delabastita and D'hulst, eds, 91–104.

Stiernstedt, W. Gordon, ed. and trans., *Amalia von Helvigs brev till Erik Gustaf Geijer* (Stockholm, 1950).

Vingedal, S.E., *Shakespeares ordmagi på svenska: En litteraturhistorisk översikt och en bibliografi* (Norrtälje, 1965).

Zilliacus, Clas, 'Notes on Metrical and Deictical Problems in Shakespeare Translation', in Gunnar Sorelius, ed., *Shakespeare and Scandinavia: A Collection of Nordic Studies* (Newark, 2002), 142–7.

3

Cold maids and dead men: Gender in translation and transition in *Hamlet*

Cecilia Lindskog Whiteley

It took nearly 200 years for Shakespeare's most famous and celebrated play to reach Sweden, and even longer for translations to appear in print. In that time, the character of Ophelia had undergone several transformations on stage. The introduction of female performers after the re-opening of the British theatres in 1660 had made possible the reincarnation of this most famous virginal character into female flesh. As Elaine Showalter argues, this shift in theatrical practice also brought gender into closer scrutiny, awakening anxiety. Partly in reaction to this, English theatrical depictions of Hamlet's female counterpart in the late eighteenth and early nineteenth centuries 'minimized the force of female sexuality and made female insanity a pretty stimulant to male sensibility'.[1] Sentimental, pictorial and de-sexualized: such was Ophelia when the first Swedish print translations of Shakespeare appeared (in 1819 and 1820). This particular Ophelia is a far cry from the intensely emotive character who would emerge later in the nineteenth century. John Everett Millais' iconic 1852 painting of a pathetic Ophelia exemplifies some of the ways in which the character was portrayed on British stages by the middle of the century. This is a different version of a Romantic Ophelia, and also the one found in the third published Swedish translation of *Hamlet* (1847), an Ophelia who embraces her madness and drowns in her emotions, similar to the way she is often read and performed in the twentieth and twenty-first centuries.[2] As such, the Swedish Ophelias of the first half of the nineteenth century broadly correlate to British trends for staging the character.

However, alongside these similarities with British representations of the character during the same period, the first two translations of *Hamlet* into Swedish can also be read in the context of a burgeoning movement of nationalist attempts to reposition and revalue Swedish culture. This Swedish enlightenment project is outlined in an essay by Olof Bjurbäck (1750–1829) accompanying his translation of 1820 (the second to be published), a text which betrays considerable anxiety about the moral stakes of literature in relation to national culture. Given this aim of establishing an elevated Swedish literary culture, what the character of Ophelia intimates about gender and sexuality becomes a point of concern in a manner akin to what is also seen in Britain. Kimberley Rhodes notes that in the British tradition of the mid-nineteenth century, 'the project of constructing an ideal womanhood [is conflated] with nationalism'; this served to make Shakespeare's heroines, and Ophelia in particular, focal points for revisions and reimaginings.[3] Similarly, the effects of this twin project of creating an elevated national culture and removing the taint of immoral content can be observed in the earliest published Swedish translations of *Hamlet*, which offer sentimental Ophelias, de-sexualized and marginalized, suitable for dissemination for the edification of the nation. This chapter seeks to bring to light the editorial and translation choices which combined to construct these scrubbed virginal characters, comparing each Ophelia to Shakespeare's own 'sweet maid', before concluding by considering the difference between the earlier two translations and Ophelia in the 1847 translation.[4] The latter was part of the first Swedish translation of Shakespeare's collected plays, motivated less by moral anxiety than by an ambition to disseminate an authorship. It resulted in an Ophelia who was much more like Shakespeare's original than her earlier sisters.

It was not only *Hamlet* but also Shakespeare as a whole that reached Sweden relatively late from a European perspective. The first print translation of a Shakespeare play into Swedish was published in 1813, by Erik Gustaf Geijer (1783–1847), poet, historian and composer as well as a famous propounder of national Romanticism.[5] Gunnar Sorelius notes that 'Scandinavia took part in the discovery of Shakespeare that was part of the early Romanticism in many areas of Europe', before claiming that 'there is no sign that [Shakespeare] was used in the formation and strengthening of a national culture'.[6] However, following in the footsteps of Geijer, Per Adolf Granberg (1770–1841) and Olof Bjurbäck both chose to frame their near-contemporaneous translations of *Hamlet* within the context of promoting a national Swedish culture of enlightenment and good taste. Initiated by the ambitions of King Gustaf III (1746–1792), late-eighteenth-century Sweden attempted to fashion itself as a cultural behemoth. This era saw the establishment of the Swedish Academy (1786), whose motto *Snille och Smak* [Genius and Taste] functioned well as shorthand for the king's ambitions for Sweden as a whole; the founding of the Royal Swedish Opera (1772) and the building of the opera house (1782); the establishment of the Royal Dramatic Theatre (1788); and the creation of a national costume (1778), this last another handy metaphor for the self-fashioning project as an exercise in (national) myth-making.[7] The aim by the early nineteenth century had developed into establishing Sweden as cultural power in its own right, rather than simply a pale French-inspired imitation. As Romantic poet Carl Fredrik Dahlgren (1791–1844) wrote in a letter to a friend the day after he had attended the first performance of Granberg's *Hamlet*:

> yesterday evening, the exterminating angel of Egypt extended his sword to Stockholm and slew the first born son of the eighteenth century. ... Now we, like Hamlet, have made amends with the father of Drama ... The French whore, with whom the Swede has so long fornicated, has been imprisoned or sent to Bedlam.[8]

The exterminating angel is the perpetrator of the final of the ten plagues of Egypt, killing all firstborn sons in the country to avenge the Egyptians' treatment of the Israelites, while the French whore (a common slur aimed at Marie Antoinette) likely referred more generally to the significant French influence on Swedish culture in the eighteenth century, an influence which Dahlgren clearly felt was corrupting and which Granberg and Bjurbäck both also wished to counteract with their translations. The stakes of the national enlightenment project in relation to Shakespeare and *Hamlet* could not be more clearly enunciated than by this Romantic rhetoric.

Unsurprising in this context, a keen awareness of Sweden's cultural position can be found in the first two translations of *Hamlet*, along with anxious traces of implied national cultural inferiority, expressed in the translators' forewords. Granberg's 1819 translation of *Hamlet* includes a foreword which states that the translator aims to 'bestow upon an enlightened nation the portrayal of the dramatic character of this genius'.[9] This clearly positions Granberg's efforts within the project of national enlightenment: he is introducing Shakespeare the Bard to an audience that wishes to consider itself culturally enlightened, yet is comparatively unfamiliar with a major international author. To reconcile the image of Sweden as a country of learning and culture with the relative anonymity of Shakespeare, Granberg explains that he sought to 'also in our country pay duty to one of the most unusual of geniuses'.[10] The point is subtle but significant: given the unusual nature of Shakespeare's genius, the Swedish cultural establishment cannot be faulted for his still being relatively unknown. Nevertheless, it is an anonymity which needs to be rectified.

The second *Hamlet* translation, an 1820 version by Olof Bjurbäck, Bishop of Karlstad, was accompanied by a 34-page essay outlining his thoughts on Shakespeare and the play, in which Bjurbäck also positions his translation as part of a national cultural concern: 'Shakespeare is among our reading Public nearly unknown; few likely possess the ability to read him in the original language'.[11] The translation, specifically intended for reading rather than performance, aims to provide access to Shakespeare's 'phenomenal Genius', even though the Bishop also states his belief that

> the majority do not possess that power and depth of emotion, not that free and lively understanding, not that ... Experience and, above all, not that *Simplicity* and *Honesty*, that *Denial of Self*, that infantile *Innocence*, which is required in order to feel and comprehend [Shakespeare].[12]

Bjurbäck, then, seems to believe that he is writing partly in vain, yet also in the hope of improving his audience. Such improvement lies primarily in morals, rather than in the expansion of a cultural canon: 'the implacable truth in Shakespeare raises its mighty voice against foolish, blind pride, shaking and obliterating the pillars of doom in inflated, wrathful, hard hearts'.[13] The Bishop is hoping to inspire readers of *Hamlet* with a warning, a humbling caution, employing the terminology of a Romantic to advocate for the importance of rationality to navigate a turbulent existence (couching a position of reason and enlightenment belief within the emerging framework of the primacy of experience that the Romantic movement brought). For Bjurbäck, *Hamlet* constitutes an ideal vehicle for such lessons: 'Fear thou, who looks upon the fool, know that thy gifts of Thinking rely on a single thread; who is there, that can promise, never to become his equal?'.[14] It is within this context of pity and empathy that

Bjurbäck discusses Shakespeare's Ophelia, claiming that 'the way in which Ophelia is portrayed in the original, when read, I defy any man with common sense and Heart, not to find most sublime'.[15] Such professed tolerance and compassion are somewhat undermined by the treatment which Bjurbäck metes out to the character.

Given her enduring cultural relevance, it is remarkable that Ophelia, in Shakespeare's original play, only appears in five scenes. As Mary Floyd-Wilson remarks, 'the cultural construct of Shakespeare's Ophelia has overridden her presence (or absence)' in the original text.[16] The current cultural construct dates to the nineteenth century, as Showalter argues: that is to say, the origins of Ophelia as a cultural cipher for attitudes about gender and sexuality coincides, historically at least, with her arrival in Sweden.[17] In spite of her relatively limited time on stage, Shakespeare's Ophelia is established as a multi-faceted character, essentially ambiguous (and therefore, to the early translators of the play into Swedish, problematic), within a Danish court in which doubts and duality are dangerous. It is a position which makes her demise an inevitability. Each of Ophelia's interactions in Shakespeare's text serves to demonstrate the impossibility of her existence, the unattainable expectations placed upon her by her father, her brother, Hamlet and by the court as a whole. In the early Swedish translations, Ophelia's agency and ambiguity are both circumscribed to produce a desexualized version of the character, much in line with English late-eighteenth-century adaptations of *Hamlet*. While her fate is never in doubt in these translations, minor changes of inflection effect major interventions in the portrayal of Ophelia, resulting in a character who abides by the rules of propriety in her new age, yet cannot be allowed to step outside a nineteenth-century Swedish system of control which is even more rigid than that of Shakespeare's original Danish court.

Floyd-Wilson argues that late-eighteenth-century British revisions of Ophelia 'invested her with a mixture of "ideal" femininity and veiled sexuality', resulting in an intriguing ambiguity, while Susan Lamb speaks of Ophelia as directed by

Garrick as marked by 'virtuous sexual desire' (virtuous, because thwarted; because thwarted, the cause of her madness).[18] The anxious impetus seemingly underlying such revisions would appear to have been shared by the early Swedish translators, who take pains to mark Ophelia as contained by patriarchal structures. One of the clearest examples of how this is effected through the use of minor alterations can be seen in Bjurbäck's translation of Polonius' 'I have a daughter – have while she is mine' (*Ham* 2.2.105). The pompous pedantry of his infamously tortured syntax notwithstanding, Polonius here acknowledges that his rights of possession are temporary, the implication being that Ophelia will become the property of her husband upon marriage. Bjurbäck's rendition of the line is close, but with one significant difference: 'Märk! jag har en dotter – *har*, ty hon är min' [Mark! I have a daughter – *have*, for she is mine] (emphasis in original).[19] The tense and pronoun work powerfully here to show that the possession is permanent, conditioned only on the father's right. It removes potential agency from the character of Ophelia, so her position in the play is easier to locate. Similar minor alterations can be found in several of Polonius' interactions with Ophelia, in Granberg's translation as well as Bjurbäck's: they fashion a father who jealously controls his daughter's personal relationships with her suitor, blaming her for being at once too forward and too innocent. Aligning with anxiety displayed in English eighteenth-century portrayals, such alterations simultaneously introduce a curiously liminal version of Ophelia, at once censored and proto-Romantic, whose emotional suffering is foregrounded, but whose morals are vigorously guarded, to a public interested in mediating a perceived conflict between sense and sensibility. When coupled with the extensive changes made to some of Ophelia's most important scenes, a pattern emerges: Granberg and Bjurbäck are both engaged in the construction of a female heroism for Ophelia, scrubbing away the taint of sexuality and transvaluing, in Wolfson's terms, melancholy into patient suffering.[20]

The stakes of Ophelia's sexuality are highlighted by Granberg in the nunnery scene (3.1), where he chooses to translate Shakespeare's key term 'honest' as 'dygdig' [virtuous], a word laden with implications of sexual morality.[21] This is a choice which once again removes some of the ambiguity of Shakespeare's original. Shakespeare's Ophelia is a performer in this scene, acting upon instruction from her father and conscious of both her performance and of being watched, complicit in the courtly machinations. The audience, too, are invited to play the role of the court, watching Ophelia's exchange with Hamlet, one which serves to illustrate the intimacy and relative power dynamics within their relationship while simultaneously emphasizing its dysfunction when outside influences are admitted. Sympathies for Ophelia on account of Hamlet's famous and unreasonable double bind – 'the power of Beauty will sooner transform Honesty from what it is to a bawd than the force of Honesty can translate Beauty into his likeness' (*Ham* 3.1.110–13) – is moderated by the opening query, Hamlet's question if she is 'honest' (*Ham* 3.1.101). The dramatic irony lies in the audience being well aware that Ophelia is not 'honest' in this scene. The lack of honesty identified by them is a taint that can gradually spread to Ophelia's sexual morals over the course of the dialogue, so that Hamlet's condemnation seemingly receives confirmation. Granberg's choice to translate 'honest' using a term laden with implications of sexual morality is a foregrounding of this motif, reinforcing the hint in Shakespeare's original that moral imperfections in female characters can spread to become sexual taints regardless of the original sin. Given this, Granberg's rendering of Hamlet's 'Get thee to a nunnery! Why wouldst thou be a breeder of sinners?' is remarkable: 'Gå i ett kloster Ophelia; hvarföre skall du blifva qvar i verlden och kanske föröka syndares antal?' [Enter a nunnery Ophelia: why should you remain in the world and perhaps increase the number of sinners?].[22] In this formulation, the cause for the multiplication of sinners is (deliberately) vague, introducing the suggestion that Ophelia may be adding to the number not (only) by giving birth to inherently sinful children, but by choosing to act in sinful ways. The change subtly alters Hamlet's generalized misanthropy into a more targeted misogyny.

Perhaps unsurprisingly for a translation which purports to aim at delivering eternal truths and with a strong Christian inflection, Bjurbäck's version of the same scene is somewhat different. The sexual implications of virtue have been replaced by a straight translation of Shakespeare's 'honest'. In the dialogue which follows, mentions of bawds, commerce and anything else suggestive of sexuality, in particular of sexuality as transactional (a major motif of the interactions between Hamlet and Ophelia, established by Polonius' exhortations to his daughter), have been scrupulously excised.[23] These decisions may serve to purify the relationship on a moral level, but come at a stylistic, as well as a narrative, cost, making the dialogue less fluent. Thus, Ophelia's question 'Kan skönheten hafva better sällskap, än ärligheten?' [Can beauty have better company than honesty?], is answered with a flat 'Fordom älskade jag er.' [In the past I loved you].[24] Removing Hamlet's musings on the inevitable corruption of female beauty, presumably because Bjurbäck wished to avoid the subject, the complexity of the relationship is rendered simplistically in the mould of a courtship operating within the laws of eighteenth-century propriety.

Similar anxiety relating to the sexual ambiguity of Ophelia's character can be found in both translations of the *Mousetrap* scene. In many respects the counterpart to the nunnery scene, this is another key moment for Ophelia in the original, Shakespeare giving us an entertaining exchange between two near-equals:

HAMLET
   Lady, shall I lie in your lap? *Lying down at Ophelia's feet*
OPHELIA
   No, my lord.
HAMLET
   I mean, my head upon your lap?

OPHELIA
Ay, my lord.
HAMLET
Do you think I meant country matters?
OPHELIA
I think nothing, my lord.
HAMLET
That's a fair thought to lie between maids' legs.
OPHELIA
What is, my lord?
HAMLET
Nothing.
OPHELIA
You are merry, my lord.
(*Ham* 3.2.108–15)

As Kimberly Rhodes notes, Ophelia's dual function in this passage, both witness (of the play and the plotting) and sparring partner to Hamlet, is a 'juxtaposition [that] expresses the duality of her character (active/passive, sexually experienced/innocent) and obscures an easy reading of her sexuality'.[25] Perhaps unsurprisingly, given the sexual subtext of many of Ophelia's lines, this is a place in which we find both Bjurbäck and Granberg making significant cuts and changes. Hamlet's initial double entendre is sanitized in both early Swedish translations, which work hard to obscure any sexual undertones.

In Granberg's translation, Hamlet's question has been amended to 'Tillåter ni att jag lutar mitt hufvud mot edert knä?' [Will you allow me to lean my head against your knee?]. While 'knä' could mean either 'knee' or 'lap', the preposition chosen ('mot' [against]) indicates that the reference is to the joint of the leg, rather than the sexually laden lap (which would logically have taken the proposition 'i' [in]), making this read like another minor intervention which serves to remove sexual ambiguity from the relationship.[26] As if to emphasize the propriety of the question, Granberg then interrupts his translation with an added stage direction immediately following

Hamlet's line: '*Polonius vinkar bifall*' [*Polonius waves assent*].²⁷ Thus, Ophelia is spared the burden of having to interpret what is, in fact, a sanitized question. In the original, her immediate refusal is highlighted by Hamlet's 'Did you think I meant country matters?', a line that functions both to introduce the sparring between Hamlet and Ophelia and to highlight her ability to identify the sexual pun. Granberg's decision to have Polonius intervene in the exchange alters this dynamic, so that the audience may be assured of Ophelia's purity. Not only does she evade the responsibility of interpreting a sexually charged double entendre, she is not even required to exercise her own judgement in relation to a suitor. These kinds of changes, serving to limit Ophelia's ability to act and judge, are a feature of Granberg's translation but are perhaps most clearly seen in this scene, where they markedly alter the tenor of Hamlet and Ophelia's exchanges, the bantering reduced to blandness:

HAMLET
   What, you seem irresolute? Are you distracted, or what were you thinking?
OPHELIA
   I was thinking of nothing.
HAMLET
   In truth a fair thought!²⁸

There is nothing here of the playful banter and sexual punning of the original. Removing these, Ophelia's ability to interact with Hamlet (in essence, her ability to function effectively in her primary relationship), is circumscribed. Moreover, Granberg's effacing of Ophelia's 'duality' (to use Rhodes' term), is one which not only affects readings of her character, but also changes Hamlet's possible motivation. Erasing the sexual aspects of the relationship means removing frustrated sexuality on the part of the prince. The focus of the interaction, the only suggested reason behind his melancholy, becomes a kind of existential meditation, one which falls neatly in line with his famous soliloquy (*Ham* 3.1.55–87).

Bjurbäck's version of the same exchange is characterized by a similar impetus to remove suggestions of impropriety. He renders Hamlet's opening question in explicit language which leaves little room for double meanings: 'Min Fröken, får jag sitta här vid Edra fötter och lägga mitt hufvud på Ert knä' [My lady, may I sit here by your feet and lay my head on your knee?][29] Once again, the choice of 'knä' rather than 'sköte' and the use of the preposition 'på' [on] rather than 'i' [in] in the Swedish translation is suggestive of a reading of 'knä' as asexual, an impression which is supported by the more elaborate and explicit phrasing in which Hamlet specifies that he is asking to place himself by Ophelia's feet. The effect is to emphasize for a reader that there can be no sexual contact from this position, a position which places Hamlet as a supplicant at Ophelia's feet. It is courtly love without either the sadism or the sex.

It is clear that the Bishop himself recognized that the original did contain sexually charged material and his response is even more repressive than Granberg's. While Granberg acknowledges in his preface that he has chosen to 'on occasion avoid and veil certain expressions', Bjurbäck has cut the dialogue about country matters in its entirety, something which he reflects upon in a footnote: 'Here follows a conversation between Hamlet and Ophelia which cannot be translated, and only explained with reference to the difference between our time and that in which Shakespeare wrote'.[30]

The notion that something in the original by necessity escapes translation is itself ambiguous: it suggests that either the language or the content, or perhaps both, cannot be rendered in Swedish. However, particularly in light of the fact that this same passage had been translated into Swedish only a year previously, albeit with significant alterations, Bjurbäck's editorial intervention becomes less a question of translatability as of his reticence to translate it. In his introduction, Bjurbäck claims that 'the reasons for excluding something will be immediately apparent', yet this textual footnote explicitly provides an explanation for the cut.[31] The footnote, in fact, serves not so much as a justification for the cut, but rather as though Shakespeare's inclusion of a scene of sexual bantering would need some justification in itself. For Bjurbäck, it is a conversation which needs to be 'explained' and excused with references to the different mores of an earlier era. As such, Bjurbäck, as Granberg before him but to an even more puritanical degree, wilfully omits any textual hints of Ophelia's sexuality, with the view of rehabilitating Shakespeare (to a greater extent than the character of Ophelia) from accusations of immorality. Bjurbäck's introduction specifically states that 'Sh-re's tongue is not the discharge of a filthy mind, but a victim of human weakness and the taste of Time', drawing a distinction between temporal mores and eternal morality, before using the past as an excuse to recommend measured self-reflection about Sweden in the early nineteenth century. 'In other respects the taste of our Time ought to be more objectionable', Bjurbäck writes, since, unlike the England of James I, nineteenth-century Sweden did not threaten harsh penalties for the invocation of God's name in literature.[32]

Bjurbäck is clear that he wants *Hamlet* to function as a 'tuktomästare' [master of castigation], an example from which readers should learn. This ambition is another justification for Shakespeare's authorship: 'Sh-re portrays the sublunary world such as it is, a mixture of evil and good, vices and virtues, ... and is thereby culpable of nearly all the faults and flaws which can be laid at the feet of an author, with the exception of that most severe fault, being *immoral*'.[33] Yet, the Bishop clearly felt that Shakespeare at least verged on immorality in his portrayal of Ophelia, the refashioning of whose character is completed in a remarkable rewriting of the funeral scene. In itself, this was not a novel approach in translations of *Hamlet*: shortening or cutting the funeral scene in its entirety (like Granberg does) was often done in British as well as Continental adaptations. For Bjurbäck's version, the changes relate to the excision of original material that hints at sexuality. This causes a subtle reconceptualization of the plot, since it also removes the sexual rivalry that Shakespeare establishes between Hamlet and Laertes. Indeed, Bjurbäck entirely removes Hamlet as an active character from the funeral itself after 5.1.211, when he and Horatio stand apart to observe the passing procession.[34] Shakespeare shows us Hamlet's reaction to Ophelia's death in an aside ('What, the fair Ophelia?', *Ham* 5.1.232), a line which Bjurbäck has cut, before the confrontation at Ophelia's grave, another significant omission. One effect is that Hamlet's grief over Ophelia is rendered invisible, removed as an additional motivation for the Prince in the final scene of the play. Overall, in Bjurbäck's version, there is no sense in which the relationship between Hamlet and Ophelia – and hence Ophelia as a character – is important enough to truly affect Hamlet.

In place of the confrontation between Hamlet and Laertes, Bjurbäck has created a more elaborate funeral ceremony for the dead Ophelia, one which delivers a message of Christian salvation for all, while simultaneously placing great importance on the construction of her as pure and absolutely virginal. After Laertes' remonstration to the priest that 'a ministering, serving angel shall my sister become when thou lay gnashing thy teeth' is rendered relatively accurately (*Ham* 5.1.231),[35] Bjurbäck makes a remarkable and extensive addition to the scene: he introduces two choirs who sing their lamentations over the dead. The overall effect is to situate Ophelia's death as well as Hamlet's struggles within an explicitly Christian context. The song references 'the torch of salvation' carrying all 'through the cold mist of madness', a message appropriate for Ophelia and Hamlet both, while Ophelia is referred to as 'the bride of Heaven',[36] born for a better world.

Bjurbäck's funeral lamentation for Ophelia represents the culmination of his reconstruction of the character. These choirs in effect replace her own voice, excised from the *Mousetrap* scene and moderated in many others. Described by the choir of maidens as 'our joy, our pride', she was the personification of immortal virtue. 'Like angels', her demise is an affront to those angels' 'blessed state'; not even in suicide is she allowed agency. Instead, she is

> Like a plant which has been moved
> To a harsh and punishing clime
> Well might it sprout and bloom,
> As its peers are seen to do,
> But it cannot reach maturity,
> But must fall away and die.[37]

In this formulation, Ophelia's suicide is a natural necessity, one which derives from the dichotomy between her 'fallen body' and 'Spirit'. This term places Bjurbäck's Ophelia within a Romantic context, reinforced by the natural imagery and pathetic inflection that he gives to the passage. Ophelia's spirit, 'descended from the abode of peace', has 'returned to its home' upon her death. Bjurbäck essentially agrees with Hamlet's misogyny in the nunnery scene but disagrees with his worldly compromise: rather than a nunnery, only a celestial, non-physical existence can accommodate a virtuous woman. As a Bishop, it is also likely that Bjurbäck felt strongly about the intimations of suicide: by representing Ophelia's death as an inevitability, the suspicion and stigma of suicide can be minimized.

In the context of amendments to Shakespeare, it is interesting to note that the passage is significant for stylistic reasons, standing out from the rest of Bjurbäck's translation as entirely distinct in its formal aspects. Throughout his translation, Bjurbäck casts aside Shakespeare's predominant blank verse, instead rendering *Hamlet* unbound in metre and rhyme. Indeed, he even remarks on his conscious decision to forgo formal metre and rhymes in favour of a free-flowing language, because 'Metre, euphony, tone, are added pleasures, but not the essential, not the most important: a body is more than clothes ... No translator is capable of showing how Shakespeare wrote verse'.[38] But this passage with the two choirs is composed of rhyming stanzas in an ABAB pattern, similar to the rhythmic quality of a hymn. Stylistically, this disrupts the text, calling attention to the section as distinct and separate. In his introduction, Bjurbäck comments in a general way about additions to the text: 'the few and brief additions shall, perhaps, not be so easily justified'.[39] This acknowledgement suggests a recognition of the significance of his interventions in Shakespeare's text (hardly brief), yet there is no attempt at justification of the most substantial of these interventions. Perhaps this suggests that Bjurbäck felt the major rewriting of Ophelia's funeral was justified within the remit of rendering *Hamlet* appropriately for his age. This he considers to be the true task of the translator:

> Where Shakespeare in Hamlet allows the ghost to appear alive, a translator can show it through an urn, in which the ashes of the murdered King are stored ... In such a deviation from Shakespeare, nothing needs to be pointed out, since the intention [with a translation] is not portray how Shakespeare thought ..., but simply to use one of Shakespeare's plays to craft another, suited to the characteristics and temperament of its time.[40]

Here, translation is the refashioning of geographically and chronologically related materials into shapes more appropriate for new ages and places. By extension, we may conclude that, for Bjurbäck, a radical rewriting of Ophelia is a fundamental part of such a process.

Whereas Bjurbäck rewrites Ophelia's life through this scene of funeral oration, Granberg chose to deal quite differently with both her funeral and death. Bjurbäck, as we have seen, embellishes the funeral in a manner which effectively functions to erase the sexual and emphasize a Christian message. Granberg, on the other hand, cuts the funeral scene altogether. Moreover, he also modifies the way in which the audience of the play comes to understand the events surrounding Ophelia's death, related in Gertrude's speech in 4.7. Following a reasonably faithful translation of the description of Ophelia's death, Granberg ends by describing her as 'the fairest ornament of virginity'. This pristine image of feminine perfection stands in stark contrast to Shakespeare's original Ophelia, a 'poor wretch' (*Ham* 4.7.180), whose female physicality is beautiful as well as pure and innocent.[41] However, the relatively unobtrusive, if significant, translation slippages make way for a more egregious decision in Granberg's rendering of Laertes' reaction to the news of his sister's drowning: 'Oh God! She died ere our father was avenged! Unhappy Ophelia! I will join you shortly. For me remains just one deed and then death'.[42] Comparing this speech to Shakespeare is illuminating: in the original lament for his sister, Laertes has none of the death-embracing posturing that he occupies in Granberg's version. Perhaps Granberg's changes were in part influenced by his decision to remove the funeral scene, which also meant cutting the confrontation between Laertes and Hamlet. This, in turn, meant cutting Laertes' assertion of his primary claim to his sister's dead body, a moment memorably performed on the stage as he leaps into her open grave. Shakespeare has Laertes literally join Ophelia in the grave, something to which a Swedish audience was not exposed. Like Bjurbäck, Granberg provides commentary on editorial choices, stating that he has cut 'several episodes superfluous to the effect', as well as scenes which 'possibly might give rise to some unpleasant impression'.[43] By extension, Granberg must have considered the funeral scene, with its visceral expressions of grief, as either superfluous to the play overall or at risk of provoking undesirable reactions. The former places rivalry as well as sexual relationships outside the remit of the play, whereas the latter suggests that Granberg was uncomfortable with displaying such matter on stage. Either interpretation places Ophelia at the centre of Granberg's censorship, the cipher for what is and is not considered to be in good taste.

The decision to cut the entirety of the original funeral reflects the significant anxiety about Ophelia's character displayed by both Granberg and Bjurbäck. As is attested by the alterations in both translations, in the early nineteenth-century Swedish context, Ophelia is the focal point of those changing mores cited by both translators as a major difference between Shakespeare's era and the nominally enlightened 'modern'

Sweden, a culturally advanced nation apparently characterized by an increased circumscription of female agency in drama. Ophelia's part has become less active, the character less a subject and more a vessel for others, as well as more clearly shaped by her patriarchal relationships.

Carl August Hagberg and the 1847 translation of *Hamlet*

The final Ophelia of this chapter, appearing nearly three decades after her two older sisters (1847), was conceived in a different social and literary climate and has maintained a cultural relevance unmatched by her predecessors. This can largely be explained by the enduring popularity of the translation by Carl August Hagberg (1810–1864), one which long remained the standard Swedish version of *Hamlet*. The longevity of the translation, however, may very well be explained in large part by Hagberg's lack of anxiety-induced interventions, part of the legacy of which is a less circumscribed Ophelia.

Hagberg belonged to a later generation of men of letters than Granberg and Bjurbäck. As a student in Uppsala in the 1820s, he encountered a Romantic tradition which he would react against in much of his later works, including in his approach to translations, as well as an interest in Shakespeare. Hagberg's friend Elias Wilhelm Ruda (1807–1833) used *Hamlet* as an example of the generally poor standard of drama in Sweden when he noted it as a 'masterpiece' which had been 'mutilated' by 'the chopping and changing of forgers' and Hagberg himself would voice a similar opinion in his own cultural magazine *Studier, Kritiker och Notiser*.[44] Reflecting in 1845 on a performance of Granberg's *Hamlet* which he had attended, Hagberg damned it as 'woefully falsified'; this comment was made after Hagberg's own translation was finished, but while he was in the midst of translating all of Shakespeare's plays and, as such, can be an indication of his own priorities.[45] Like Bjurbäck, Hagberg's translation work was partly motivated by 'an almost patriotic duty' and his biographer, Karin Monié, argues that the effort of translating Shakespeare's complete works was 'intimately connected with his idea about Sweden, the motherland and its culture'.[46] These motivations are neatly mirrored in Bjurbäck's introduction to his translation. The similarities in patriotic motivation notwithstanding, however, each translator's underlying principles would come to affect their adaptations of Shakespeare's original in different ways. We have already seen how Bjurbäck's moral anxiety, in combination with patriotic ambition, resulted in significant interventions in his translation: Hagberg, on his part, had attacked leading Swedish romantics on the basis of immorality.[47] However, when it came to translations, his commitment to accuracy overrode the moral cast of thought and his ruling impetus was to render Shakespeare complete.

Hamlet was the first of Shakespeare's plays translated by Hagberg and would come to form part of the first translation of Shakespeare's collected plays into Swedish. Unsurprisingly, given Hagberg's commitment to 'elevated philology', his version is much more reminiscent of Shakespeare's original than the earlier two print attempts.[48] It is rendered in a blank verse less fluent and versatile than Shakespeare's, but efficient nonetheless. Hagberg's editorial interventions are similarly minimized. The result is more recognizably a translation of the original, rather than an alternative to it.

A brief comparison of Hagberg's handling of the nunnery and *Mousetrap* scenes serves as an illustration of how far his adaptation departs from the earlier translations, as well as of the extent and impact of the earlier interventions. Where Shakespeare's 'honest' in *Hamlet* 3.1 was a loaded term for Granberg and a neutral one for Bjurbäck, Hagberg opts for 'ärbar' [honourable], a word with interestingly dual connotations – of valour as well as virtue – that combine the subtext of both of Bjurbäck's and Granberg's choices. While honourability could contain sexual virtue, however,

Hagberg does not include Ophelia among the number of inevitable sinners, choosing instead to render Hamlet's original misanthropy. Similarly, in the *Mousetrap* scene, Hagberg reflects the ambiguity in the original text, translating Hamlet's request 'Lady, shall I lie in your lap?' (*Ham* 3.2.108) as 'Min fröken, får jag ligga i ert sköte?' [My lady, may I lie in your lap?].[49] Where the first two translations chose 'knä', Hagberg opted for a noun which – like the original – carries connotations of physical embrace: 'sköte' can indeed mean lap, but also a woman's womb or bosom. The exchange between Hamlet and Ophelia which follows in the original has been kept (not excised as in Bjurbäck), but with a small modification. Having allowed for the ambiguities of 'sköte' rather than 'knä', Hagberg sticks with this term, resulting in a similar effect as when the original Hamlet muses that it is 'a fair thought to lie between maids' legs' (*Ham* 3.2.112), but without the explicit vulgarity. Hagberg renders this line as 'Det är en skön tanke att ligga i jungfrusköt' [It is a pleasurable thought to lie in a maiden's lap/bosom]: the adjectival choice acknowledges how the line glosses Hamlet's earlier pun in the original, fully cognisant of the sexual implications and steering away from Granberg's existentialist scrubbing.[50] Unlike in either of the earlier translations, Ophelia is allowed to interact with a more complex Prince: responding to complexity also allows her to claim her own.

Hagberg makes no cuts to Shakespeare's text on either moral or stylistic grounds and, as a consequence, Ophelia is allowed to reclaim her duality. This difference is clearly demonstrated in the translations of Gertrude's recounting of Ophelia's death. Important as an instance in which Ophelia is constructed through the narration of a female, rather than male, character, this speech also lies at the centre of later nineteenth-century conceptions of Ophelia:

> There is a willow grows askant the brook
> That shows his hoary leaves in the glassy stream.
> Therewith fantastic garlands did she make

Of cornflowers, nettles, daisies and long purples,
That liberal shepherds give a grosser name
But our cold maids do dead men's fingers call them.
There on the pendent boughs her crowned weeds
Clambering to hang, an envious sliver broke,
When down her weedy trophies and herself
Fell in the weeping brook. Her clothes spread wide
And mermaid-like awhile they bore her up,
Which time she chanted snatches of old lauds
As one incapable of her own distress,
Or like a creature native and endued
Unto that element. But long it could not be
Till that her garments, heavy with their drink,
Pulled the poor wretch from her melodious lay
To muddy death.

(*Ham* 4.7.164–81)

Themes of madness and innocence join associations mobilized by the imagery of gender, flowers, and water, to portray a richly textured Ophelia. She has knowledge of the 'grosser name' but, as a 'cold maid', opts to use a different term, one which foreshadows the embrace of death. Innocence in this formulation is the exercise of judgement, rather than the lack of knowledge, a useful counterpoint to Granberg's decision to circumvent Ophelia's judgement in the *Mousetrap* scene. Symptomatic of their shared censorship ambition, Granberg and Bjurbäck both neatly omit any mention of these suggestive 'long purples' in Gertrude's speech. Hagberg, however, does not shy away. Instead, he allows uncouth labourers, coarse language and phallic plants to co-exist in the same sphere as Ophelia: 'Dem råa herdar giva grövre namn, / Men blyga jungfrur kalla "dödmäns fingrar"' [Those that unrefined shepherds give grosser name, / But shy virgins call 'dead men's fingers'].[51] With a rehabilitated Ophelia, *Hamlet* regains its complexity and richness. No longer a mediation between Enlightenment and proto-Romanticism or between the temporal and eternal, it can emerge as a truly Shakespearean play. This, in turn, rather than any ideological motivation to support a burgeoning movement for female emancipation, seems to have been Hagberg's primary motivation.

The first Ophelias in print in Sweden are shaped by deliberate and extensive editorial interventions by translators motivated by impulses to restrain 'subversive or violent possibilities' and, above all, to curb and contain female sexuality.[52] These efforts share many similarities with near-contemporaneous attempts to refine Shakespeare in Britain, perhaps best exemplified by Garrick's Jubilee.[53] The one-dimensional maidens produced by Granberg and Bjurbäck, however, serve an additional purpose: they are revisionist models of virginity, certainly, but within the cultural context of national romanticism. Both translators conspicuously position themselves within the context of (further) educating an enlightened nation, one whose enlightenment in respect of women's sexuality must be curtailed and redirected. Their brave attempts notwithstanding, neither of their Ophelias would emerge as the Swedish iconic 'sweet maid'. That recognition must be granted to Hagberg's mid-nineteenth-century edition of *Hamlet*, which, because of its commitment to translating, rather than rewriting, Shakespeare, fashioned the modern Ophelia as Sweden knows her today.

Notes

1   Showalter, 'Representing Ophelia', 82. See also Ronk, 'Representations of Ophelia', *passim*.
2   Showalter, 'Representing Ophelia', 86–7.
3   Rhodes, *Ophelia and Victorian Visual Culture*, 21.
4   Shakespeare, *Hamlet*, 5.1.234. All quotes from Shakespeare's original are taken from the Arden Shakespeare Third Series, ed. Anne Thompson and Neil Taylor, and will henceforth be referenced parenthetically within the main text.
5   For discussion of Geijer as a translator of Shakespeare, see Lindell's and Hägglund's chapter in the present volume.

6   Sorelius, 'Introduction', 9. For an historical overview on Shakespeare in Sweden up until the early twentieth century, see Swan, 'Shakespeare in Sweden'; also, Molin, *Shakespeare och Sverige*.

7   The Swedish Academy was instituted by Gustaf III after its French counterpart and is today best known as the body which selects the Nobel laureates in literature, but among its other duties is the stewardship of the Swedish language. The national costume was an example of the unification of cultural and financial interests, in which Gustaf's ambitions for a culturally distinguished nation could be joined with his efforts to curb the nation's excessive spending on luxuries. The initiative received significant attention outside of Sweden as well, with Voltaire, who was much admired by Gustaf III, commenting that: 'Nations should be themselves. They should only imitate each other in what is good and never in what is capricious'. Quoted in a letter from Gustav Philip Creutz to Gustaf III, 29 March 1778, in von Proschwitz, *Gustaf III*, 162. All translations from Swedish are my own.

8   Carl Fredric Dahlgren, letter to H. J. Öfverberg dated 27 March 1819, quoted in Molin, *Shakespeare*, 102.

9   Granberg, *Hamlet*, 2.

10 Granberg, *Hamlet*, 2.

11 Bjurbäck, *Hamlet*, 1.

12 Bjurbäck, *Hamlet*, 1.

13 Bjurbäck, *Hamlet*, 4.

14 Bjurbäck, *Hamlet*, 24.

15 Bjurbäck, *Hamlet*, 25–6.

16 Floyd-Wilson, 'Ophelia and Femininity', 397.

17 Showalter, 'Representing Ophelia', 83.

18 Other critics, such as Showalter and Rhodes, argue that eighteenth-century Ophelia was far less ambivalent than the character would be in the nineteenth century, not finding the same leniency in subtexts that Floyd-Wilson and Lamb do. Floyd-Wilson, 'Ophelia and Femininity', 397; Lamb, 'Applauding Shakespeare's Ophelia', 117; Showalter,

'Representing Ophelia', 83–4; Rhodes, *Ophelia and Victorian Visual Culture*, 51.
19 Bjurbäck, *Hamlet*, 87.
20 Wolfson, 'Romanticism & Gender & Melancholy', 445.
21 Granberg, *Hamlet*, 41.
22 Granberg, *Hamlet*, 41.
23 On the ambiguity of Polonius' commercial language, see Bross, *Versions of Hamlet*, 184–7.
24 Bjurbäck, *Hamlet*, 113.
25 Rhodes, *Ophelia and Victorian Visual Culture*, 58.
26 Lending further weight to a reading of Hamlet's request as asexual is the choice made by Granberg and Bjurbäck both to avoid translating 'lap' as 'sköte', the term which would be preferred in the third translation and which carries similar connotations to those of Shakespeare's original 'lap'. See the discussion on Hagberg's translation (below) for more detail.
27 Granberg, *Hamlet*, 48.
28 Granberg, *Hamlet*, 48.
29 Bjurbäck, *Hamlet*, 122.
30 Granberg, *Hamlet*, 1; Bjurbäck, *Hamlet*, 122.
31 Bjurbäck, *Hamlet*, 32.
32 Bjurbäck, *Hamlet*, 3.
33 Bjurbäck, *Hamlet*, 3, 2.
34 It is worth noting the material difference between Shakespeare's and Bjurbäck's renderings of the funeral scene as a spectacle observed by Hamlet and Horatio. In Bjurbäck's version, Hamlet effectively disappears for the rest of the scene: since he has no further lines or stage directions, he is functionally invisible in a closet drama. In performance, on the other hand, Hamlet and Horatio remain on stage, their presence perpetuating the claustrophobic sense of ever-present watchers that permeates the Danish court, while they simultaneously remain active characters in their own right. Hamlet is not a bystander, but an observer whose observations prompt his actions later in the scene.
35 Bjurbäck, *Hamlet*, 186.

36 Apart from its obvious connotations with a nun, 'himlabruden' also had a contemporaneous usage relating to music, the arts and a gendered non-corporeal existence, which Bjurbäck may be mobilizing in this passage. Abraham Hülphers (1734–1798) refers to heaven as a place 'Where angels in their millions / Sing with the Bride of Heaven' in the foreword to his survey of ecclesiastical music and Erik Johan Stagnelius (1793–1823), Romantic poet, would use the same term in his sonnet 'Tystnaden' [Silence], published posthumously in 1830 but likely composed around 1820 (according to Paula Henriksson), to refer to a mystical state of silence and bliss, figured as female, which 'halts the rude sounds / that dare disrupt the sabbath of the soul' to instead bring about 'joyous wedding choirs'. See Hülphers, *Historisk Afhandling*, 27; Stagnelius, *Samlade Skrifter*, 88, 304.

37 Bjurbäck, *Hamlet*, 187.

38 Bjurbäck, *Hamlet*, 33.

39 Bjurbäck, *Hamlet*, 33.

40 Bjurbäck, *Hamlet*, 3.

41 For more on the eroticism of the representation of Ophelia in this scene, see Berry, *Shakespeare's Feminine Endings*, 26–8.

42 Granberg, *Hamlet*, 80.

43 Granberg, *Hamlet*, 1.

44 Ruda, *En tysk resandes ströfverier*, 98. It is interesting to compare this blistering critique with the effusive praise for the same version expressed by Dahlgren only a decade earlier, a *volte face* that is in line with the new generation's reaction against the Romantics which would also be symptomatic of Hagberg's standpoint in numerous cultural debates.On the literary climate in Uppsala during Hagberg's student years, see Monié, *Ord som himlen når*, 236.

45 Quoted in Monié, *Ord som himlen når*, 238.

46 Monié, *Ord som himlen når*, 241; 250.

47 Monié, *Ord som himlen når*, 190–4.

48 Speech by Hagberg on his installation as Professor at Lund university in 1844, quoted in Monié, *Ord som himlen når*, 150.

49 Hagberg, *Hamlet*.

50 Hagberg, *Hamlet*.
51 Hagberg, *Hamlet*, 412. As a testament to his commitment to an accurate translation of sexually charged symbols in full, rather than one which censors perceived as sexual impropriety, Hagberg also supplies a note to 4.5 (Ophelia's distribution of flowers), in which he specifies that the columbines given are 'a symbol of lust and illicit desire'. Hagberg, *Hamlet*, 455.
52 Showalter, 'Representing Ophelia', 83.
53 On Garrick and his 1769 Shakespeare Jubilee, see Cunningham, *Shakespeare and Garrick*, and Deelman, *The Great Shakespeare Jubilee*.

Works cited

Berry, Philippa, *Shakespeare's Feminine Endings: Disfiguring Death in the Tragedies* (London, 1999).
Bjurbäck, Olof, trans., *Hamlet* (Stockholm, 1820).
Bross, Martina, *Versions of Hamlet: Poetic Economy on Page and Stage* (Leiden, 2017).
Cunningham, Vanessa, *Shakespeare and Garrick* (Cambridge, 2008).
Deelman, Christian, *The Great Shakespeare Jubilee* (London, 1964).
Floyd-Wilson, Mary, 'Ophelia and Femininity in the Eighteenth Century: "Dangerous conjectures in ill-breeding minds!"', *Women's Studies*, 21/4 (1992), 397–409.
Granberg, Per Adolf, trans., *Hamlet*, assisted by Gustaf Fredrik Åkerhielm (Stockholm, 1819).
Hagberg, Carl August, trans., *Shakespeares Dramatiska Arbeten*, i: *Hamlet* (Lund, 1847).
Hülphers, Abraham Abrahamsson, *Historisk Afhandling om Musik och Instrumenter* (Västerås, 1773).
Lamb, Susan, 'Applauding Shakespeare's Ophelia in the Eighteenth Century: Sexual Desire, Politics, and the Good Woman', in Susan Shifrin, ed., *Women as Sites of Culture: Women's Roles in Cultural Formation from the Renaissance to the Twentieth Century* (London, 2002), 105–23.
Molin, Nils, *Shakespeare och Sverige intill 1800-talets mitt: En översikt av hans inflytande* (Göteborg, 1931).

Monié, Karin, *Ord som himlen når: Carl August Hagberg – en levnadsteckning* (Stockholm, 2008).

Proschwitz, Gunnar von, *Gustaf III: Mannen bakom myten* (Lund, 1992).

Rhodes, Kimberly, *Ophelia and Victorian Visual Culture: Representing Body Politics in the Nineteenth Century* (London, 2017).

Ronk, Martha, 'Representations of Ophelia', *Criticism*, 36/1 (1994), 21–43.

Ruda, Elias Wilhelm,. *En tysk resandes ströfverier på svenska parnassen* (Stockholm, 1830).

Shakespeare, William, *Hamlet*, ed. Ann Thompson and Neil Taylor, rev. edn (London, 2016).

Showalter, Elaine, 'Representing Ophelia: Women, Madness, and the Responsibilities of Feminist Criticism', in Geoffrey H. Hartman and Patricia Parker, eds, *Shakespeare and the Question of Theory* (London: Routledge, 1986), 77–94.

Sivefors, Per, 'Trade Routes, Politics and Culture: Shakespeare in Sweden', in Janet Clare and Dominique Goy-Blanquet, eds, *Migrating Shakespeare: First European Encounters, Routes and Networks* (London, 2021), 189–208.

Sorelius, Gunnar, 'Introduction', in *Shakespeare and Scandinavia: A Collection of Nordic Studies* (Newark, 2002), 9–16.

Stagnelius, Erik Johan, *Samlade Skrifter*, ed. Paula Henrikson, F (Stockholm, 2011).

Swan, Gustaf N., 'Shakespeare in Sweden', *Publications of the Society for the Advancement of Scandinavian Study*, 2/1 (1914), 50–2.

Wolfson, Susan J., 'Romanticism & Gender & Melancholy', *Studies in Romanticism*, 53/3 (2014), 435–56.

4

The poetics of adaptation and politics of domestication: *Macbeth* and J. F. Lagervall's *Ruunulinna*

Jyrki Nummi, Eeva-Liisa Bastman and Erika Laamanen

Introduction

Jacob Fredrik Lagervall's *Ruunulinna: A Tragedy* (1834), an adaptation of Shakespeare's *Macbeth*, is the first five-act tragedy in Finnish. The play is an early example of the explicit

---

An earlier version of this chapter was published in Finnish as Jyrki Nummi, Eeva-Liisa Bastman and Erika Laamanen, 'Adaptaation Poetiikkaa: *Macbeth* ja Lagervallin *Ruunulinna*', *Synteesi* [Journal of the Finnish Semiotic Society], 1–2 (2016), 4–21. Grateful acknowledgement is made to Eero Tarasti and the journal for permission to make this revised version available in an English translation by Nely Keinänen. The translator gratefully acknowledges Donald Adamson, who helped with the translations of the poetry. Citations to Lagervall's works are to page numbers and will appear parenthetically in the text; *Ruunulinna* will be identified as *R* and *Satu Sallisesta* as *SS*.

effort in Finland to integrate different sources of cultural identity, such as history, mythology and folklore, into a literary form. Lagervall's dramatic adaption of Shakespeare's play is thus localized into the Finnish context.

Shakespeare arrived in Finland in the eighteenth century via the tours of travelling companies. The company of Carl Gottfried Seuerling, a German actor and theatre director who primarily worked in Sweden, went as far north as Oulu, performing a *Romeo and Juliet* which had premiered in Sweden in 1776. In the summer of 1819, the company of Karl Gustav Bonuvier, a Swedish actor and director, performed *Hamlet* in Turku, according to newspaper announcements.[1] The source text for *Ruunulinna* is considered to be the Swedish-language translation of Erik Gustaf Geijer (1813), which was also an inspiration for Finns (compare Lindell and Hägglund's chapter in this volume).[2] Geijer's Swedish translation was influenced by Schiller's version of *Macbeth*.[3]

In the early nineteenth century, especially in theatre and opera, adaptation was an established and accepted way of transferring novels to the stage, drama to prose and, of course, anything could be turned into an opera.[4] *Ruunulinna* was at first greeted favourably and its pioneering qualities were well regarded.[5] But opinions about the play changed drastically at the turn of the twentieth century, when modernist conceptions of art valuing originality spread over Europe. This generation of patriotic, young Finnish artists worked to establish a national identity by adopting the latest international trends and applying them in their work.

In the early twentieth century, critical opinion held that *Ruunulinna* consisted of childish scribblings, revealing a peripheral, primitive and shameful underside of Finnish culture, in a time when well-known cosmopolitan artists such as the painter Albert Edelfelt and composer Jean Sibelius moved gracefully in the international art world and their works commanded attention beyond national boundaries.[6] The tension between native and foreign, between the Finnish and the European cultural heritage, dominates the long-standing problem of identity in Finnish culture.[7]

A cultural–political programme to Europeanize Finnish culture was established in the mid-nineteenth century. In the 1840s, J. V. Snellman, an important figure in the Finnish national awakening, had called for a 'national literature' programme, which aimed to create a Finnish-language literary culture in part through the adaptation of foreign models.[8] August Ahlqvist, a professor of Finnish at the Imperial Alexander University in Finland (University of Helsinki), who published poetry under the pseudonym A. Oksanen, wrote a poem for a university awards ceremony in 1869 in which he introduced the great models to be followed:

> Come muse of Finland, welcome, hear our call,
> And enter Finland's spacious lecture hall!
> Here is a place reserved with honour due
> To one who was a stranger hitherto,
> Among the muses who from ancient times
> Brought forth the finest verses, epics, rhymes –
> Muses who to the greatest did appear,
> Inspiring Dante, Göthe and Shaskespeare [sic].[9]

In his celebratory verse, Oksanen locates Finnish poetry in European literary traditions. He celebrates the indigenous poetic style of *Kalevala* verse, but nevertheless directs the Finnish muse to sit alongside the muses of the European classics – Shakespeare, Dante and Goethe.

At the climax of the poem, the speaker reminds the Muse how important it is for the development of Finnish poetry that it be in contact with European literary models:

> From Europe surely you must lessons learn,
> If European 'tis your wish to be.
> There lies the path: that to her style you bend,
> Your own ancestral songs with hers to blend.
> So if poetic minds you seek to please
> And win the prize, her instruments you'll seize.[10]

In his poem, Oksanen raises the often-discussed centre/periphery problem: how should Finnish culture be developed in relation to foreign innovations and influences? In the early stages of building a national consciousness, Finns had a strong need to build their cultural, economic and political institutions in accordance with those of old European nation-states, as well as to make their own contributions to European history and its achievements. According to the programme, Finnish literature, which was then still in its infancy, had a responsibility to develop and adapt foreign models and, in so doing, create a national artistic repertoire and thus contribute to Finnish nation-building efforts. Lagervall's *Ruunulinna* is an early manifestation of this awakening national consciousness, an example of fulfilling this responsibility.[11]

In recent years, *Ruunulinna* has been examined from the point of view of translation theory and discussed in terms of its relationship to the development of Finnish literary language.[12] Before that, in the early decades of the twentieth century, it was studied from a dramaturgical point of view, with most attention paid to its unfitness for the modern stage.[13] Our focus here is not to analyse the play as an independent and unique work of art, but rather to consider it as an adaptation of Shakespeare's *Macbeth*, looking at the ways in which Shakespeare's play was appropriated into the cultural, historical and political environment of Finland at the time. We show how Lagervall shapes Shakespeare's drama, how he domesticates a play written in iambic pentameter in early modern English, telling a story set in Scotland and fits it onto Finnish soil, at the same time building an early view of Finnish history through the fictional events depicted in his play.

As an adaptation, *Ruunulinna* follows two loose textual strategies: transposition and commentary. The former is a *serious* (contra *playful*) transformation according to Gerard Genette's functional typology of hypertextual relations.[14] The commentary is, like a prologue, epigraph, footnote and epilogue, a *threshold* text (Fr. *seuil*) surrounding the proper text in Genette's typology of paratextual relations.[15] Within

Genette's framework the text of *Ruunulinna* is a serious adaptation of Shakespeare's *Macbeth* (in other words, not playful, parodic or polemical). By contrast, an afterword appended to the play by the author is a commentary on the playtext.

Ruunulinna's status in Finnish literature and especially in Finnish theatre history has not yet been adequately addressed in scholarship, to say nothing of its significance in the development of Finnish Shakespeare.[16] The role of Lagervall's play in terms of literary history is here examined from a broad perspective by analysing it as the work of an author who identified himself as a Finn and who was trying to understand the function of literature in his own language in the newly awakening cultural and political community. We ask what materials *Macbeth* and *Ruunulinna* offer for building the identity of a people who were just beginning to claim their rightful place among the nations of Europe? In order to answer this question, we first examine the structural and thematic connections between Lagervall's play and *Macbeth*. We then turn to more specific analyses of Lagervall's language, looking at how he adapted the trochaic metre used in the Finnish national epic in response to Shakespeare's iambic pentameter. Finally, we consider the effects of genre and the choices that Lagervall made when domesticating a Renaissance play to fit on Finnish soil.

Macbeth in the landscape of the Finnish national epic, *Kalevala*

Historical drama

While attention has been paid to *Ruunulinna*'s dramaturgical faults, little attention has, as yet, been paid to the play's genre, more specifically to the ways that Lagervall shapes Shakespeare's tragedy of mind into an historical drama.

Amidst the upheavals of the early nineteenth century, European literature still strongly adhered to traditional genre classifications. Although the long-standing genres maintained by the *ancien régime* disappeared in practice, replaced by new arrivals, the hierarchical ordering of genres seems to have remained strong. New labels were stuck onto old forms but, at the same time, all the empty spaces in the old system were filled with new forms: classical tragedy was replaced by melodrama, while vaudeville and farce took the place of classical comedy.[17] These changes spread all over Europe, beginning in the large cultural centres, Paris and London, making their way quickly to Scandinavia as well.[18] At the same time, there was a deep change in the European mentality: all conceptions of human behaviour were historicized.[19]

In 1809, Finland's rupture with Sweden and her annexation as an autonomous Grand Duchy in the Russian empire, brought into greater relief the hitherto rather vague, heraldic but not yet administrative, concept of Finland and led to the need for literary and historical descriptions.[20] Historical drama provided Lagervall, a veteran of the 1809 war, the possibility of serving his country on the literary front. With its depictions of earlier historical periods, events and persons, historical drama presents history as an overwhelming force, which nations can use to create their own identity. The genre could easily be shaped to present the image Lagervall wanted to create of the Finnish people: speaking Finnish but dressed in Shakespearean garb.

History, myth and folklore

The central feature of historical drama is temporal distance from the events being depicted. Setting the play far in the past guarantees authenticity, increasing the believability of the characters, events and circumstances. The assumption is that historical distance both filters and illuminates: unlike the present, which is complex and difficult to grasp, it is possible to depict historical events and people more objectively.

The past in *Ruunulinna* differs from the past in *Macbeth*, in that the former contains two complementary dimensions shaping the view of the Finnish past, history and myth. The events of *Ruunulinna* are set in Karelia, in the village of Kurkijoki. In his afterword to the play, Lagervall discusses his place names, including their etymology and comments on the current state of Kurkijoki. For example, the author asks whether the prevalence of the surname *Laulaja* [Singer] implies that in the distant past the villagers worked as singers in ancient temples and courts. In his commentary, Lagervall deliberately creates connections between two epochs.

The Finnish setting is established in part through historical place names, as in a scene describing the armies of generals Ruunulinna and Sallinen, who defeat an army led by Harakkalinna [Magpie Castle], who was trying to overthrow the king. Their forces are composed of regiments named for all of Finland's provinces:

> Turmoil reigned in Häme's troops,
> Savo lads could not advance,
> Savo's bravest boys were stalled,
> Blocked behind the river bend
> Hapless Häme quite undone.
> Aunus came to save the day,
> Many from Karelia fell;
> All Kajaani's troops were slain. (R,11)

Such lists composed of parallel structures are familiar from folk poetry and Lagervall uses them to create as broad a picture as possible of Finland and Finns.

In addition to authentic historical locations, historical dramas also focus on actual historical persons, most often monarchs and rulers, who are considered interesting in part because of their status. No matter what roles they play, they are captivating and significant public figures. Georg Lukács has drawn attention to the different status of historical figures in drama and fiction. In historical drama, monarchs and rulers are usually central figures, whereas in historical novels they usually appear in minor roles, with much less visibility.[21]

In *Ruunulinna*, the counterpart to Duncan is Rostio. Rostio's name is from Christfried Ganander's *Mythologia Fennica*, an encyclopaedic listing of key events and figures in Finnish mythology (1789) and a key source for the historical–mythological world of *Ruunulinna*. Indeed, Lagervall was not the only writer working with nationalist themes who was inspired by Ganander. *Mythologia Fennica* was also a key work for Elias Lönnrot (1802–1884), known in Finland as the collector of the poems in the Finnish national epic, *Kalevala*, published in 1835, a year after *Ruunulinna*. In *Mythologia Fennica*, Rostio is an ancient Finnish king who, after his death, was worshipped as a god.[22] In *Ruunulinna*, Rostio is usually anachronistically called a Grand Duke, a title which only began to be officially used for the ruler in 1809, the year Finland became a Grand Duchy in the Russian empire.

Lagervall has named his protagonist Ruunulinna, a name which combines the Finnish words for crown [*kruunu*] and castle [*linna*], both metonyms for power and sovereignty. In Shakespeare's play, the name of the main character is recognizably Scottish, but Lagervall's choice has more symbolic and figurative meanings: 'CrownCastle' foreshadows the early events of the play, as we follow the protagonist from the battlefield to the castle where he is crowned king. By contrast, the other characters have very typical Eastern–Finnish names, such as the counterpart to Macduff, who is called Sallinen, or the counterpart to Banquo, who is given an invented ancient Finnish name, Suuvuoro (literally *suu* [mouth] + *vuoro* [turn], SpeakingTurn). Lagervall also gives the wife of Ruunulinna her own name, Pirjo, an ordinary woman's name, in contrast to Lady Macbeth, who has her husband's name.

In *Ruunulinna* all the main characters are fictional, but there are two military leaders, Sallinen and Mullinen, whom Lagervall introduces as the mythical forefathers of historical figures. Sallinen is presented as the ancestor of Erkki Sallinen (1680–1758), a peasant leader who led a battle against the

Cossacks in border skirmishes with Russia in the 1740s.[23] In Lagervall's work, Macduff is thus turned into the ancestor of an early Finnish national hero, who functions in the play as the counterpart to Ruunulinna. Allusions to real historical figures are one way drama can create links to history and remind viewers of the historical veracity of what is being told and depicted.[24] Through the use of historical figures and actual place names, the line between fiction and reality is blurred.

In addition to these historical and fictional elements, Lagervall also weaves in mythological elements, which also function as national reminders of Finland's historical past and present. A good example of mixing of mythological past and national spirit is the frontispiece to the play, which interestingly does not depict Ruunulinna or any of the other characters in the play. Instead, it depicts a traditional rune singer playing the kantele, a folk instrument (see Figure 4.1) which, in the early nineteenth century, became a symbol of the voice of the Finnish people.[25] In poetry and art, the kantele became a symbol of the cultural and artistic skills of the people.[26]

A second mythological element in Lagervall's play is the witches. While in *Macbeth*, the witches represent the supernatural, in *Ruunulinna*, the witches are named after figures described in Ganander's *Mythologica Fennica*. Unlike the witches in *Macbeth*, they do not practise witchcraft as such, but are akin to evil supernatural figures from folklore. As with the name 'Ruunulinna', some of their names carry metaphorical meanings while all carry the feminine ending *tar/tär*, marking them as female: *Syöjätär* [Devouress], *Mammotar* [Snake Mother], *Vaiviatar* [Distress] and *Kivutar* [Pain]. In the cast of characters, however, they are referred to as 'the witches'. *Vaiviatar* is the only one in Ganander's text who is identified as a witch: she is 'an old witch-woman, who was thought to have been the foster mother to a wolf'.[27]

In addition to the witches, Lagervall adds two more folkloric figures to the cast of *Macbeth*, whose names are also from Ganander. *Lemmes* and *Luonnatar* are forest spirits who question the witches' plans and warn Ruunulinna about their

FIGURE 4.1 *The frontispiece of* Ruunulinna.

evil intentions. Their warnings, however, fall on deaf ears: neither the witches nor, indeed, Ruunulinna pay any attention to them. Despite these additions, however, Lagervall has not attempted to radically change the original plot, so the effect of the added characters on the play's events is negligible.

Shakespeare's witches are based on traditional European beliefs about witchcraft but, at the same time, the play questions whether the witches should be interpreted as supernatural figures or hallucinations. Stephen Greenblatt notes the connection between genre and the theatricality of witches. As he explains, '*Macbeth* manifests a deep, intuitive recognition that the theatre and witchcraft are both constructed on the boundary between fantasy and reality, the border or membrane where the imagination and the corporeal world, figure and actuality, psychic disturbance and objective truth meet.'[28]

Witchcraft becomes a means of depicting the complexity of the human mind as well as the power of the imagination. In *Ruunulinna*, as in *Macbeth*, encounters with the supernatural are used to highlight the protagonist's choices, but in rather different ways. In *Macbeth*, the witches initiate internal thought processes which lead to action. In *Ruunulinna*, by contrast, the spirits are allegorical figures, good and evil personified. The choice between them is played out dramatically: both good and evil spirits compete for the protagonist's attention. This is a long-standing dramatic convention and can be seen in the medieval morality play *Everyman*, as well as in Marlowe's *Doctor Faustus*. In this sense, *Ruunulinna* follows the allegorical representations familiar from the morality play tradition.

In *Ruunulinna*, supernatural beings appear for longer stretches than in Shakespeare's play. In *Macbeth*, for example, in the first scene the witches are on stage for 14 lines, whereas the corresponding scene in *Ruunulinna* is 73 lines. This multiplication of the witches' part is in part due to the parallelism inherent in the Kalevala metre, where it is common to repeat in other words what has just been said. But at the same time, the more prominent role of the witches is testament to how seamlessly folklore and mythological elements are woven into works creating and depicting a Finnish national past. Lagervall's depiction of the past is at once realistic and unreal. The events take on a mythological aura, adding authority to the folklore traditions awakened in the play.

Changes to the plot and soliloquies

In Lagervall's hands, Shakespeare's 'tragedy of mind' is turned into a national romantic historical drama, performed through the medium of folk poetry. By analysing in more detail the kinds of changes Lagervall made to the structure and content, we can begin to trace the significant differences between his adaptation and Shakespeare's original. Lagervall preserves *Macbeth*'s plot, but re-arranges some of the scenes. For example, Act 2 of *Ruunulinna* is divided into 11 scenes, while there are only four in *Macbeth* (see the appendix to this chapter for a list of scenes). The large number of scenes in Act 2 is partly the result of Lagervall's having shifted material from Shakespeare's Acts 1 and 3, which allows him to avoid changes in location. The first act of *Ruunulinna* takes places on the battlefield, Acts 2 and 3 in Ruunulinna's castle, Act 4 in Sallinen's camp and Act 5 back in the castle.[29]

Lagervall has taken the most freedoms with the soliloquies, many of which have been moved, shortened, or removed. These changes reflect a shift in emphasis from the interior world of the protagonist to external events. Macbeth's soliloquy 'Is this a dagger which I see before me' (2.1.33–64) is reduced to four lines, which Ruunulinna recites while looking at his dagger (*R*, 43–4). At the same time, the dagger, which Macbeth only imagines, becomes a real thing, the instrument of murder. In addition, Macbeth's monologue on hearing of his wife's death ('She should have died hereafter', 5.5.16–27) is reduced to two lines:

> No bead of breath to grace your lips,
> Not one more day of life to live? (R, 98)

While some soliloquies are either eliminated or so reduced as to become unrecognizable, Lagervall compensates by expanding the text in other ways. Many of these extensions are achieved through adding parallel structures. For example, Lady Macbeth's soliloquy beginning 'The raven himself is hoarse' (1.5.40–54) is expanded by adding parallel variations on Lady Macbeth's invocation of the 'spirits / That tend on mortal thoughts' (*Mac* 1.5.40–41):

> Come ye pangs of conscience cold,
> Terrors that make all afeared,
> Barren beings of horror spun
> Deathly beasts that make men quake,
> Come, ye spectres one by one,
> Turn my mind from my intent! (R, 35)

The monologue has become the opposite of the original: in Shakespeare's version, Lady Macbeth asks the spirits to make her cruel and unrepentant, so she can carry out her plan. By contrast, Pirjo calls upon spirits to prevent her from turning her thoughts into action.

The use of these parallel phrases makes these soliloquies repetitive and a bit simplistic. There is no room here for reflection, nor for the use of ambiguous descriptive language. Through the use of repetition, short lines can expand into longer monologues. When Lady Macbeth reacts to the news of Duncan's visit, she has a ten-line speech beginning 'O never / Shall sun that morrow see' (1.5.60–1), whereas *Ruunulinna*'s Pirjo responds with a longer monologue, again emphasizing the mythological and folkloric elements. Pirjo greets her esteemed guest in a friendly and polite manner, but then tells herself that the Grand Duke will never leave her castle. He will be driven into a trap like a wolf or bear:

> Never shall you leave this place
> Move beyond these castle walls,
> Never shall you see your home
> Never shall you find your nest,
> Lay your body down to rest.
> Seldom wolf the hunter seeks,
> Nor does bear with butcher bide,
> Beast unto his slayer slink
> Willing go to meet his fate.
> Now the same awaits you here,
> Straight into my trap you've slid.
> Your journey here was ill-advised,
> My home the place of your demise. (R, 29).

Instead of the maternal metaphors of Lady Macbeth's 'The raven himself' speech, Lagervall gives Pirjo hunting metaphors, creating a mythical and heroic frame.

Lagervall's changes to Macbeth's final monologue in Act 5 also highlight the Finnish heroic context. In Shakespeare's version, the soliloquy shows the cruel and ruthless ruler in a more sympathetic light, as alone and hopeless. In *Ruunulinna* the monologue has been moved to before Pirjo's death (which is accidental) and the moving of Anajoki (Birnam) Wood. Ruunulinna is thus never depicted at the height of despair, but retains his resolve to the bitter end. He is not broken by adversity or hardship, as giving up is never an option:

> Never shall I quake with fear,
> Nor affliction lead to grief;
> Words can never bring me woe,
> Nor shall speech my purpose foil.
> ....
> Never shall I leave this land,
> Never quit my castle home,
> Kurkijoki ne'er forsake.
> Only cowards fly the coop,
> Hapless howls their sole defence.

> Steadfast in my own abode
> Rest I shall with curtains drawn:
> Resolvéd to await my fate,
> Let my foul deeds bring reward (R, 94).

The fallen hero is thus granted a return of honour, allowing him to display bravery in the face of certain defeat. Despite losing his final battle, Ruunulinna dies as a king:

> 'Spite of all a king I die,
> Lordly as my spirit flies. (R, 118).

Thematic changes

Many of Lagervall's changes are formal and are not motivated by thematic concerns. Nevertheless, some changes do affect the overall themes of the play. Robert Lanier Reid, who analyses the structure of *Macbeth* in relation to the psychological development of the main character, argues that the play is built around three cycles, of which each depicts a certain psychic stage. The dramaturgy of *Macbeth*, according to Reid, consists of a three-part structure:

> [A]cts 1 and 2 present, in a continuous sequence, the regicide and its immediate consequences; act 3 shows the murder of Banquo and then its impact on Macbeth at the banquet, acts 4 and 5, another continuous cycle of action, presents the slaughter of Macduff's family, then its social and psychological consequences.[30]

The three murders Macbeth commits – the murder of an authoritative, paternal ruler; the murder of a brother-like friend and finally, the murder of a mother and her children – represent three primary relationships which are destroyed, one after another. In this sense, the play deconstructs the infrastructure of human psychology.[31]

Lagervall's adaptation breaks the symmetry of this three-part structure. The play focuses on the murder of the ruler, which is the only murder that Ruunulinna himself commits. The second, the murder of a friend, i.e. Banquo/Suuvuoro, is not depicted in Lagervall's play. Instead, the murderers report to Ruunulinna that they have done the deed. At the same time, a new murder is planned, as Ruunulinna wishes to get rid of a general loyal to the previous ruler. These plans, however, are not realized in the play. The third murder, that of Lady Macduff and her children, is removed entirely from Lagervall's adaptation. *Ruunulinna* thus focuses primarily on the murder of the Grand Duke, which has the effect of making the final murders seem unnecessary. The elimination of the Macduff family also results in a change of motivation, as there is no longer a personal need for revenge. In other words, there is no place for individual tragedy in Lagervall's interpretation, which focuses much more on nationalist concerns.

So, instead of the three sets of murders in *Macbeth*, there are only two murders in *Ruunulinna*. Therefore, there is less of an escalating spiral of violence which inevitably leads to the protagonist's destruction, but it is there rather as a possible development or intention. Lagervall has also left out Lady Macbeth's sleep-walking scene (5.1), where her dream state allows us to see her remorse and pangs of conscience. The removal of this scene demonstrates the ways that Lagervall's adaptation is less interested in internal psychological processes, which he views as sub-plots that can easily be cut. Instead, the drama focuses primarily on external events, while the analogies that are created between different characters are secondary.

The analogical relationship between Ruunulinna and Sallinen, for example, is the main way in which the national romantic frame is emphasized. Both of them are esteemed generals, but they differ in their attitudes to power. Like Macbeth, Ruunulinna has an infinite lust for power and wants the crown no matter the cost. By contrast, Sallinen is offered the crown at the end of the play, but refuses it. Sallinen's role is thus quite different from that of the Scottish Macduff.

In addition to being a character in *Ruunulinna*, Sallinen is the main character in an epic poem which Lagervall published in 1831. In this story, Sallinen is found as a baby in the forest and Joukahainen (the enemy and, in some versions, brother of Väinämöinen, the hero of *Kalevala*) takes him home; Väinämöinen becomes his godfather. Väinämöinen names the child Sallinen and predicts he will become a celebrated leader:

> He for Finland will fend well,
> Make the state secure and strong,
> Keeping our Karelia bright,
> Our Savo secure and safe.
> Peace he'll keep in Aunus fair,
> Häme suffer no duress,
> Life in Lapland shall he raise,
> Food unto the folk provide. (SS, 9)

In the final battle, Ruunulinna, unlike Macbeth, does not face a nobleman who wishes to revenge the bloody murders of his king and family, but rather a mythic national hero who has been given the task of protecting his people.

In creating his characters, Lagervall follows the same principles we examined in terms of monologues and structural changes. National, historical, mythical and ideological ideals are emphasized, while individual, psychological and tragic features are played down. Unselfishly serving one's country and fulfilling any tasks required are presented as the highest goals. In addition to Sallinen, these ideals can also be seen, for example, in the castle guard, who speaks with Officer Rataskilpi just before the revelation of the Grand Duke's murder. The guard has not been able to sleep during the night, as his job was to guard the duchy itself:

> How could I lay me down in bed,
> Let myself be lulled to sleep,
> Finland's realm – its guard am I,
> And its state I must protect. (R, 53)

Rataskilpi asks him: 'How are you the guardian of the Finnish realm, protector of the state?' and the guard responds:

> Don't I guard the Finnish state,
> And protect the Finnish realm,
> While in this keep lies the king,
> Our Grand Duke, the honoured one? (R, 53)

Through its repeated phrases, the dialogue makes clear that the guard understands his duty: he is not guarding the life of the king, or his dynasty, but rather he is a protector of the Finnish realm. This dialogue also epitomises the play's theme, in accordance with historical drama, but, at the same time, reveals something very personal and topical for Lagervall: What is the fate of the Finnish people when caught in the midst of complicated power politics?

The traditions of folk poetry

Kalevala metre before the *Kalevala*

As part of his nationalist goals, Lagervall also chose to write his play in the metre of old Finnish folk poetry, which was undergoing a renaissance in the nineteenth century.[32] The so-called Kalevala metre is trochaic tetrameter and there are restrictions on the first accented syllables of words. In addition, as you may have noticed in the examples above, there is abundant use of parallelism and alliteration.

The use of this metre profoundly shapes the play and, to a large extent, its dramatic force grows out of the use of parallel structures and repetition:

> Ruunulinna to his steed
> Spake a multitude of words,
> Hurled commands of what to do,

> Strong commands unto his colt
> Whom it was they'd meet that day
> Whom they needed most to see. (R, 14.)[33]

Kalevala metre was developed from an ancient metre used by eastern Finns living near the Baltic Sea and is estimated to be up to 2,500 years old. It received its current name only after the publication of the *Kalevala* and today this name is used, however anachronistically, to describe the metre used in old folk poetry and its variations. Classic Kalevala metre is said to be the version that Lönnrot later used in the *Kalevala*.[34]

Kalevala metric verse was originally sung and is strongly linked to the oral tradition.[35] Its devices function mainly as aids to memory, as is typical of older metres.[36] Before the spread of literacy and writing skills in Finland, Kalevala metre was a way of transferring knowledge from one generation to the next. When it became possible to produce written documents, the metre became unnecessary. As writing skills became more widespread, it declined in use.[37]

Beginning in the sixteenth century, alongside traditional folk metres, newer poetic forms and metres began to emerge. These were mainly based on Germanic models and contained features foreign to Kalevala metre, such as specific rhyming patterns and stanza structures. Kalevala metre and these foreign metres coexisted for centuries and hybrid forms also developed.[38] Little by little, the newer metres began to replace the older ones and, by the beginning of the nineteenth century, the significance of the Kalevala metre had decreased in Finnish poetry. But with the advent of national ideals, new attention was paid to these older forms and this is what inspired Lagervall to experiment with them in his dramatic text. The publication of *Kalevala* one year after *Ruunulinna* consolidated the position of the old metre in Finnish poetry, even if it had changed considerably. Kalevala metre became 'an archaic, but nevertheless usable metre for written poetry'.[39]

The metre of *Ruunulinna* and its functions

We can examine the metre of *Ruunulinna* from two perspectives. Firstly, we can ask why Lagervall chose this metre instead of another: what is its ideological function? Poetic metres carry associations and significances stemming from the earliest ways they were used[40] and we can analyse the poet's way of imitating and developing the methods used by his predecessors and his attitudes towards these methods.[41] The ideological significance of *Ruunulinna's* Kalevala metre grew out of national ideas prevalent at the time Lagervall was writing his play. Poetic metre can also have multiple functions within a text. Through the use of metre, a poet can, for example, emphasize a specific moment (deictic function), imitate an aspect of the text (mimetic function) or allude to previous uses of the same metre (intertextual function).[42]

In classical Kalevala metre, a verse is made up of eight syllables in a pattern of accented and unaccented beats. Certain limitations on the first syllable of individual words and where they can appear in the line, however, differentiate it from normal trochaic verse. So, for example, according to these rules, a long first syllable can only be in the rising, accented position, while a short first syllable can only be in a falling, unaccented position.[43] These so-called 'length rules' create two types of verse, whose variation creates the characteristic rhythms of Kalevala metre.[44]

Even more than these metrical rules, the use of parallelism and alliteration are typical features of the Kalevala poetic form. In *Ruunulinna*, both are used throughout the text. Parallelism, repeating the same idea using different words in the following line, is indeed so prevalent that it becomes problematic in the play. For example, when he has killed the king, Macbeth says the following: 'Will all great Neptune's ocean wash this blood / Clean from my hand?' (*Mac*, 2.2.62–3). By contrast, due to the parallelism, in *Ruunulinna* it takes four times the number of lines to depict the same thing:

There's no breaker from Nais Bay,
Wave from Vuolijoki's flow,
Aura River's current fierce,
Billows from Lake Ladoga,
Swell and surge from Saimaa Lake
That these clothes of mine shall cleanse,
Make my fingers fair again
Make my hands again be pure,
Wash away these drops of blood. (R, 47)

In general, the parallelism prolongs the play and makes it difficult, if not impossible, to depict complex thought.[45] Alliteration and rhyme have traditionally been seen as incompatible, in that alliteration has been seen as a characteristic Finnish technique, whereas rhyme has come from foreign models. Lagervall, however, uses both of them, sometimes in the same line.

At times, *Ruunulinna* also deviates from classical Kalevala metre.[46] Short or incomplete lines, i.e. those with fewer than eight syllables, are a simple but effective way to break the classic rhythm which, to a large extent, is tied to the eight-syllable structure. Before the Kalevala metre was formalized it was, in fact, rather common to leave off the final unaccented syllable.[47] In *Ruunulinna*, by contrast, the full eight syllables are the norm and exceptions are used to create variation. For example, Lagervall will sometimes use a seven-syllable line, a trochaic tetrameter catalectic, whose rhythmic force is quite different from the full eight-syllable line (see footnote 48 for the original Finnish):

Finland's greatest Grand Duke, hear
Outrage from the Tervu plain.
Late last week the enemy,
Smote our troops with swords unleashed
Slew unholy numbers dead,
Faithful folk of yours they killed,
Honoured vassals serving you,
Finest of your friends they felled
Laid your dear defenders low.[48] (R, 16–17)

In these trochaic tetrameter catalectic lines, there is a pause between each line, given that the line ends on an accented syllable and the next line also begins with an accented syllable. Due to the stresses, the ends of each line are emphasized, which makes the line especially suitable for the expression of strong emotions. In the quotation above, Rataskilpi is telling Rostio, the Grand Duke, about the destruction wrought by the enemy: the seven-syllable lines give the impression that Rataskilpi is agitatedly speaking in a loud voice. Perhaps not coincidentally, this is also the metre Shakespeare uses for the witches in *Macbeth*.

As mentioned above, as Finnish was being established as a literary language, writers also experimented with other metrical systems, including iambic, which is not natural to Finnish. Iambic passages can even be distinguished in the text visually. In *Ruunulinna*, there are usually three or four iambic feet and end rhyme is often used. In Finnish, broken-off words are used to provide the unaccented first syllable and, in this English translation, we have tried to produce a similar effect with shortened words in other positions:

> This comp'ny riding at the helm
> Protects and guards the Finnish realm,
> Proudly the wounds of war they bear
> Example giv'n beyond compare,
> So tell we now without fanfare
> The foe is broken and ensnared. (R, 9)

These iambic lines are part of a dynamic prosodic system, where the placement of accented and unaccented syllables depends on their relative weight. In these iambic lines, the normal rules of Kalevala metre do not apply and there are no limitations on the first syllables. Disregarding the so-called 'length rules' might also lead to the lines becoming normal trochees or trochee-dactyls:

> Killed by his guard without a doubt!
> Now in my mind is naught but grief

> From such great sorrow no relief.
> How can I understand this deed
> Oh sure my eyes do me mislead.
> I stumble in a fevered rage
> I flounder in a foul malaise.[49] (R, 55)

In this example, Pirjo is pretending to be shocked at hearing of the king's murder. The rhythm is also prosaic until it shifts to iambs. In *Ruunulinna*, unlike *Macbeth*, the characters never speak in pure prose.

Shifts in metre in the middle of scenes is often a sign of changes in the speaker's tone, attitude or reactions. The metre changes to iambic, for example, when Ruunulinna repeats the witches' prophecy (R, 24) or when Rataskilpi notices that Rostio has been murdered (R, 54). The Kalevala metre changes to trochee-dactylic when Kieri, Ruunulinna's aide, begins to stutter in fright when he tells of the approach of Sallinen and his troops. He switches to Kalevala metre when Ruunulinna becomes angry with him, and orders him to speak more clearly and to sing what he has to say (the latter also a reference to the *Kalevala*, where the heroes sing) (R, 94–5). In Lagervall's version, the drunken porter of *Macbeth* is done in such a way that he also takes on an intertextual function: as Suomalainen points out, *Ruusulinna's* guard speaks in a way which 'reminds us of old hymnals' – which can also be seen as an allusion to Schiller's adaptation of *Macbeth* with its singing Pförtner.[50]

Most deviations to the Kalevala rhythm, however, appear at the beginnings of scenes. The beginnings of 1.2 and 1.3, as well as 2.1, 2.3 and 2.5 all include one or more of the variations mentioned above, or combinations of them. For example, at the beginning of 1.2, the short dialogue between the Grand Duke and his soldier is iambic, but when Rostio turns to speak to Parviainen, the meter changes to classical Kalevala, which is used until the end of the scene. The iambic section seems to work as some kind of opening to the scene. Lagervall uses changes in rhythm to highlight changing situations, as well as to create broader rhythmic variations between scenes.

The metre is most unstable during the witch scenes (1.1, 1.4, 1.5, 2.6, 2.9, 2.10, 2.11), which links *Ruunulinna* metrically to Shakespeare's play. The metre changes quickly from Kalevala metre to iambic and from iambic to trochaic-dactylic. In addition, there are variations in line lengths. In a sense, the metre is responding to the presence of the witches: where the witches are, there is chaos. In 2.9, however, where the witches are chanting their spells and preparing their magic potion, there is a long sequence of nearly flawless classic Kalevala metre. In addition, 2.11 is in Kalevala metre, despite the presence of the witches, although it is only one speech.

Metrical variations in *Ruunulinna* follow the plot and thematic development. Midway through the play, the variations stop almost entirely. The short first scene of Act 3 is still iambic, but the end of the play is entirely in classical Kalevala metre, with two small exceptions (R, 79, 94). This shift in metre seems to reflect the main turning point in the play. At the beginning of Act 3, Ruunulinna is at the height of his power, but Sallinen and his troops are on the way and his victory over Ruunulinna is just a matter of time. The witches also disappear after the second act. Given that the presence of the witches led to much of the chaotic metrical situation at the beginning of the play, the metrical instability disappears along with them.

Kalevala metre searching for its form

In the early nineteenth century, efforts to create a national Finnish culture led to debates about older Finnish poetic metres. Henrik Gabriel Porthan had earlier published a monumental study of Finnish folk poetry (in five parts, 1776–1778), in which he wrote about the Kalevala metre normatively, but his way of thinking had not yet caught on.[51] In Lagervall's day, commentators still approached the Kalevala metre theoretically, as it lacked official norms and, in principle, anyone could express an opinion on the matter. Lively debates connected to the Finnish language and poetic metre were carried out on the pages of newspapers and Lagervall himself engaged in a correspondence on these topics with Lönnrot, who was collecting Finnish folk poems and would publish *Kalevala* the following year.[52] Reviews of *Ruunulinna* also reveal the spirit of the times: Lagervall's metrical choices were either praised or criticized depending on what the critic felt was good Finnish.[53]

At the beginning of the nineteenth century, writers were thus still experimenting with the Kalevala metre and could use it quite creatively.[54] In his short study, *Anmärkningar uti finska skaldekonsten* [Notes on Finnish Poetry, 1816], Jaakko Juteini did not attempt to describe how Kalevala metre had been used in traditional folk poetry, but instead tried to create a guide for contemporary poets wishing to use it. Juteini's poetic experiments themselves were not widely admired, but critics appreciated the ways he attempted to develop rather than formalize Kalevala metre.[55]

In *Ruunulinna*, Lagervall took advantage of the metrical freedoms of his age. While the play remains close to folk poetry, he also chooses to deviate from classical Kalevala metre, in part by absorbing metrical influences from Shakespeare's play. In this way, Lagervall adds foreign features to Kalevala metre and also breaks some of its rules, which distance *Ruunulinna* from Finnish folk traditions and brings it closer to European traditions. By combining two metrical traditions, domestic and foreign, Lagervall is able to create metrical variations which function on multiple levels.

At the end of the play, the Kalevala metre itself is thematized. In 5.7, Ruunulinna has been defeated and the days of oppression are finally behind them. Sallinen and the new Grand Duke Juurikki are bidding each other farewell. In his final speech, Juurikki asks Sallinen to tell his story to future generations, so they can learn from it:

Hear ye now my last request,
Go thou, Sallinen, my friend:

> Tell this tale to lands afar
> Tell it to the world at large,
> Let it shine to folk unborn
> So that they example take,
> Let their hearts by it be moved. (R, 116)

The text alludes to the original function of the Kalevala metre, as an aid to memory and thus a way to preserve and pass on inherited knowledge. In the same way, Lagervall asks his play to perform some of the same work as done in folk poetry: pass on collected wisdom from one generation to the next in the form of poetry.

Unser Shakespeare

At the turn of the eighteenth and nineteenth centuries, interest in the translation and domestication of Shakespeare was especially high in Germany, which had adopted the English dramatist as one of their own, 'unser' Shakespeare.[56] In *West-Eastern Divan* (1819), Goethe divides Shakespeare translations into three epochs: in the first, prose translations allow people to become familiar with the original texts; in the second, the translator attempts to domesticate the foreign text and present it as his own transplantation, from one country to another:

> The translator endeavors to transport himself into the foreign situation but actually only appropriates the foreign idea and represents his own. I would like to call such an epoch parodistic, in the purest sense of the word. It is most often men of wit who feel drawn to the parodistic. The French make use of this style in the translation of all poetic works ... for every foreign fruit there must be a substitute grown in their own soil.[57]

The third epoch is a transformation of the first and second. In this stage, the aim to achieve a perfect, identical version of the original, so that one is not a replacement of the original but rather is simply in its place.[58]

Lagervall's *Ruunulinna* is closest to Goethe's second strategy – at least to the extent that the adaptation can be considered a translation. When *Ruunulinna* was published, the Kalevala metre had not yet been formalized with its own set of rules and Lagervall was able to use the metre quite freely, with variations. But the publication of *Kalevala* the following year meant a turning point in the use of Kalevala metre. The variant of the metre used by Elias Lönnrot, who collected and edited the volume, became the norm, with the result that creative uses and variations began to be thought of simply as mistakes. With time, Lagervall's experimentations with verse forms were rejected and then finally forgotten.

Ruunulinna is written in the language of the *Kalevala*. While folk characters are not prominent in the play, they are powerfully present in the play's language. In his epilogue, Lagervall explains that he deliberately chose themes and language heard in Finnish language sayings, folk poetry and nursery rhymes. Lagervall's principles closely reflect a leading metaphor of the age, as seen in Herder's *Stimmen der Völker in Liedern* (1807), that folk poetry can be seen as the voice of the people, in which one can hear the spirit of the people. Beginning in the 1760s, folk poetry was increasingly linked to literature in modern Europe. The literarization of folk poetry was a conscious process, fed by a number of political, ideological and aesthetic texts.[59] Writers were inspired to imitate the earliest poetry ('natural poetry') and to set this poetry against the classical tradition. The set-up is illustrated most clearly in Lönnrot's forward to his *Kanteletar*, a collection of old Finnish songs (1840). According to Satu Apo, the concept of natural poetry was like a gospel to educated people living on the peripheries of Europe. Their remoteness, backwardness and the lack of high-quality literature could now be interpreted positively: the folk songs and stories handed down through generations were natural poems, which had preserved their purity.[60]

Folk poetry also often functioned to encourage people to continue folk traditions and languages and strength was sought from the past. By domesticating a Shakespearean tragedy, Lagervall was depicting the status of a newly elevated nation in the midst of a political crisis. He drew inspiration from Karelian history, folk poetry and folk beliefs. From history came the generals – Ruunulinna, blinded by ambition and Sallinen, who unselfishly serves his country. The witches, who have features of both Finnish evil spirits as well as the European and English conceptions of witches drawn from Shakespeare's play, are depictions of the darker sides of the human mind. In *Ruunulinna*, however, the supernatural is not only associated with evil, as the witches are opposed by nature spirits who represent goodness, honour and justice.

The allegorical mode of presentation simplifies the psychological complexity of the play's main characters. In addition, the Kalevala metre, along with its typical features such as parallelism, make the target text somewhat declamatory and repetitious, unlike the original. Lagervall, like Shakespeare, has named his play for the main character. However, in Lagervall's version, an important theme is the significance of the Finnish people and nation, even as others try to erase them from history, as opposed to Shakespeare's play, which focuses on the main character's traits and internal struggles.

When writing his historical drama, why did Lagervall choose *Macbeth* as his model, a play both historically and geographically distant, a Renaissance tragedy depicting medieval English (and Scottish) courts? The answer is connected to three features of Shakespeare's play – its generic status, its dramatic energy and its literary quality.

Genre transformations are a key way of updating and situating a play in a new literary tradition. *Macbeth* offered

Lagervall the possibility to dramatize his own historical goals and aims. Of the three main sub-genres of historical drama – conspiracy, tyranny and martyr plays – *Macbeth* includes the first two in its repertoire. Of these, conspiracy plays have primarily been historical. An assassination plot, which provides a clear motive for action, provides a dramatic frame for a historical plot at the same time creating an historical process which lends itself to drama.[61]

Lagervall had a sharp eye in choosing Shakespeare's *Macbeth* to adapt and domesticate, as many of his contemporaries were already calling Shakespeare one of the greatest dramatists and the play was being translated into other languages by leading writers and translators, such as Schiller and the Swedish Erik Gustaf Geijer. The power struggle that Lagervall invents in Kurkijoki, situated in the eastern part of Finland, is a dramatic creation through which a relatively unfamiliar location grows in the reader's mind to represent Finland.

The significance of *Ruunulinna*'s intrigue, assassination and power struggle lies in the fact that it does not describe actual historical events or a specific period of time; rather, through its conflict and juxtapositions it, in effect, invents a significant event in Finnish history. By harnessing the dramatic power of *Macbeth*, Lagervall is able to infuse his plot with intensity and significance.

Although the parallelism required of the Kalevala metre expands the text and destroys its dramatic possibilities onstage, nevertheless the use of the epic form has a significant function, as it renders all the descriptions and stories great, heroic and magnificent.[62] A similar effort can be seen in Schiller's translation of *Macbeth*, which at heart is an effort to turn Shakespeare's play into a classical Greek tragedy, a form which Schiller admired.[63]

The literary value of the source text is of crucial importance to the success of any adaptation. At the same time, the adaptation itself reinforces the canonical status of the source.[64] An adaptation may approach the source text in a satirical, parodic, polemic or defiant way, but these textual strategies do not in any way lower the status of the original text and, indeed, can do the opposite. Literature in a less-spoken language has the possibility to enter the realm of 'world literature' only by subjecting itself to its prevailing outlines and rules.[65] These literatures need to create analogies to world literature but, at the same time, must create something 'unique' and 'original'. In Finnish literary history, only Lönnrot's *Kalevala*, with its skilful marketing as something unique and original, has managed to successfully fulfil these requirements.[66]

In the eyes of modern Finns, the language and style of *Ruunulinna* might seem comic. We may indeed well ask whether the play was even meant to be taken seriously. In his epilogue, Lagervall tells the reader that the material and themes of his tragedy come from Shakespeare, who set his own play in Scotland. Lagervall refers to Walter Scott who, in his *History of Scotland*, said that these events had never happened there. Lagervall asks where they might have happened and answers: 'In our country [i.e. Finland]'. At the time, Shakespeare's popular tragedy had already been translated into many languages and this also made him want to translate it into Finnish. But what was Lagervall trying to say?

This question can be answered in two ways. Lagervall's response might be seen as a playful way of parodying older forms of politically motivated historical writing, where all significant historical events, Biblical peoples and societies were seen as returning the speaker or writer to his own land. In this sense, the play can be seen as a kind of Rudbeckian parody.[67] The other possibility is to understand Lagervall's response as referring to the canonical qualities and status of the original play. 'In our country' in this sense would imply that *Macbeth* could have happened anywhere. The drama is universal and Lagervall's Finnish adaptation derives its power from Shakespeare's canonical light.

4.2 Appendix: A structural comparison between *Macbeth* and *Ruunulinna*

Shakespeare, *Macbeth*

Act I, scenes 1–7
1: Witches
2: Duncan, Malcolm, Donalbain, Lennox
3: Witches, Macbeth, Banquo
4: Duncan, Macbeth — *Prophecy of witches*
5: Lady Macbeth, Macbeth
6: Duncan, Banquo, Lady Macbeth
7: Macbeth, Lady Macbeth — *King arrives*

Act 2, scenes 1–4
1: Banquo, Fleance, Macbeth
2: Macbeth, Lady Macbeth
3: Porter, Macduff, Lennox, Macbeth — *King murdered*
4: Ross, Macduff

Act 3, scenes 1–6
1: Banquo, Macbeth *Planning murder*
2: Lady Macbeth, Macbeth
3: Murderers, Banquo *Banquo murdered*
4: Macbeth, Lady Macbeth, guests, ghost of Banquo
5: Noidat — *Party*
6: Lennox, lords

Act 4, scenes 1–3
1: Witches, Macbeth
2: Lady Macduff, her son *Murder of Lady Macduff and her children*
3: Macduff, Malcolm, Ross

Act 5, scenes 1–8
1: Doctor, Lady Macbeth
2: Lennox, Angus etc.
3: Macbeth, Doctor
4: Malcolm, Siward, Macduff, Angus, Ross, Lennox, soldiers
5: Macbeth, Seyton, messenger *Lady Macbeth's suicide*
6: Malcolm, Siward, Macduff
7: Macbeth, Young Siward, Macduff
8: Macduff, Macbeth, Malcolm, Siward, Ross *Macduff kills Macbeth*

Lagervall, *Ruunulinna*

Act 1, scenes 1–6
1: Mammotar, Vaiviatar, Kivutar, Lemmes, Luonnatar (witches)
2: Grand Duke Rostio, generals Kallo, Savisuu, Parviainen
3: Rostio, Parviainen, Rataskilpi
4: Syöjätär and witches
5: Witches, Lemmes and Luonnatar, Ruunulinna and Suuvuoro
6: Ruunulinna, Suuvuoro, Rataskilpi

Act 2, scenes 1–11
1: Grand Duke Rostio, Pirjo
2: Ruunulinna, Pirjo
3: Ruunulinna, Pirjo
4: Ruunulinna, Suuvuoro
5: Ruunulinna, Pirjo, Porter
6: Ruunulinna, Pirjo, witches
7: Ruunulinna, Suuvuoro, Rataskilpi, Pirjo, Marja
8: Ruunulinna, Pirjo *Planning the murder of Suuvuoro*
9: Witches
10: Witches, Ruunulinna
11: Witches, Ruunulinna, Pirjo

Act 3, scenes 1–2
1: Ruunulinna, Pirjo
2: Ruunulinna, Pirjo and guests, murderers, and the ghost of Suuvuoro *News of Suuvuoro's murder*

Act 4, scenes 1–3
1: Juurikki, Sallinen
2: Juurikki, Sallinen, Simanainen
3: Sallinen, Parviainen, soldiers

Act 5, scenes 1–9
1: Ruunulinna, Pirjo, Marja, Doctor Savisuu
2: Ruunulinna
3: Ruunulinna, Kieri
3 (sic): Ruunulinna, Kieri ja Marja *News of Pirjo's death*
4: Ruunulinna, Juurikki
5: Ruunulinna, Sallinen
6: Ruunulinna, Sallinen, Haapalainen, Parviainen
7: Sallinen, Juurikki, Haapalainen, soldiers
8: The same and Ruunulinna *Ruunulinna dies*

Notes

1. Hirn, 'Alati kiertueella', 35.
2. See Paloposki, 'Shakespearea suomeksi', 130–1.
3. Geijer had spent the years 1809–1810 in Britain; he therefore spoke fluent English and did not need to depend on the German translation. Schiller's English skills were lacking and he relied heavily on earlier prose translations of his esteemed predecessors Wieland and Eschenburg (Donner, *Svenska översättningar*, 7). For a detailed comparison of these translations, see Donner *Svenska översättningar*, 7–20; see also Lindell and Hägglund's chapter in the present volume.
4. See Sassoon, *Culture*, 567–91.
5. For the early reception of the play in the press, see *Helsingfors Morgonblad*, 9 March 1835; *Sanan Saattaja Wiipurista*, 9 September 1835 and 23 September 1836; *Sanan-Lennätin*, 1 March 1856. J. V. Snellman mentions the play positively in *Kallavesi*, 29 August 1846.
6. See, e.g., Krohn, *Suomalaisen kirjallisuuden vaiheet*, 242. In Lauri Suomalainen's concise monograph (1903), the critique of Lagervall has already turned into sarcastic derision. In the twentieth century, this negative view only intensified. See also Tarkiainen, *Suomalaisen kirjallisuuden historia*, 144–5; Haarla, 'Suomenkielisen'; Haahtela, 'Piirteitä J. F. Lagervallin', 409–10.
7. See Knuuttila, *Tyhmän kansan teoria*, 161.
8. For the programme of national literature, see Nummi, 'Se ainoa ja tarpeellinen', 12–17.
9. The spelling of Shakespeare had not yet been regularized.
10. Oksanen, 'Tervehdyssanoja', 140.
11. See Klinge, 'Onko Täällä Pohjantähden' and Knuuttila, *Tyhmän kansan teoria*.
12. See Paloposki, 'Shakespearea suomeksi'.
13. See Haarla, 'Suomenkielisen'; Nummi, 'Kullervon tausta', 30–2.
14. Genette, *Palimpsestes*, 24–30.
15. Genette, *Paratexts*, 1–5.

16 Neither the most recent Finnish literary history (Varpio and Huhtala, eds, *Suomen kirjallisuushistoria*) nor the most recent history of Finnish theatre and drama (Seppälä and Tanskanen, eds, *Suomen teatteri ja draama*) mentions Lagervall's first tragedy in Finnish.

17 See, respectively, Steiner, *The Death of Tragedy*; Segal, *The Death of Comedy*.

18 On changes in opera and theatre markets in the early nineteenth century, see Sassoon, *Culture*, 232–89. On changes in opera and theatre in Scandinavia in the same epoch, see Marker and Marker, *History*, 96–128.

19 See Lindenberger, *History*.

20 Klinge, *Historiankirjoitus*, 14. Lagervall was not the first to examine this subject, but was preceded by a slender tradition of fictional descriptions in which Finland was seen as a geopolitically separate state unit and as a culturally and ethnically diverse region. These include the poem 'Finlands Odling', published by Franzén in 1800 in *Åbo Tidning*, as well as Runeberg's first poetry collection *Dikter* (1830) and the essay 'Några ord om nejderna, folklynnet och lefnadssättet i Saarijärvi socken' (1832) published in *Helsingfors Morgonblad*. For Franzén's poem describing the history of Finland, see Klinge, *Napoleonin varjo*, 325–35. For the Saarijärvi writings, see Karkama, *Vapauden muunnelmat*, 59–70.

21 Lukács, *The Historical Novel*, 150–62; Lindenberger, *Historical Drama*, 70–2.

22 Ganander, *Mythologia*, 79.

23 Syrjö, 'Erkki Sallinen'.

24 Lagervall also creates the impression of reality by using footnotes. The footnotes explain unknown dialectal words and tell of Sallinen's historical connections to real life. The use of references is a means of reinforcing the impression of authenticity and blurring the boundaries between fiction and truth.

25 An anonymous critic writing in 1835 mentions the image: 'There is a Karelian sitting on a rock by the lake getting ready to play his kantele. It's a charming image' (Anon., 'Arvostelu'). The reviewer does not refer to the kantele player as Väinämöinen, the hero of the Finnish national epic, who

later became a prototype of a kantele player and singer. For the character of the poet-singer in the visual arts and the development of the subject in the early nineteenth century, see Stewen, 'Unohdetut kuvitelmat Kalevalasta', 66–9.

26 For the *kantele* motif in Finnish literature, see Haavio, 'Kantele-topiikka'.
27 Ganander, *Mythologia*, 100.
28 Greenblatt, 'Shakespeare Bewitched', 32.
29 Lagervall created the metalanguage used to describe drama in Finnish: the English 'act' translates into *tapaus* (literally 'case'), 'tragedy' into *murhekuvaus* ('grief description') and 'dramatis personae' into *jäsenet* ('members'). *Kohtaus*, used by Lagervall for 'scene', has since become established in the Finnish language.
30 Reid, *Shakespeare's Tragic Form*, 112.
31 Ibid., 112.
32 There is an unpublished Swedish translation of *Ruunulinna* by Carl Niclas Keckman, an important literary figure in early Fennophile activities during the 1830s. The Swedish translation is handwritten on the interleaves of the printed *Ruunulinna*. The translation (Keckman, *Rättelser*) is only available on microfilm in the Finnish Literature Society Library and is very hard to read. Keckman assisted Elias Lönnrot and edited the first *Kalevala*. Keckman translated from several languages into Finnish and Swedish and was able to write Kalevala metre in both Finnish and Swedish, thus testifying to the general enthusiasm towards the Finnish cause amongst literary intellectuals at the time in Finland. See Pääkkönen, *Ahkeroimia*, 81–91.
33 In trying to reproduce the metrical feel of the Finnish quotations, we have mainly used a trochaic catalectic form, leaving out the final unaccented syllable.
34 See Kallio, 'Kalevalamitta oppineiden', 3; Leino, 'The Kalevala Metre', 56.
35 See Leino, 'The Kalevala Metre', 56.
36 See Haynes, 'Metre and Discourse', 242.
37 Leino, 'The Kalevala Metre', 72.

38 Asplund, *Murros*, 41; Leino, 'The Kalevala Metre', 72–3.
39 Leino, 'The Kalevala Metre', 57.
40 See Lankinen, 'Runomitta', 426.
41 Haynes, 'Metre and Discourse', 248–9; Lankinen, 'Runomitta', 417.
42 Haynes, 'Metre and Discourse', 243–7; Lankinen, 'Runomitta', 409–11, 423.
43 A syllable is long if it ends in a consonant (-kas), a long vowel (-aa) or a diphthong (-ai). It is short if it ends in a single vowel (-a, -ta).
44 The first foot of the verse is exceptional, as it can contain two to four syllables and is not subject to the 'length rules'.
45 See Leino, 'The Kalevala Metre', 58–9.
46 In his early study of Lagervall from 1901, Lauri Suomalainen criticised these variations in poetry, although he doubted that they were intentional, possibly even 'imitating Shakespeare' (Suomalainen, 'Jaakko Fredrik Lagervall', 61).
47 See e.g. Kallio, 'Kalevalamitta oppineiden', 4.
48 To give an idea of the pattern, the original Finnish lines read 'Suomen suurta Ruhtinaa / Tervehitään Tervussa: / Jossa viimoviikolla / Harakkaristi miekalla, / Tavattomast tapatti, / Hävyttömäst hävitti, / Teijän paraat palveliat, / Ylimäiset ystävänne, / Poltti teijän puoltajanne' (*R*, 16–17).
49 'Varmaan tappanna vahtinsi! / Mieleni muuttuu murheesta / Ja tästä surust suuresta / Ympäri käy minull ymmärrys, / Silmäni peittää pimeys. / Niin hoiperran kuin horkassa / Ja kohmon tässa kolkassa.' (*R*, 55)
50 See Suomalainen, 'Jaakko Fredrik Lagervall' 14–15; Schiller, *Macbeth in Schillers Bearbeitung*, 34–5.
51 See Haapanen, *Suomalaiset runomittateoriat*, 8.
52 For the correspondence between Lagervall and Lönnrot, see Haahtela, 'Piirteitä J. F. Lagervallin', 417–24.
53 See Anon., 'Arvostelu'; Anon., 'Ruunulinnasta'; Anon., 'Muutama sana Juteinin'.
54 See Kallio, 'Kalevalamitta oppineiden', 18–19; Haapanen, *Suomalaiset runomittateoriat*, 11–12.

55 Haapanen, *Suomalaiset runomittateoriat*, 13–16.
56 See McCarthy, 'The "Great Shapesphere"', 1–12.
57 Goethe, 'Translations', 64.
58 Ibid., 65.
59 Apo, 'Kansanlaulujen' 216.
60 Apo, 'Kansanlaulujen', 229.
61 For sub-genres of historical drama, see Lindenberger, *Historical Drama*, 30–53.
62 For the role of 'magnification' in historical drama, see Lindenberger, *Historical Drama*, 54–94.
63 Dröse, 'Schiller'.
64 Sanders, *Adaptation*, 8–9.
65 Lefevere, *Translation*, 76.
66 See Honko, 'Kalevala'.
67 Olof Rudbeck Senior (1630–1702) was a Swedish scientist and scholar who represented a particular reckless patriotic ('Rudbeckian') research that combines etymology, myths and history in proving the glorious past of his home country.

Works cited

Anon, 'Arvostelu: Ruununlinna', *Sanan Saattaja Wiipurista* (9 September 1835).
Anon, 'Ruunulinnasta', in *Sanan Saattaja Wiipurista* (23 January 1836).
Anon, 'Muutama sana Juteinin ja Major Lagerwallin kirjoitus – sekä runoelma – tawasta', in *Sanan-Lennätin* (1 March 1856).
Apo, Satu, 'Kansanlaulujen ääni 1700-luvun kirjallisuudessa', in Sakari Ollitervo and Kari Immonen, eds, *Herder, Suomi, Eurooppa* (Helsinki, 2006), 216–64.
Asplund, Anneli, *Murros, muutos ja mitta: Metriikan, rakenteen ja sisällön välisistä suhteista suomalaisissa kansanlauluissa*, unpublished licentiate thesis, University of Helsinki, 1997.
Donner, H. W., *Svenska översättningar av Shakespeare's Macbeth, i: Schillers inflytande på Geijers översättningar*, Acta Academiae Aboensis, 20 (Turku, 1950).

Dröse, Astrid, 'Schiller zähmt Shakespeare: Der Weimarer Macbeth (1800/1801) in Licht der Kulturtransfer-Forschung', in John McCarthy, ed., *Shakespeare as German Author: Reception, Translation Theory, and Cultural Transfer* (Amsterdam, 2018), 132–54.
Ganander, Christfrid, *Mythologia Fennica* (1798; 4th edn, Helsinki, 1984).
Genette, Gérard, *Palimpsestes: Literature in the Second Degree*, trans. Channa Newman and Claude Doubinsky (Lincoln, 1997).
Genette, Gérard, *Paratexts: Thresholds of Interpretation*, trans. Jane E. Lewin (Cambridge, 1997).
Goethe, Johan Wolfgang von, 'Translations' (1819), trans. Sharon Sloan, in L. Venuti, ed., *The Translation Studies Reader* (2nd edn, New York, 2004, 64–6).
Greenblatt, Stephen, 'Shakespeare Bewitched', in Tetsuo Kishi, Roger Pringle and Stanley Wells, eds, *Shakespeare and Cultural Traditions: Selected Proceedings of the International Shakespeare Association World Congress, Tokyo 1991* (Newark, 1994), 17–42.
Haahtela, Sampo, 'Piirteitä J. F. Lagervallin oikeakielisyysharrastuksista', *Virittäjä*, 40 (1936), 409–25.
Haapanen, Toivo, *Suomalaiset runomittateoriat 1800-luvulla* (Helsinki, 1926).
Haarla, Lauri, 'Suomenkielisen alkeis-näytelmän muotokamppailua', *Naamio*, 5, (1931), pp 97–100.
Haavio, Martti, 'Kantele-topiikka', in *Kalevalaseuran vuosikirja*, 50 (Porvoo, 1970), 85–122.
Haynes, John, 'Metre and Discourse', in Ronald Carter and Paul Simpson, eds, *Language, Discourse and Literature: An Introductory Reader in Discourse Stylistics* (London, 1989), 233–56.
Hirn, Sven, 'Alati kiertueella', in *Teatterimme varhaisvaiheita vuoteen 1870* (Helsinki, 1999).
Honko, Lauri, 'Kalevala: aitouden, tulkinnan ja identiteetin ongelmia', in Lauri Honko, ed., *Kalevala ja maailman eepokset*, Kalevalaseuran vuosikirja, 65 (Helsinki, 1987), 125–80.
Kallio, Kati, 'Kalevalamitta oppineiden käytössä uuden ajan alun Suomessa', *Elore*, 22 (2015). Available at: www.elore.fi/arkisto/1_15/kallio.pdf, accessed 5 January 2016.
Karkama, Pertti, *Vapauden muunnelmat: J. L. Runebergin maailmankatsomus hänen epiikkansa pohjalta* (Helsinki, 1982).

Keckman, C. N., *Rättelser, Rör Ruunulinna*, manuscript on the interleaves of J. F. Lagervall's *Ruunulinna* (Helsinki, 1834).

Kiuru, Silva, 'Ensimmäisten suomenkielisten näytelmien kielestä', *Virittäjä*, 1 (2001), 59–73.

Kjellin, Gösta, '1800-talet möter Shakespeare', in Johan Wrede, ed., *Finlands svenska litteraturhistoria*, i: *Åren 1400–1900* (Helsinki, 1999) 373–4.

Klinge, Matti, 'Onko Täällä Pohjantähden alla Suomen kansallisromaani?', in Yrjö Varpio, ed., *Väinö Linna: Toisen tasavallan kirjailija* (Helsinki, 1980), 234–43.

Klinge, Matti, *Napoleonin varjo: Euroopan ja Suomen murros 1795–1815* (Helsinki, 2009).

Klinge, Matti, *Historiankirjoitus ja historiakulttuuri keisariaikana* (Helsinki, 2010).

Knuuttila, Seppo, *Tyhmän kansan teoria – näkökulmia menneestä tulevaan* (Helsinki. 1993).

Krohn, Julius, *Suomalaisen kirjallisuuden vaiheet* (1897; Helsinki, 1953).

Kustfinne, 'Ruunulinna Murhekuvaus', in *Helsingfors Morgonblad* (9 March 1835).

Laitinen, Kai, *Ikkunat auki Eurooppaan: kirjojen virrassa – tutkielmia ja esseitä kirjallisuudesta ja lukemisesta* (Helsinki, 1999).

Lagervall, J. F., *Ruunulinna: Murhekuvaus 5: sätapauksessa* (Helsinki, 1834).

Lagervall, J. F., *Satu Sallisesta* (Helsinki, 1831).

Lankinen, Pasi, 'Runomitta ja moniäänisyys', in Markku Haakana and Jyrki Kalliokoski, eds, *Referointi ja moniäänisyys* (Helsinki, 2005), 406–28.

Lauerma, Petri, 'Gustaf Renvall suomen kirjakielen standardoijana', *Sananjalka*, 47 (2005), 119–57.

Lefevere, André, *Translation, Rewriting and the Manipulation of Literary Fame* (London, 1992).

Leino, Pentti, 'The Kalevala Metre and its Development', in Anna-Leena Siikala and Sinikka Vakimo, eds, *Songs beyond the Kalevala: Transformations of Oral Poetry* (Helsinki, 1994), 56–74.

Lindenberger, Herbert, *Historical Drama: The Relation of Literature and Reality* (Chicago, 1975).

Lindenberger, Herbert, *The History in Literature: On Value, Genre, Institutions* (New York, 1990).

Lukács, Georg, *The Historical Novel*, trans. Hannah and Stanley Mitchell (1937; Harmondsworth, 1969).
McCarthy, John A, (2018) 'The "Great Shapesphere": An Introduction', in John A McCarthy, ed., *Shakespeare as German Author: Reception, Translation Theory, and Cultural Transfer* (Amsterdam, 2018), 1–76.
Marker, Frederick J and Lise-Lone Marker, *A History of Scandinavian Theatre* (Cambridge, 1996).
Nummi Jyrki, 'Se ainoa ja tarpeellinen: Lyhyt johdatus kansalliskirjallisuuteen', *Kirjallisuudentutkijain seuran vuosikirja*, 50 (1997), 9–55.
Nummi, Jyrki, 'Modernist Asymmetries: Centre, Periphery, and Juhani Aho's Yksin', in Traian Sandu et al, eds, *Ouest-Est: dynamiques centre-périphérie entre les deux moitiés du continent* (Paris, 2012), 363–80.
Nummi, Jyrki, 'El cisne y el bardo: lo europeo y lo local en la literatura finlandesa', *Quimera: Revista de litteratura*, 362/1 (2014), 11–14.
Nummi, Jyrki, 'Kullervon tausta ja vastaanotto', in *Aleksi Kivi: Kullervo—näytelmä viidessä näytöksessä*, ed. Jyrki Nummi et al. (Helsinki, 2014), 16–49.
Oksanen, A. [August Ahlqvist], 'Tervehdyssanoja 31 p. Toukok. v. 1869 seppelöidyille Filosofian Majistereille', in *Säkeniä: Kokous runoelmia*, v (1869; Helsinki, 1898).
Pääkkönen, Irmeli, *Ahkeroimia. Piirteitä Carl Niclas Keckmanin elämäntyöstä*. Publications of the Department of Finnish, Saami and Logopedics 26 (University of Oulu, 2005). Available at: http://jultika.oulu.fi/files/isbn9514278577.pdf.
Paloposki, Outi, 'Shakespearea suomeksi ensi kerran: Ruunulinna', in H. K. Riikonen et al, eds, *Suomennoskirjallisuuden historia*, i (Helsinki, 2007), 130–2.
Reid, Robert Lanier, *Shakespeare's Tragic Form: The Spirit in the Wheel* (Newark, 2000).
Sassoon, Donald, *The Culture of the Europeans: From 1800 to the Present* (London, 2006).
Sanders, Julie, *Adaptation and Appropriation: The New Critical Idiom* (London, 2006).
Schiller, Friedrich, trans., *Macbeth in Schillers Bearbeitung herausgegeben von E. von Sallwürk* (Bielefeld, 1921).
Segal, Erich, *The Death of Comedy* (Cambridge, MA, 2001).

Seppälä, Mikko-Olavi and Katri Tanskanen, eds, *Suomen teatteri ja draama* (Helsinki, 2010).
Shakespeare, William, *Macbeth*, ed. Sandra Clark and Pamela Mason, The Arden Shakespeare, Third Series (London, 2015).
Snellman, J. V., [untitled], in *Kallavesi* (29 August 1846).
Steiner, George, *The Death of Tragedy* (London, 1961).
Stewen, Riikka, 'Unohdetut kuvitelmat Kalevalasta kuvataiteessa', in Ulla Piela, Seppo Knuuttila and Pekka Laaksonen, eds, *Kalevalan kulttuurihistoria* (Helsinki, 2008), 66–81.
Suomalainen, Lauri, 'Jaakko Fredrik Lagervall: kirjallisuushistoriallisia piirteitä', in *Suomi: kirjoituksia isänmaallisista aineista*, i (Helsinki, 1903).
Syrjö, Veli-Matti. 'Erkki Sallinen: kansallisbiografia-verkkojulkaisu', in *Studia Biographica*, iv (Helsinki, 2006).
Tarkiainen, Viljo, *Suomalaisen kirjallisuuden historia* (Helsinki, 1934).
Varpio, Yrjö and Liisi Huhtala, eds, *Suomen kirjallisuushistoria*, i (Helsinki, 1999).

5

Søren Kierkegaard's adaptation of *King Lear*

James Newlin

In 1851, eight years after his intensely original, prolific literary career began, the Danish writer Søren Kierkegaard published a short piece explaining his idiosyncratic literary strategy. 'On My Work as an Author' details the objective of what Kierkegaard calls his 'authorship', an *oeuvre* consisting of both signed and pseudonymous writings.[1] The pieces published under Kierkegaard's own name – such as the *Upbuilding* discourses and 'On My Work as an Author' itself – are 'exclusively religious writing' directly addressed to a devoutly Christian audience.[2] By contrast, the series of texts that Kierkegaard called his 'indirect communication' targets a more sceptical audience. These pseudonymous works inventively juxtapose literature, criticism, philosophy and theology, with the aim of 'deceiv[ing their reader] into the truth'.[3] By unsettling the reader's expectations

---

A draft of this chapter was presented at the fortieth annual meeting of the Society for Comparative Literature and the Arts in 2014. Support for this project was provided by the University of Florida and Webber International University. Special thanks to Erin Crump, and to Richard Burt, Terry Harpold, Eric Kligerman and R. Allen Shoaf for their comments and suggestions.

about how a published book 'should' work, the indirect communication uncannily guides Kierkegaard's reader to a more intuitive understanding of his famous spheres of existence, or life stages: the aesthetic, the ethical and the religious.[4]

By 'aesthetic', Kierkegaard often means 'Romantic'.[5] Kierkegaard's university dissertation was an extended critique of Romantic irony, particularly as espoused by Friedrich Schlegel. Yet, in pseudonymous works like *Either/Or*, Kierkegaard does not mount an attack on Romanticism so much as perform a kind of uneasy parody of Romantic forms that seems as much an homage to as a satire of the fragmentary, animated *Romane* of Schlegel and Novalis. In an expanded version of 'On My Work as an Author', published posthumously, Kierkegaard clarifies that this appropriation of Romantic tropes is an act of Socratic irony – therefore a kind of ironizing of Romantic irony – meant to take the aesthetically orientated reader's 'delusion' 'at face value', in order to 'deceive' them into 'what is true'.[6]

Kierkegaard shared with the Romantics a passionate admiration for Shakespeare's drama, and scholars have long considered the legion of references to Shakespeare in Kierkegaard's writings.[7] But the extent to which Kierkegaard is not only alluding to Shakespeare's dramas, but may also be actively rewriting them, much as he adapted Romantic literary forms and tropes, has not yet been studied. In this chapter, I hope to prove that Kierkegaard authors a thoughtful adaptation of Shakespeare's *King Lear*, buried within the two volumes of *Either/Or* and their quasi-sequel *Stages on Life's Way*. In a series of brief, though significant, allusions, Kierkegaard's characters re-enact the narrative of *Lear*, sequentially restaging the love test, storm and prison scenes. As the reader moves through these works, they not only move through clarifications of the aesthetic, the ethical and the religious life stages, but they also move through the narrative of *King Lear*.

Kierkegaard's *King Lear* is certainly not a traditionally faithful adaptation of the play.[8] Most notably, in his reworking of *Lear*'s narrative, Kierkegaard does not depict Cordelia's senseless death. Though it was common for stage productions of *Lear* to end on a cheerful note,[9] Kierkegaard knew the play primarily as a reader of the acclaimed (and largely faithful) Schlegel-Tieck translation.[10] Unlike the stage productions that conclude with Cordelia reviving, Kierkegaard does not correct the play's devastating ending so much as he stops short of it, leaving the narrative suspended. This suggests, paradoxically, Kierkegaard's close attention to *Lear*'s conclusion and his awareness that the play's nihilistic vision does not align with his religious one. Such an understanding is also reflected in Kierkegaard's journals.

Lear appears at the nexus of the major concerns of Kierkegaard's early literary output: his complicated debt to Romanticism and his creative reworking of his personal biography. More to the point, tracing Kierkegaard's adaptation of *Lear* shows the extent to which Shakespeare informs Kierkegaard's strategies as an author. I begin with a close reading of the sequential allusions to *King Lear* in the two volumes of *Either/Or* and *Stages on Life's Way*, clarifying the role *Lear* plays in Kierkegaard's strategy of indirect communication. But Kierkegaard's interest in *Lear* is not just rhetorical. Judging from his references to the play in his journals, it seems to me that *King Lear* affected Kierkegaard as personally as any other work of literature. I close by considering the parallels that Kierkegaard draws in his journals between the situation of *Lear* and his own family, in order to hypothesize why he may have concluded his adaptation of the play so abruptly.

'Flattery requires great care': Love tests in *King Lear* and *Either/Or* Part I

A brief summary of *Either/Or* is necessary to qualify the role that *Lear* plays in the two volumes of this unusual text. The title page of the first volume informs us that the work is '*A Fragment of Life*', edited by a character named Victor Eremita.

In his preface, Eremita recounts how he came into possession of 'two groups' of papers by happenstance; he found them inside a writing desk he had purchased. Despite the 'marked external difference' between the two sets of papers, Eremita decides to edit and publish them together.[11]

The first volume, primarily authored by a figure Eremita calls 'A', is by far the more diverse set of writings. The writings attributed to A include a number of aesthetic essays which consist of a series of aphorisms (the 'Diapsalmata'); a long critical reading of Mozart's *Don Giovanni* ('The Immediate Erotic Stages'); another long reading of *Antigone* ('The Tragic in Ancient Drama Reflected in the Tragic in Modern Drama'); a series of more abstract critical assessments of female characters from Goethe and Mozart (the 'Silhouettes'); a review of a contemporary comedy by Augustin Eugène Scribe; and a 'venture in a theory of social prudence' called 'The Rotation of Crops'.

However, A is not only an author, but also claims to have come into possession of and edited a series of papers himself: 'The Seducer's Diary'. Supposedly written by a figure named Johannes, the diary depicts his elaborate seduction of a young woman. In his diary, Johannes the Seducer details his overly aestheticized pursuit of his beloved. He stalks her through the streets of Copenhagen and manipulates one of her other admirers. He eventually proposes to her but, for Johannes, an erotic connection is only as desirable as it is transient. Once a beloved stops resisting, there is nothing to a romantic relationship but 'weakness and habit' (1.445). So he slyly persuades her to become disillusioned with the idea of marriage so that *she* calls off the engagement, before he finally seduces and abandons her.

A's introduction to the diary comments upon its contents – despite his own romanticization of Don Juan figures, he finds himself appalled (1.310) – and includes extracts from letters written by the object of Johannes's affection. The first volume of *Either/Or* includes at least four named voices: Eremita, A, Johannes and Johannes's beloved. By contrast, the next volume is made up almost entirely of two formal letters written to A from 'B'. Within these letters, B reveals his occupation (judge) and his name (Wilhelm, hereafter 'William', per the standard English translation by Edna and Howard Hong). The titles of his letters ('The Esthetic Validity of Marriage' and 'The Balance Between the Esthetic and Ethical in the Development of Personality') indicate that the purpose of this volume is to guide the reader along the continuum of Kierkegaard's spheres of existence. While William's letters trace the overlap and points of transition between an aesthetic and an ethical life, he also gestures towards the final, religious stage. Like Eremita and A before him, William is not only an author, but also an editor (of sorts). In his final letter addressed to A, Judge William introduces a copy of an as-yet-undelivered sermon written by an unnamed pastor called 'The Upbuilding That Lies In the Thought That In Relation To God We Are Always In The Wrong'.

We can already see how Kierkegaard upends a reader's expectations of a 'published' work. *Either/Or* is not 'by' Søren Aabye Kierkegaard, it is 'by' anywhere from two to five different people, but edited and introduced by someone else. This unusual presentation of the text reflects Kierkegaard's own expectation that it may – and perhaps should – go largely unread. In 'On My Work as an Author', Kierkegaard makes clear that his strategy of indirect communication is intended to 'shake off' those who are unlikely to adopt his religious conception of individuality.[12] By contrast, his ideal reader, the 'single individual', should not agree with virtually any of *Either/Or*. The ethical and the aesthetic alike are essentially too 'interesting' and rational in contrast with the simple, though absurd and paradoxical, religious.[13] This sort of negative construction of the text – a conceiving of the work as *Neither/Nor* – is directly communicated in Eremita's preface, which warns: 'read [the two volumes] or do not read them, you will regret it either way' (1.14).

By presenting each of these volumes as a stumbled-upon assortment of documents that are, in some cases, partially written or deserve to be only partially read, Kierkegaard is clearly ironizing the Romantic fragmentary form.[14]

Kierkegaard's interest in Romantic forms is closely aligned with his treatment of Shakespeare, a principal subject of Romantic reading. Kierkegaard's Shakespeare is, in many ways, a German Shakespeare, received through the *Shakespearomanie* phenomenon which permeated German literary culture in the nineteenth century.[15] Not surprisingly, Kierkegaard's cryptic adaptation of *King Lear* begins in the most overtly 'Romantic' section of *Either/Or*: 'The Seducer's Diary'.

In the midst of his elaborately constructed 'erotic somersault' (1.426), Johannes considers the significance of his beloved's name: Cordelia Wahl. But, as if doubly reflecting the reader's position, Johannes recognizes and aestheticizes his beloved's resemblance to Lear's daughter, while failing to acknowledge the extent to which *he* then resembles Lear:

> Cordelia! That is really a splendid name – indeed, the same name as that of King Lear's third daughter, that remarkable girl whose heart did not dwell on her lips, whose lips were mute when her heart was full. So also with my Cordelia. She resembles her, of that I am certain. But in another sense her heart does dwell on her lips, not in the form of words but in a more heartfelt way in the form of a kiss. How ripe with health her lips! I have never seen lips more beautiful.
>
> (1.336)

In Johannes's recounting of *Lear*'s details, a slippage seems to occur where Cordelia's inability to 'heave / My heart into my mouth' is joined with Lear's final, hysterical hallucination that his daughter has revived ('Look on her: look, her lips').[16] Even if this conflation of *Lear*'s beginning and ending is intentional on Kierkegaard's part, I doubt that it is what Johannes intended. It is, however, fitting, considering his inevitable discarding of Cordelia Wahl. Precisely where Johannes's monstrous aesthetics are meant to illuminate something poetic about Cordelia, he inadvertently indicates something about himself: namely, that he is a character in a fictional world that inverts the fictional world of *King Lear*. In a complete reversal of Shakespeare's narrative, 'The Seducer's Diary' begins with an awareness of love and concludes with the misguided and cruel rejection of a devoted Cordelia. In another conflation of the beginning of *Lear* with its ending, we might also equate Johannes's love for his Cordelia's muteness with Lear's praise for the 'excellent thing in woman', a gentle, soft voice, that the king only recognizes when she is dead and completely mute (*KL* 5.3.270–1).

Lear and Johannes's shared admiration for a woman's silence is obviously misogynistic but, in Johannes's case, it also wilfully delusional. This is nothing like the silence that Kierkegaard celebrates elsewhere in the authorship, as a virtuous counterpart to the 'chatter' of modern life. In fact, it's not really silence at all. What Johannes identifies as his Cordelia's silence reflects his own perspective or actions, whether observing her from a distance or by leaving her letters unopened. So, Johannes's inadvertent praise of Cordelia's silent 'lips' is either ghoulish – since it likens his Cordelia to *Lear*'s Cordelia when she is dead – or it is a fairly obvious misreading of the play's opening scene. The Cordelia of *King Lear* is emphatically *not* silent. Saying 'nothing' is not the same thing as saying nothing:

LEAR
    what can you say to draw
A third more opulent than your sisters? Speak.
CORDELIA
    Nothing, my lord.
LEAR
    Nothing?
CORDELIA
    Nothing.
        (*KL* 1.1.85–9)

Cordelia will go on to gloss not only her response at length, but also that of her sisters' initial claims: 'Why have my sisters husbands, if they say / They love you all?' (*KL* 1.1.99–100).

In other words, Cordelia is diagnosing Goneril and Regan's overemphatic *epideixis* as 'nothing', a pure rhetorical exercise. While we may rightly consider Goneril and Regan's initial praise of Lear to be disingenuous and self-serving, it is also highly conventional. Goneril's claim to 'love [Lear] more than word can wield the matter' is a familiar appeal to the *topos* of inexpressibility (55), while Regan's reply to love Lear even more than that (Goneril 'comes too short') (72) is just as familiar an appeal to the *topos* of outdoing.[17] Again, Cordelia comments on the predictability of these *topoi* in her own reply. Her claim that she 'cannot heave / [her] heart into [her] mouth' – the passage that so delights Johannes – ironically responds to Regan's claim that the 'very deed of love' is named within her 'true heart' (69, 70).

The greater Cordelia Wahl's resemblance to Lear's favourite daughter, the more the reader associates Johannes himself with the mad king. Both Johannes and Lear share an obsession with flattery. However, while Johannes dissects the role of flattery as a device of seduction, it is clear that he also shares Lear's obsessive desire to be praised:

> Yesterday she told me there was something royal in my nature. Perhaps she wants to defer to me, but that absolutely will not do. To be sure, dear Cordelia, there is something royal in my nature, but you have no inkling of the kind of kingdom I have dominion over. It is over the tempests of moods. Like Aeolus, I keep them shut up in the mountain of my personality and allow one and now another to go out. Flattery will give her self-esteem; the distinction between what is mine and what is yours will be affirmed; everything will be placed upon her. Flattery requires great care. Sometimes one must place oneself very high, yet in such a way that there remains a place still higher: sometimes one must place oneself very low. The former is more proper when one is moving in the direction of the intellectual; the latter is more proper when one is moving in the direction of the erotic.

(1.400)

Earlier, before having met Cordelia, Johannes addresses his own 'storms of passion' much like Lear in the storm ('roar away, you wild forces, roar away, you powers of passion'), while insisting that he could manage these 'as calmly as the king of the mountain' (1.324–5). Likewise, with his 'royal nature', the not entirely convincing claim to reign over the 'tempests' in his mind and the obsession with flattery – both giving and receiving – Kierkegaard conflates Johannes with Lear precisely at the moment that Johannes enacts what is, in essence, a love test.

Johannes's plan to begin an engagement that is then broken by his beloved followed by a final tryst certainly differs in specifics from the public expression of Lear's 'darker purpose' (*KL* 1.1.35). Yet there are illuminating parallels between both characters' need for a public display of affection.[18] Both Lear and Johannes need the display to appear natural and unprompted, even though it is thoroughly familiar to the point of trope. Cordelia's utterance of 'nothing' confronts Lear with the facts of what he wanted all along – perhaps the thought of what lies between her legs as well as the bare *auxēsis* of her praise – but with his 'arrangement', Johannes does not actually give his Cordelia such an opportunity. In contrast to the Cordelia in *Lear*, he acts as though Cordelia Wahl actually says nothing, rather than 'nothing'. In order to preserve this illusion even after achieving what he calls 'the ultimate' (1.368), he finds a way to keep her silent, by sending back her later letters unopened (1.311).

Johannes's decision to read some, but not all, of Cordelia's letters is emblematic of Kierkegaard's critique of Romanticism. 'The Seducer's Diary' is delivered in a parody of the fragmentary Romantic style. But here the so-called 'Romantic Agony' of *Lucinde* is presented as a constructed performance, rather than a spontaneous, passionate expression. On the contrary, in a seduction, 'everything must be properly arranged' (1.342). Rather than a genuine expression of inwardness, Johannes's pursuit of his beloved is performed *via* an intentionally unrepresentative fragmentation of texts and *lives* read as texts.

As a part of his broader goal of presenting an 'ironic revision of Romantic irony' itself,[19] Kierkegaard creates an aesthetic character who, quite predictably, admires Shakespeare's *Lear*, to show how a character of that type closely and obliviously resembles Shakespeare's foolish and narcissistic Lear.

However, just because the next stage of existence – the ethical – offers a correction to the aesthetic life view does not mean that the ethical is wholly preferable to the aesthetic. In the next volume of *Either/Or*, Kierkegaard shows us another figure who fails to read *Lear* closely and thereby ignores what the play and the aesthetic stage have to teach us about the insularity of religious experience.

Total absorption in oneself: Storms and heaths in *King Lear* and *Either/Or* Part II

This unexpected distance between the ethical and the religious – and the unexpected proximity of the ethical and the aesthetic – is demonstrated in the second volume of *Either/Or*. Judge William believes himself to be religious. However, the very length and rigour of his arguments in favour of the aesthetic and ethical validity of marriage suggest that he cannot achieve the religious in Kierkegaard's understanding of the term. It is precisely William's *defence* of marriage that indicates his failure to become a single individual – that paradoxical figure who is 'higher than the universal'[20] – and thus certainly higher than any couple.

If the aesthetes A and Johannes were conventional admirers of Shakespeare, then the ethicist William is just as predictably dismissive of the Bard.[21] For B/Judge William, Shakespeare is only a producer of 'old sayings' like 'to be or not to be' that hold for the person who lives aesthetically but not for others: 'all such imaginary gymnastic constructing is equivalent to sophistry in the realm of knowledge' (2.253). But we should hardly assume that Kierkegaard shares William's opinion. In a moment that closely recalls the critical missteps of Johannes the Seducer, William misses the allusion to Shakespeare's *King Lear* in the very sermon he implores A to read so closely![22] This missed reading shows not only that the ethical life view is as prone to missteps as is the aesthetic; it also reveals the unexpected synchrony between the aesthetic life of living poetically and the religious stage.

The references to *Lear* are placed quite deliberately in *Either/Or*. In both instances, the allusion to *Lear* appears at the very end of the volume, in a section authored by an entirely new voice that is introduced to us by the volume's primary editor–author. The first volume of *Either/Or* depicted a Lear-of-sorts crafting a love test, while the second portrays a Lear-of-sorts out in the storm. The unnamed pastor who closes volume two prefaces his sermon on 'upbuilding' with the following description:

> 'The heath in Jylland [Jutland]', [the pastor] says, 'is a real playground for me, a private study room beyond compare. I go out there on Saturday and meditate on my sermons, and everything unfolds for me. I forget every actual listener and gain an ideal one; I achieve total absorption in myself. Therefore, when I step into the pulpit, it is as if I were still standing out there on the heath, where my eyes see no human being, where my voice rises to its full power in order to drown out the storm'.
>
> (2.338)

The Danish intelligentsia who read the first and second editions of *Either/Or* would have recognized the Jutland heath's cultural resonance as a particularly 'romantic spot' (1.6).[23] (As we will see, the region also held personal significance for Kierkegaard.) Yet, with the figure of a minister aiming to 'drown out the storm', Kierkegaard also seems to have another literary heath in mind.

The figure of the pastor addressing the storm seeking an 'ideal' listener, as opposed to the 'actual' congregation, and associating that 'ideal' listener with achieving 'total absorption' in himself is an adaptation of the figure of Lear madly 'contending with the fretful elements' (*KL* 3.1.4). Read in concert with the first volume's explicit reference to the figure of Cordelia, this allusion surely must be intentional. Lear argues or 'contends' with the storm, but he does not think that he wins such an argument:

> I tax not you, you elements, with unkindness.
> I never gave you kingdom, called you children;
> You owe me no subscription. Why then, let fall
> Your horrible pleasure. Here I stand your slave,
> A poor, infirm, weak and despised old man,
> But yet I call you servile ministers,
> That will with two pernicious daughters join
> Your high-engendered battles 'gainst a head
> So old and white as this.
> (*KL* 3.2.16–24)

Lear's characterization of the elements as 'servile ministers' that are merely attending to the will of his 'two pernicious daughters' speaks to the delusion that Lear shares with Johannes the Seducer. Lear gave up 'the name and all th'addition to a king' precisely when he tried to retain *only* 'the name, and all th'addition' without 'all the large effects/That troop with majesty' (*KL* 1.1.137, 132–3). Likewise, there is nothing particularly natural about what Johannes calls a 'royal nature'; it is guaranteed by signifying 'effects'. Where Johannes thinks that he can govern the tempests of his own moods – through variations of flattery, sometimes placing himself high, sometimes low – Lear sees those actual tempests governed, in effect, by Goneril and Regan. Of course, they would not be in such a privileged place of governance had he not given them that kingdom, given them 'all' (*KL* 2.2.439). It is not until he is confronted with what he assumes is 'the thing itself' in the figure of Poor Tom that Lear seems to understand that the elements are beyond the mastery of his (former) kingdom, asking his 'philosopher', 'What is the cause of thunder?' (*KL* 3.4.150–1). In other words, while he may not blame the elements for 'unkindness', while he calls himself their 'slave', the argument with the storm reveals his literally maddening self-absorption.

In 'Fear and Trembling', Kierkegaard more directly links the religious sphere with what most people would call insanity or foolishness.[24] But the final volume of *Either/Or* celebrates the divine illogic of the religious life view by implicitly linking that experience with Lear's. An ethical thinker like Judge William is blind to both. Lear argues with the storm, but admits that he cannot really blame it for his woes, because it only serves the will of his two pernicious daughters. For the pastor, there is a similarly absurd conclusion: religious upbuilding begins with an awareness that 'lies in the thought that in relation to God we are always in the wrong' (2.346). Lear's debate with the elements arrives at a conclusion of sorts. His claim that he 'tax[es] not' the storm with 'unkindness' is outrageous, but nonetheless reflects an epistemological understanding of the world in keeping with the 'royal nature' that he still privileges. For the pastor, a similar, affected 'total absorption in myself' out on the heath, speaking with the storm, leads to an on-going dialectic of humility which negates deliberation: 'it was not through deliberation that you became certain that you were always in the wrong, but the certainty was due to your being built up by it' (2.350).

After a lengthy volume praising marriage, we abruptly return to an image of solitariness, celebrating the religious as an experience of radical insularity. Structurally, this means that the second volume of *Either/Or* mirrors the first, to show how the pastor's 'total' self-absorption ironically recalls something like the egoistic self-absorption of Lear and Johannes. This shows that the aesthetic stage is, in some curious way, closer to the religious than the ethical: both are forms of 'living poetically' (1.304).[25] Kierkegaard indicates as much at the outset of *The Point of View*, when he clarifies that 'the religious is present from the very beginning [of his authorship]. Conversely, the esthetic is still present even in the last moment'.[26] In other words, the insights of the mad Lear in the storm are infinitely preferable to the narcissistic delusions of the Lear who coordinates the love test of the first act. However, the two are related.

This synchronicity between living poetically and living religiously appears to have troubled Kierkegaard.[27] It certainly troubles the conflicted lover in *Stages on Life's Way*, a quasi-sequel to, a critical assessment of, and an adaptation of *Either/Or*. It is also the volume that concludes Kierkegaard's covert adaptation of *King Lear*.

Expressions of madness: Dreams of prison in *King Lear* and *Stages on Life's Way*

That Kierkegaard gradually unfolds a series of allusions to moments from *King Lear* which follow the play's sequence of events suggests that he is intentionally adapting the play across the novelistic works that he called 'the indirect communication'. That this adaptation is somewhat buried and staged in terms of *misreading* suggests that Kierkegaard thinks about his adaptation of *Lear* as a kind of synecdoche for *Either/Or* as whole. Kierkegaard's characters fail to read either text adequately, missing both the depth of the allusions to Shakespeare's play and the respective merits of the aesthetic and ethical life stages.[28]

This kind of dramatic misreading is further complicated in *Stages on Life's Way*, which features characters from Kierkegaard's pseudonymous novels, as well as other characters who have read those books. Naturally, *Stages on Life's Way* further ironizes the framework of the unreliable editor that Kierkegaard uses in *Either/Or*. If Victor Eremita warned that you will 'regret' either reading or not reading *Either/Or*,

Stages on Life's Way goes one step further. Its purported editor, Hilarius Bookbinder, appears to have barely read the book he is publishing![29]

Unsurprisingly, *Stages on Life's Way* concludes with yet another supposedly found and edited diary: 'Guilty/Not Guilty'. Yet the diary's fabulous frame narrative – the journals were found sunk at the bottom of a lake like hidden treasure – is undercut by the title page, which labels the whole piece an 'imaginary construction by Frater Taciturnus' (185). 'Guilty/Not Guilty' is, then, explicitly *not* a found-and-edited text, such as A claimed 'The Seducer's Diary' to be. It is an overtly authored text. It is also clearly an adaptation. The title clearly alludes to *Either/Or*; Taciturnus refers throughout his accompanying letter to Kierkegaard's *Repetition* – yet another account of a broken engagement. In short, the text declares itself to be a literary adaptation of Kierkegaard's earlier narratives by one of his particularly careful readers.

'The Seducer's Diary', with the rest of *Either/Or*, was written in the wake of Kierkegaard's own broken engagement to Regine Schlegel (*née* Olson). The caddish Johannes reflects the persona Kierkegaard himself affected in order to persuade Regine that he was not worthy of her. 'Guilty/Not Guilty' somewhat sets the record straight (at one point even reproducing Kierkegaard's original farewell letter to Regine word-for-word).[30] Like Kierkegaard, Quidam, the diarist of 'Guilty/Not Guilty', ends his engagement to pursue a religious life. Still, Taciturnus's letter provides a critique of Quidam's diary, in light of Kierkegaard's stages of existence. He argues that Quidam seeks the religious aesthetically, and therefore cannot find comfort in either religious or erotic passion. Quidam is thus 'suspended' between the stages.

Yet, Taciturnus's note to the reader is probably most famous for diagnosing another fictional character's inability to reach the religious stage. In an appendix to his letter, curiously placed right in the middle, Taciturnus discusses Shakespeare's *Hamlet*. Taciturnus concludes that *Hamlet* is not a 'religious drama', but only because no play ever quite could be. Were the play to end differently – with Hamlet 'collaps[ing] into himself and into the religious until he finds peace there' after successfully completing his revenge plot – that would be one thing. But 'a drama, of course, can never come from' so extended an account of interiority (454).

If Frater Taciturnus's reading of *Hamlet* emphasizes Shakespeare's inadequacy in representing the religious, he also considers the points of contact between religious feeling and the aesthetic – even 'demonic' – life view. What Frater Taciturnus envisions as an un-stageable drama would be a circumnavigating of the ethical stage. A demonic aesthete authors a plan that he is resolutely capable of carrying out. Yet this resolution gradually transforms into a new form of total self-absorption, much like what the pastor had described as occurring out on the Jutland heath. In other words, perhaps *Hamlet* would be a religious drama were it only a little more like *King Lear*.

In addition to reworking the narrative at the centre of 'The Seducer's Diary', 'Guilty/Not Guilty' concludes the subtle, buried restaging of *King Lear* that was begun in that earlier piece. As Kierkegaard guides his reader through the plot of *Lear*, he does not display what Christy Desmet calls 'technical' fidelity to the play.[31] This seems intentional, given his interest in portraying characters who misread, or miss reading, the play's details. But Kierkegaard's strategy changes somewhat in 'Guilty/Not Guilty', where he demonstrates a deeper *emotional* fidelity to the play. Quidam is the one character in Kierkegaard's adaptation who appears to grasp what it means to resemble a character from *King Lear*. As a result, he is the one most affected, even tormented, by the play's imagery:

> And yet if I were just sitting with her, just that I dared to be in her presence, that I dared to do everything even if it is nothing – that would still be a relief, a relief that, like a smoldering, is an uninterrupted dull pain but not so much a suffering. Then she would confuse everything; she would

believe that as before we were sitting in the boat on that lake we sailed together, and then we would exchange, if not winged words, then expressions of madness, and would understand each other in madness, and speak of our love as Lear wanted to speak with Cordelia about the royal household and ask for news from it.

(264)

When Lear speaks of his desire for a life in prison with his beloved daughter, it seems to be a new, albeit calmer, expression of his deluded mind which was supposedly cured when he was reunited with Cordelia at the end of Act 4. Whereas the pastor alludes to the synchronicity between mania and the religious, Quidam is explicitly aware that Lear's desire is the stuff of madness:

> No, no, no, no. Come, let's away to prison;
> We two alone will sing like birds i'th' cage.
> When thou dost ask me blessing, I'll kneel down
> And ask of thee forgiveness. So we'll live,
> And pray, and sing, and tell old tales, and laugh
> At gilded butterflies, and hear poor rogues
> Talk of court news; and we'll talk with them too –
> Who loses and who wins, who's in, who's out,
> And take upon 's the mystery of things
> As if we were God's spies
> (KL 5.3.8–17)

King Lear repeatedly depicts moments where characters mistake 'nothing' for everything. Quidam seems to recognize that any relief that Lear feels arrives in the form of a hallucination. The king first daydreams of the fantasy of gossiping over courtly nothings and he will eventually hallucinate hysterically that Cordelia is actually breathing (KL 5.3.308–9). But those breaths are not real; they are a nothing which Lear treats as though it is everything. When he orders that we 'look there, look there' at this nothing – a nothing that Johannes the Seducer inadvertently celebrated when he praised his Cordelia's silent lips – Lear is consumed.

Quidam is likewise obsessed with nothingness. Quidam understands that treating nothing as though it is everything can feel like a relief, when it is an expression of madness. This seems to me to be very much in the spirit of *Lear*. But Quidam neither embraces the delusions of this passionate romantic love, nor does he wholly abandon it and leap into the religious stage. As such, he seems more aware than most of Kierkegaard's figures that the aesthetic life view is unfulfilling, yet its resemblance to the religious makes it that much more difficult to leave behind:

> What is the point of all my concerns and plans and efforts? What am I achieving? Nothing. But I am not going to stop for that reason. Precisely for that reason I am not going to stop, for when a person does everything and it is of no help, then he can be sure that he is acting with enthusiasm. Therefore I do not disdain this nothing ...
>
> (306)

Ultimately Quidam's 'great' act of turning away from his beloved causes him to 'topple' inwardly, worrying at length over the implications of giving up 'everything' to accomplish what looks like nothing. Frater Taciturnus, with his pronouncement that 'the negative is higher than the positive', seems to suggest that Quidam's problem is that he welcomes nothingness as proof of the accomplishment of his suffering – the final entry in the diary claims that '*Guilty/Not Guilty*' 'contains nothing ... sometimes it is the hardest life that deals with nothing' (397) – and therefore he does not go far enough. The religious stage is just that much farther than, that much less than, nothing, and by settling for nothing, Quidam remains demonic.

Kierkegaard invokes *Richard III* to illustrate the 'demonic' in 'Fear and Trembling'.[32] However, that is not quite how Quidam refers to *Lear*. He alone seems to read *Lear* faithfully, not because it speaks to the religious stage, but because it does not, and is therefore parallel to his own condition. Other figures in Kierkegaard's *oeuvre* change earlier narratives and details at will, adapting previous texts as they see fit. Why, then, does Quidam not simply change *Lear* to fit what it is he wants to say about the religious stage? Why does he alone, out of all of these figures, understand that Lear is completely mad, but is probably happier that way, so to want to resemble him or learn from him would also be mad?

Poor Quidam's diary ends 'for the time being' (397), so Kierkegaard's adaptation of *Lear* also ends in suspension. He does not bring his reader to the final, nearly apocalyptic, moments of the play and its horrifying, inverted *pietà*. There, a father holds his daughter in place of a mother holding her son and resurrection is deemed impossible just as it is anticipated.[33] Instead, Quidam leaves us with Lear's twisted delight at being led off to prison.

Numerous readers have drawn parallels between Kierkegaard and that other melancholy Dane, Hamlet.[34] However, there is much to suggest how deeply *King Lear* affected Kierkegaard. Reading his fragmented version of *Lear*, we gain a sense that Kierkegaard may have been resistant to recognizing something in reading the play in its entirety. References to *King Lear* in Kierkegaard's journals and papers offer suggestions of what that something may be.

'As if we saw into the depths': *King Lear* in Kierkegaard's journals

Hans Peter Barfod, the first and much-criticized editor of Kierkegaard's journals and papers, aimed to arrange the contents of his edition in chronological order. However, he was apparently so struck by the following entry that he broke with this planned arrangement and placed it at the very beginning of his edition:

Then it was that the great earthquake occurred, the frightful upheaval which suddenly drove me to a new infallible principle for interpreting all the phenomena. Then I surmised that my father's old-age was not a divine blessing, but rather a curse, that our family's exceptional intellectual capacities were only for mutually harrowing one another; then I felt the stillness of death deepen around me, when I saw in my father an unhappy man who would survive us all, a memorial cross on the grave of all his personal hopes. A guilt must rest upon the entire family, a punishment of God must be upon it: it was supposed to disappear, obliterated by the mighty hand of God, erased like a mistake, and only at times did I find a little relief in the thought that my father had been given the heavy duty of reassuring us all with the consolation of religion, telling us that a better world stands open for us even if we lost this one, even if the punishment the Jews always called down on their enemies should strike us: that remembrance of us would be completely *obliterated*, that there would be no trace of us.[35]

Glued to this passage is an entry entitled '25 years old', which consists entirely of a transcription of the speech from *Lear* cited in Quidam's diary, where Lear fantasizes about life in prison with Cordelia.[36]

The 'great earthquake' passage is 'one of the most disputed of all Kierkegaard's journal entries'.[37] It is virtually impossible to know for certain what Kierkegaard is referring to when he mentions a 'great earthquake'. However, when these passages are read together, Lear's delusion, a pathetic rebuttal to Cordelia's observation that they 'have incurred the worst' (*KL* 5.3.4), is a counterpart to Kierkegaard's own vaguely reported epiphany about his father, Michael, and the melancholy that they shared. Even at their clearest, the journals can be as indirect as any example from Kierkegaard's pseudonymous writings. Whether Kierkegaard affixed these passages, or whether they were glued together by Barfod or somebody else, is uncertain.

Still, *somebody* noticed the parallels between these two passages and affixed them together and perhaps it was Kierkegaard. Other entries in the journals offer a reason why Kierkegaard may have associated his father's 'curse' with the story of *King Lear*. While it is unclear what Kierkegaard specifically means by the 'great earthquake', it is possible that he is referring to an incident from his father's youth. Exasperated from hunger and poverty, Michael cursed God in a dramatic fashion; the memory caused him guilt for decades to come and he repeatedly recounted the narrative for Kierkegaard and his brother, Peter. The anecdote had a profound effect on Søren, and its setting was particularly resonant:

> How appalling for the man who, as a lad watching sheep on the Jutland heath, suffering painfully, hungry and exhausted, once stood on a hill and cursed God – and the man was unable to forget it when he was eighty-two years old.[38]

When Kierkegaard turned to *Lear* at the end of *Either/Or* to write of a pastor out on the Jutland heath, with a 'voice [rising] to its full power in order to drown out the storm', he likely had Michael in mind as well.

Whether or not this is the 'great earthquake' that Kierkegaard discussed in the entry from 1838, both he and his father struggled for a long time with the anxiety borne erruptively from this moment out on the Jutland heath. While the narratives of broken engagements in 'The Seducer's Diary' and 'Guilty/Not Guilty' encourage us to associate Lear and Cordelia with Søren and Regine, the journals seem to suggest that Shakespeare's tragedy reminded Kierkegaard of his complicated relationship with his father.

In both *Lear* and the journal entry, insight is compared to the brutality of nature, expressed with a sublime image ('hurricano', earthquake). In both *Lear* and this entry, the effects of the father's misdeeds are felt by his children. There is some consolation to be found in religion, but there is also anxiety and scepticism in the face of the obliteration that is prophesized. In this entry, Kierkegaard confesses to 'only at times' finding comfort in the promise of a better world. *Lear* offers no such comfort.

King Lear may be a play about anxiety, in the Kierkegaardian sense of what is bequeathed by original sin – which is to say, somebody else's sin. In this sense, Kierkegaard's *Lear* is inexorably intertwined with Kierkegaard's relationship with his own father:

> King Lear's fate can be accounted for as Nemesis. His fault is the madness with which the play begins, of summarily requiring his children to declare the depth of their love for him. Children's love for their parents is a bottomless mystery, rooted as well in a natural relationship. An event can therefore be the occasion which reveals its depth, but it is unseemly, impious, and culpable to wish curiously and selfishly to dissect it, as it were, for the sake of one's own satisfaction. Such a thing is tolerable in an erotic relationship (when the lover asks the beloved how much she loves him), although even here it is pandering.[39]

What is a great earthquake if not an event that painfully reveals unseen depths? The excerpt from *Lear* attached to the 'great earthquake' entry is taken from Ernst Ortlepp's translation. There, Lear's dream that he and Cordelia will shuffle off to prison to discuss the 'mystery of things/As if [they] were God's spies' (*KL* 5.3.16–17) becomes a more general claim to speak of mysterious things, 'as if we saw into the depths' (*das Tiefste*).[40] For Kierkegaard, *King Lear* addresses quite painfully which depths of intersubjective relationships should be revealed and which concealed. Or, rather, for Kierkegaard, the play addresses which of those depths were revealed *to him* specifically.

Of course, Kierkegaard similarly dissected his love for Regine Schlegel at length and was never satisfied with what he uncovered. As a result, his

God-relationship, is in many ways the happy love of my unhappy and troubled life. And even though this love story (if I dare to call it that) has the essential mark of the true love story, that only one can completely understand it, and to only one does a person have absolute joy in telling it, to the beloved, therefore here the one by whom one is loved – it nevertheless is enjoyable to speak of it to others also.[41]

The notion that love can only be expressed between individual lovers is the model for Kierkegaard's own identification of his readership as one other *single* individual. Though he writes that it is 'impious' for a parent and child to communicate this way, Kierkegaard seems to have found an echo of this quandary of communication in Lear's dream of prison, in suspension, Quidam-like, waiting for the revelation that Cordelia will, in fact, 'come no more/Never, never, never, never, never' (*KL* 5.3.306–7).

Conclusion

The bleakness of *Lear*'s conclusion is beyond the scope of Quidam's diary. Yet there is one more moment in the indirect communication that may be touched by *Lear* and which may engage this final revelation that Cordelia will 'never, never, never, never, never' rise again. In 'Fear and Trembling', Johannes de Silentio remarks that 'great Shakespeare' can 'say everything, everything, everything just as it is':

Why did you never articulate this torment [i.e. Abraham's *horror religiosus*]? Did you perhaps reserve it for yourself, like the beloved's name that one cannot bear to have the world utter, for with his little secret that he cannot divulge the poet buys this power of the word to tell everybody else's dark secrets. A poet is not an apostle; he drives out devils only by the power of the devil.[42]

Frater Taciturnus suggests that Shakespeare withholds a portrayal of the religious because no drama could ever accurately depict the inwardness of the religious stage. Johannes de Silentio suggests here that Shakespeare's avoidance of the religious is more strategic; rather than reveal his own 'secret' inward torment, he sublimates it into an unmatched, though demonic, aesthetic achievement.[43]

If when Johannes de Silentio speaks of Shakespeare's ability to communicate 'everything, everything, everything' he inverts the conclusion of *King Lear*, then he goes further than Quidam's diary to the point where Lear sees the disintegration of language itself. Lear, at the play's close, finally faces the nothing that has come of nothing ('no, no, no life'; 'Never, never, never, never, never', *KL* 5.3.304, 307) and can only respond by 'howl, howl, howl, howl!'-ing and directing those around him to look at something that is not really there (*KL* 5.3.255). Johannes de Silentio may wonder why Shakespeare can say 'everything, everything, everything' but does not show the religious despair and anxiety that Abraham must have felt. Other figures in Kierkegaard's writings suggest that Shakespeare simply could *not* express such a feeling dramatically. The truth is that, in *Lear*, Shakespeare shows us something else and something worse: the void that Johannes de Silentio feared would prove that everything leads to despair and that Abraham suffered for nothing.

Perhaps what Kierkegaard shares with Hamlet is not melancholy, but certainty. As the psychoanalyst Jacques Lacan puts it, in his own idiosyncratic reading of the play, Hamlet *knows*.[44] Though both Hamlet and Kierkegaard are not without doubt, at heart they both believe in the existence of something beyond what is 'dreamt of in your philosophy' (*Ham* 1.5.166). Lear and *Lear* also demonstrate a vision of existence with certainty, but one which suggests that what awaits us – unless you mercifully hallucinate otherwise ('look there, look there!') – is nothing. Whatever comfort or joy there may be is founded upon the nothingness of discourse, be it philosophy, poetry or the 'pandering' that Kierkegaard objected to in any love-relationship other than the one he claimed to share with God.

Notes

1. Kierkegaard, 'On My Work as an Author', 6. Kierkegaard indicates that the authorship begins with *Either/Or* (1843), thereby distinguishing this sequence of texts from his earlier writing, such as his dissertation, *The Concept of Irony* (1841).
2. Kierkegaard, 'On My Work', 8.
3. Kierkegaard, 'On My Work', 7.
4. Discussions of Kierkegaard's spheres of existence are legion; for a clear introduction, see Evans, *Kierkegaard*.
5. McDonald, 'Kierkegaard and Romanticism', 94.
6. Kierkegaard, *The Point of View*, 53.
7. See Rasmussen, 'William Shakespeare'; Ruoff, 'Kierkegaard and Shakespeare'; and Ziolkowski, *The Literary Kierkegaard*, 183–212. Though he seems to focus more on *Hamlet* than *Lear*, see also Stewart, '*Lear* in Kierkegaard'.
8. For conflicting takes on the value of 'fidelity' in the study of adaptation of Shakespeare's drama, see Lanier, 'Shakespearean Rhizomatics' and Desmet, 'Recognizing Shakespeare'.
9. Nahum Tate's much-derided, happy-ending version of *King Lear* dominated the British stage until Macready's more faithful production in 1838. Nineteenth-century productions of *Lear* at the Vienna Burgtheater concluded with Cordelia reviving. See Williams, *Shakespeare on the German Stage*, 115–19. A translation of Tate's *Lear* appeared in Danish near the end of the eighteenth century, but attempts to stage it fizzled out. See Ruud, *Shakespeare in Denmark*, 84 and Jensen, 'Shakespeare in Denmark', 93.
10. Kierkegaard appears to have favoured the Schlegel-Tieck translation, but he also owned Ernst Ortlepp's German translation and the Danish translations by Peter Foersom and Peter Frederik Wulff. See Rasmussen, 'William Shakespeare', 208–12, for a bibliography of texts by and referencing Shakespeare owned by Kierkegaard.

    Niels Lyhne Jensen claims that between 1830 and 1849, 'Shakespeare was only played twice on the national stage' in Denmark, and productions drawing upon Foersom's direct translations of Shakespeare's verse were 'rejected in favour of insipid and governessy adaptations' until the 1860s. See Jensen, 'Shakespeare in Denmark', 94. It seems unlikely that Kierkegaard saw much Shakespeare on stage, though he does praise Johanne Luise Heiberg's performance as Juliet in his 1847 essay, 'The Crisis and a Crisis in the Life of an Actress', 321–2.

At any rate, Kierkegaard could not have seen *Lear* on the Danish stage by the time of *Either/Or*'s composition in 1841 and 1842; a production flopped in 1816 and *Lear* was not staged again until 1851. See Ruud, *Essay*, 90. Nor could Kierkegaard have seen a stage production of Shakespeare during his few visits to Berlin between 1841 and 1845. According to Williams, the only significant Berlin production in that time was Ludwig Tieck's staging of *A Midsummer Night's Dream* in 1843; see Williams, *Shakespeare*, 183–5 and 223. While Kierkegaard was in Berlin during 1843, his trip began and ended in May; Tieck's production premiered that October. See Garff, *Søren Kierkegaard*, 229–32 and Patterson, *The First German Theatre*, 121.

11 See Kierkegaard, *Either/Or Part I* and *Either/Or Part II*. Subsequent citations in text, indicated by volume number followed by page number.

12 Kierkegaard, 'On My Work', 9.

13 See also Rasmussen, *Between Irony and Witness*, 43–4. On Kierkegaard's complicated treatment of the concept of the 'interesting', see Stokes, *Kierkegaard's Mirrors*.

14 Friedrich Schlegel's *Lucinde*, for example, is also a collection of fragments of epistolary, critical and narrative writing which, in its seeming disorder, 'affirm' 'the right to a charming confusion'. See Schlegel, *Lucinde*, 45. See also Rasmussen, *Between Irony and Witness*, 26–31 for a reading of *Either/Or* as a continuation of the attack on *Lucinde* begun in Kierkegaard's dissertation, *The Concept of Irony*.

15 See Ziolkowski, *Literary Kierkegaard*, 188–9.

16 Shakespeare, *King Lear*, Arden Shakespeare Third Series, 1.1.91–2, 5.3.308. Subsequent citations in text; all citations taken from Arden Shakespeare Third Series.

17 For an account of these *topoi*, see Curtius, *European Literature*, 159–65.

18 In a letter to Cordelia, Johannes writes: 'Erotic love loves secrecy – an engagement is a disclosure; it loves silence – an engagement is a public announcement; it loves whispering – an engagement is a loud proclamation, and yet, with my Cordelia's help, an engagement will be a superb way to deceive the enemies' (1.388).

19 Rasmussen, *Between Irony and Witness*, 27.

20 Kierkegaard, 'Fear and Trembling', 70.

21 For A's praise of Shakespeare, see Kierkegaard, *Either/Or*, 1.28.

22 Judge William pays more attention to Shakespeare in *Stages on Life's Way*. There, the married man should resemble 'a deceiver portrayed by Shakespeare' (meaning Iago). William also praises Desdemona for her 'sublime lie' and 'angelic patience' (140, 142), implicitly suggesting that the ideal couple in Shakespeare would *not* be Romeo and Juliet (168), but rather an Iago paired with a Desdemona! Subsequent citations in text. See Ziolkowski, *Literary Kierkegaard*, 191–6.

23 The Jutland heath would be the subject of a popular poem by Hans Christian Andersen in 1859. For a discussion of the heath's agricultural transformation and its impact on the Danish literary imagination, see Olwig, 'Literature and "Reality"'.

24 Kierkegaard, 'Fear and Trembling', 16–17. See also Llewelyn, 'On The Borderline of Madness' and Westphal, 'Kierkegaard and the Logic of Insanity'.

25 Sylvia Walsh considers the parallels and distinctions between Kierkegaard's aesthetic and religious stages at length: 'the truly poetic is identified with the religious', but 'the notion of "living poetically" in a Christian manner is sketched in contrast to a romantic mode of living poetically'. See Walsh, *Living Poetically*, 16.

26 Kierkegaard, *Point of View*, 30.

27 In a journal entry written as he was sketching 'Guilty/Not Guilty', Kierkegaard writes: 'If I had had faith, I would have stayed with Regine. Thanks to God, I now see that. I have been on the point of losing my mind these days.' See Kierkegaard, *Søren Kierkegaard's Journals*, 5664. All journal entries cited by entry number.

28 By not only portraying but also embedding a process of misreading in these volumes, Kierkegaard is targeting the passionate, fragmented – but therefore *selective* – style of reading associated with Romanticism. But it bears mentioning that the perils of misreading are also central to *King Lear*; Gloucester's fortunes fall as a result of his failing to catch the deceit in Edmund's 'invent[ed]' letter (1.2.20).

29 A member of the intelligentsia that Hilarius calls 'Mr. Literatus' sends several books and manuscripts to be bound, but dies before Hilarius finishes the job. While Hilarius occasionally reads from 'the book' for diversion, he confesses that, 'I cannot say that there was much diversion, for I did not understand very much.' Later, his children's tutor – someone who 'had entirely abandoned studying to be a pastor since he found out that he was an esthete and a poet (I think that is what he calls it)' – borrows the book and encourages Hilarius to publish it (4). Hilarius confesses that he is uncertain of both the quality of the work or its likelihood to draw a profit and turns the matter over to the 'fair-minded reader' (6).

30 See Garff, *Søren Kierkegaard*, 186.

31 On this distinction between technical and emotional fidelity, see Desmet, 'Recognizing Shakespeare', 47.

32 Kierkegaard, 'Fear and Trembling', 105–6.

33 Maynard Mack offers a more optimistic reading of Lear as a kind of secular 'Mary bending over another broken child' in his *King Lear in Our Time*, 116.

34 For example, see Lowrie, *A Short Life of Kierkegaard*, 143. See also Lisi, 'Hamlet: The Impossibility of Tragedy/The Tragedy of Impossibility'.

35 Kierkegaard, *Søren Kierkegaard's Journals*, 5430.

36 Kierkegaard, *Søren Kierkegaard's Journals*, 5429. Also grouped with these entries are quotations from Goethe and the Danish poet Christian Winther. See the account in Garff, *Søren Kierkegaard*, 131–8.

37 Garff, *Søren Kierkegaard*, 132.

38 Kierkegaard, *Søren Kierkegaard's Journals*, 5874.

39 Kierkegaard, *Søren Kierkegaard's Journals*, 1165.

40 Ortlep's translation, as transcribed in the journals, reads: 'Wir sprechen von geheimnissvollen Dingen, / Als ob wir in das Tiefste sie durchschauten'. In Kierkegaard, *Søren Kierkegaard's Journals*, 5429.
41 Kierkegaard, *Point of View*, 71.
42 Kierkegaard, 'Fear and Trembling', 61.
43 See also Kierkegaard's essay, 'The Difference Between a Genius and an Apostle'.
44 Jacques Lacan, 'Desire', 19. On the connections between Lacan's and Kierkegaard's readings of *Hamlet*, see Duquette, '*Pour faire une hamlette*'.

Works cited

Curtius, Ernst Robert, *European Literature and the Latin Middle Ages*, trans. Willard R. Trask (1948; 7th edn, Princeton, 1990).

Desmet, Christy, 'Recognizing Shakespeare, Rethinking Fidelity: A Rhetoric and Ethics of Appropriation', in Huang and Rivlin, eds, *Shakespeare and the Ethics of Appropriation*, 41–57.

Duquette, Elizabeth, '*Pour faire une hamlette*: Freud, Kierkegaard, Lacan', *Literature and Psychology* 49/1–2 (2003), 1–38.

Evans, C. Stephen, *Kierkegaard: An Introduction* (Cambridge, 2009).

Garff, Joakim, *Søren Kierkegaard: A Biography*, trans. Bruce H. Kirmmse (Princeton, 2007).

Huang, Alexa and Elizabeth Rivlin, eds, *Shakespeare and the Ethics of Appropriation* (New York, 2014).

Jensen, Niels Lyhne, 'Shakespeare in Denmark', *Durham University Journal*, 56 (1963–4), 93.

Kierkegaard, Søren, 'The Crisis and a Crisis in the Life of an Actress', in *Christian Discourses and The Crisis and a Crisis in the Life of an Actress*, trans. Howard V. and Edna H. Hong (1847; Princeton, 1997), 303–25.

Kierkegaard, Søren, 'The Difference Between a Genius and an Apostle', in *The Book on Adler*, trans. Howard V. and Edna H. Hong (1849; Princeton, 1998), 173–88.

Kierkegaard, Søren, *Either/Or Part I* and *Either/Or Part II*, trans. Howard V. and Edna H. Hong (1843; Princeton 1987).

Kierkegaard, Søren, 'Fear and Trembling', in *Fear and Trembling and Repetition*, trans. Howard V. and Edna H. Hong (1843; Princeton, 1983).

Kierkegaard, Søren, 'On My Work as an Author', in *The Point of View*, trans. Howard V. and Edna H. Hong (1851; Princeton, 1998).

Kierkegaard, Soren, *The Point of View*, trans. Howard V. and Edna H. Hong (1851; Princeton, 1998).

Kierkegaard, Søren, *Søren Kierkegaard's Journals and Papers*, ed. and trans. Howard V. and Edna H. Hong, assisted by Gregor Malantschuk, 7 vols (Bloomington, 1967–78).

Kierkegaard, Søren, *Stages on Life's Way: Studies by Various Persons*, trans. Howard V. and Edna H. Hong (1845; Princeton, 1988).

Lacan, Jacques, 'Desire and the Interpretation of Desire in *Hamlet*', in Shoshana Felman, ed., *Literature and Psychoanalysis: The Question of Reading: Otherwise* (Baltimore, 1982), 11–52.

Lanier, Douglas, 'Shakespearean Rhizomatics: Adaptation, Ethics, Value', in Huang and Rivlin, eds, *Shakespeare and the Ethics of Appropriation*, 21–40.

Lisi, Leonardo, 'Hamlet: The Impossibility of Tragedy/The Tragedy of Impossibility', in Jon Stewart and Katalin Nun, eds, *Kierkegaard's Literary Figures and Motifs: Gulliver to Zerlina* (Farnham, 2016), 13–38.

Llewelyn, John, 'On the Borderline of Madness', in Elsebet Jegstrup, ed., *The New Kierkegaard* (Bloomington, 2004), 88–11.

Lowrie, Walter, *A Short Life of Kierkegaard* (Princeton, 1965).

Mack, Maynard, *King Lear in Our Time* (Abingdon, 1966).

McDonald, William, 'Kierkegaard and Romanticism', in John Lippitt and George Pattison, eds., *The Oxford Handbook of Kierkegaard* (Oxford, 2013), 94

Olwig, Kenneth Robert, 'Literature and "Reality": The Transformation of the Jutland Heath', in Douglas C. D. Pocock, ed., *Humanistic Geography and Literature: Essays on the Experience of Place* (Totowa, 1981), 47–65.

Patterson, Michael, *The First German Theatre: Schiller, Goethe, Kleist and Büchner in Performance* (New York, 1990).

Rasmussen, Joel D. S., *Between Irony and Witness: Kierkegaard's Poetics of Faith, Hope, and Love* (New York, 2005).

Rasmussen, Joel D. S., 'William Shakespeare: Kierkegaard's Post-Romantic Reception of "the Poet's Poet"', in Jon Stewart, ed., *Kierkegaard and the Renaissance and Modern Traditions*, iii: *Literature, Drama, and Music* (Burlington, 2009), 185–213.

Ruoff, James E., 'Kierkegaard and Shakespeare', *Comparative Literature*, 20/4 (1968), 343–54.

Ruud, Martin, *An Essay Toward a History of Shakespeare in Denmark* (Minneapolis, 1920).

Schlegel, Friedrich, *Friedrich Schlegel's Lucinde and the Fragments*, trans. Peter Firchow (1799; Minneapolis, 1971).

Shakespeare, William, *Hamlet*, ed. Ann Thompson and Neil Taylor, Arden Shakespeare Third Series (New York, 2006).

Shakespeare, William, *King Lear*, ed. R. A. Foakes, Arden Shakespeare Third Series (London, 1997).

Stewart, Stanley, '*Lear* in Kierkegaard', in Jeffrey Kahan, ed., *King Lear: Critical Essays* (New York, 2008), 278–96.

Stokes, Patrick, *Kierkegaard's Mirrors: Interest, Self, and Moral Vision* (New York, 2010).

Walsh, Sylvia, *Living Poetically: Kierkegaard's Existential Aesthetics* (University Park, 1994).

Westphal, Merold, 'Kierkegaard and the Logic of Insanity', *Religious Studies*, 7/3 (1971), 193–211.

Williams, Simon, *Shakespeare on the German Stage*, i: *1586–1914* (Cambridge, 1990).

Ziolkowski, Eric, *The Literary Kierkegaard* (Evanston, 2011).

6

'A blot on Swedish hospitality': Ira Aldridge's visit to Stockholm in 1857

Per Sivefors

When the African-American actor Ira Aldridge arrived in Stockholm on 21 May 1857, rumours of his visit had already been circulating for a few weeks.[1] First reported in the Stockholm press, the news was clearly considered interesting enough to be picked up by various local newspapers around the country.[2] Prior to the visit, there had been unfounded rumours that Aldridge had died in a railway accident,[3] while his arrival was noted in the press on 22 May.[4] By the next day, according to reports in the Stockholm *Fäderneslandet*, Aldridge had been received by the English consul and the local bookshops already had his portrait for sale.[5] It was on the initiative of the director of the Royal Theatre, Gunnar Olof Hyltén-Cavallius, that Aldridge – who had previously performed in front of the Queen of Sweden in Switzerland in 1854 – was now invited to play Othello in a production of Shakespeare's play. It was agreed that Aldridge would perform in English whereas the Swedish actors spoke Swedish, using the (then) recent translation by Carl August Hagberg.[6] The multilingual approach was noted and sometimes became the object of jokes in the press;[7] for convenience, a booklet was published with Aldridge's lines in Swedish so the audience could follow his acting.[8] As it turned out, Aldridge would also star as Shylock in *The Merchant of Venice*, again at the Royal Theatre, during his six-week visit to Stockholm.

The preliminary reports in the press generally tend to mention both Aldridge's skin colour and the fact that he was going to perform in 'Shakespeare's immortal masterpiece *Othello*', often using similar turns of phrase. It is evident that this combined referencing of race and the cultural capital attached to Shakespeare's name created a great deal of interest in Stockholm and the rest of the country. Indeed, the conjunction of Shakespeare and debates on race may have begun three years earlier. A production of *The Merchant of Venice* had been performed in 1854 which, Ann Fridén argues, can be related to the fact that at exactly this time, a bill in the Swedish parliament proposed that Jewish rights of settlement be expanded. By presenting a Shylock without caricaturing or stereotyping, this production could, according to Fridén, be seen as supporting Jewish emancipation.[9] She goes on to observe that Aldridge's performances in Stockholm three years later is another powerful example of how Shakespeare's plays could be related to current political problems in Sweden in the 1850s. Discussing the press debate in the wake of Aldridge's visit, Fridén suggests that at least one of the negative reviews Aldridge received was racist, which was also commented on by a more positive reviewer in another of the major dailies at the time. The debate was, no doubt, very much caught up in discussing Aldridge's race.

However, as this chapter will demonstrate, the debate, which, in fact, echoed throughout the country in various local newspapers, did not simply play out along lines of anti-racism and racism, but was also strongly rooted in a clash over aesthetic ideals. While reviewers often brought up the question of Aldridge's blackness and how to categorize it, they were deeply divided as to his acting.[10] What is more, the lines of division cannot be neatly categorized in terms of aesthetically conservative and racist versus aesthetically radical and anti-racist. Instead, some of the most positive responses to Aldridge's performances are the most deeply entrenched in racial categorization whereas some that are more hostile reject or play down race as a category. As we will see, the discussion of aesthetic ideals in the reviews – which was extensive and wide-ranging – cannot be separated from the sometimes casual, sometimes elaborate referencing of race. In order to discuss this connection, the present chapter will begin by contextualizing the production from the perspective of changes in theatrical practice and, in particular, in debates over the nature of acting in the middle of the nineteenth century. It is from that context that we can understand how aesthetic discussions were implicated in aspects of race. In other words, the many references to Aldridge's blackness in the press cannot be understood without first grasping the terms of the debate on acting and the nature of theatrical illusion.

By this time, *Othello* had a brief history on the Swedish stage: it had been performed by a French troupe in Stockholm in 1802 and, for the first time in Swedish, in 1827 at the Royal Theatre in a production that was cancelled after eight shows and widely panned in the press.[11] It is therefore safe to say that the 1857 production was the most successful and widely publicized of Shakespeare's play in Sweden thus far. It is unsurprising that it occurred at this particular moment in time as the 1850s and 1860s were, in many ways, a turning point in the history of Shakespeare on the Swedish stage, both quantitatively and qualitatively.[12] The royal monopoly on theatre and opera in Stockholm had been abolished in 1842, which resulted in the establishment of more venues and Hagberg's best-selling translations of the plays (1847–1851) no doubt helped to propel an interest in Shakespeare even if they were far from always used in the actual productions.[13] It also seems that new acting styles were often what attracted audiences and reviewers: eschewing classical declamation and passionate Romanticism in favour of more psychologically realistic performances that critics described as balanced and measured, actors like Edvard Swartz as Hamlet (1853) and Georg Dahlqvist as Shylock (1854) were apparently key to the success of Shakespeare at the Royal Theatre.[14] In the context of the present chapter, it can be noted that both these actors went on to act with Aldridge in the *Othello* production: Swartz as Rodrigo and Dahlqvist as Iago.[15]

It is clear that there was an ongoing change in acting styles and ideals at the time, both in Sweden and the rest of Europe. Alan Downer suggests that by 1860 'the critical public was prepared to accept a literal interpretation of Shakespeare's oft-quoted precept, to 'hold the mirror up to nature'.[16] It was, of course, a bone of contention just what 'nature' might mean in the context of theatre and such controversies also spilled over into the Nordic countries. For example, in Denmark, at the Christiansborg Court Theatre, Frederik Høedt's company was noted for its attempts at realistic acting and settings. Commenting on these, the actress Johanne Luise Heiberg, herself a notable pioneer of a more psychologically orientated style, later complained of actors who 'cough, sneeze, blow their noses, scratch their heads, spit across the boards of the floor, all in reverence to truth and nature'.[17] As Marker and Marker suggest, this should not simply be seen as new ideals clashing with old ones: even an innovator like Strindberg would later reject a 'photographic' ideal of representation.[18] But it is nonetheless clear that, to many Swedish critics, Aldridge's acting represented a style that was both unorthodox and aimed for 'truth'. Indeed, the first reviewer for *Aftonbladet* commented on 'the freedom with which [Aldridge] moved on the stage and interacted with his fellow players, without any pedantic fear of even turning his back at the audience whenever required by the acting or plot'.[19] At this time, turning one's back at the audience clearly signified unorthodoxy: it was, for example, one of the shocking practices introduced at the Christiansborg Court Theatre.[20]

This is not to say that the Royal Theatre was a trailblazer in theatrical innovation. Indeed, at the time of Aldridge's visit, it was the privately run Mindre Teatern, led by Edvard Stjernström, which had a repertoire in line with the increasingly fashionable bourgeois realism. The fact that productions of Shakespeare were as frequent there as at the Royal Theatre, where Aldridge performed, indicates that Shakespeare had now become a significant factor in middle-class education. Conversely, there may have been a certain unease at the Royal Theatre about taking on Shakespeare, which could, as Fridén suggests, be ascribed to the fact that many Shakespearean plays were considered unacceptable in their representation of kings and the nobility, as well as in their general depiction of morals.[21] At the same time, even this august institution was affected by changing ideals; the production of *Macbeth* in 1858 – the year after Aldridge's visit – was, according to Fridén, a display of mostly outdated classical convention.[22] Aldridge thus performed at an arena which embodied an ongoing conflict between different aesthetic norms and, as we will see, the reviews reflect that.

What, then, did the audience see at the performances of *Othello*? Despite the short time for rehearsals, this much-publicized event at the Royal Theatre was an upscale production. While some of the decorations had been recycled from the 1854 *Merchant of Venice*, Aldridge's costume was, in the words of one reviewer, 'most sumptuous and splendid'.[23] The first show was sold out and obviously made an impression despite the fact that it was a bilingual performance; indeed, the enthusiastic reviewer for *Aftonbladet* notes that 'it must of course seem somewhat strange to hear a role executed in English when the other ones were performed in Swedish; however, the interaction was far better than could be expected under such circumstances'.[24] As for staging, the available documentation indicates that the producers aimed for a relatively contemporary style. Gösta Bergman, who briefly compares this production of *Othello* to the failed one in 1827, suggests that the acting 'has become three-dimensional in quite a different way and the lines could not have been spoken directly to the audience'.[25] Bergman emphasizes that the two productions embody a shift away from schematic groupings and abstract representation of space towards a freer, more natural type of arrangement; arguably, this approach may have blended well with Aldridge's unconventional style and body language. Indeed, the previously mentioned print in *Illustrerad Tidning* depicts Aldridge bending over backwards beside the smothered Desdemona, his back to the audience and arms and face moving expressively upwards.[26] It is clear that the space of the stage allowed him to move about freely.

When it came to Aldridge's performance, reactions were extremely mixed and, as previously noted, spawned a fierce debate in the newspapers. What unites the reviews is their emphasis on aesthetic categorization. As previously noted, the reviewer for *Aftonbladet* acknowledges Aldridge's unconventional behaviour such as turning his back on the audience; however, the same reviewer explicitly juxtaposes it to the acting style of the Royal Theatre, 'where from old times an artificial and unnatural manner ... lingers on like an old and seemingly ineradicable sourdough, and where, with particular frequency, one addresses one's lines and pathetic exclamations to the stalls or the amphitheatre or either side of the boxes, instead of to the other actors'. The reviewer, writing in the major liberal newspaper of the country, clearly pits Aldridge as an innovator against the stale mannerisms of traditional acting. Conversely, the reviewer B-n in *Post- och Inrikes Tidningar*, while full of praise for Aldridge, suggested that the actor was not sufficiently free from the ballast of tradition. 'We do not hesitate to call Mr. A. a *great* actor', B-n declares, citing Aldridge's combination of fiery temperament and 'careful study of the spirit and letter of the part'. It is true, B-n continues, that Aldridge's acting 'displays some of the vices of the English tragical school: a clerically slow declamation of the verse and an exaggeratedly solemn manner in movements and gestures'. However, such flaws were 'balanced by an inner life and wealth of content that are among the finest rarities of the stage'. Othello's passionate outbursts were not examples of bad acting: the character is, the reviewer notes, 'already deeply shaded by the poet's hand' – ultimately, therefore, Aldridge's performance only reflects what is there in the part.

Such assessments may demonstrate that Aldridge's acting was hard to classify according to common categories. Classical and stately it was not, nor was it necessarily 'natural' according to the criteria of ordinary bourgeois realism.[27] And it is here, then, in this perplexity, that we can finally begin to trace just how intimately aesthetic and race were entwined in the responses. For example, in some cases the reviewers tended to see Aldridge's acting as a deliberate, cultivated style whereas others located it more explicitly in his 'nature'. Among the latter, we have an article in *Snällposten*, dated 11 July 1857, which compares Aldridge favourably to N. P. Nielsen, a well-known Danish actor who had also made a guest appearance at the Royal Theatre in June 1857. Relaying a conversation he had had with Aldridge during an interval at the Royal Theatre, the author describes him as follows:

> [Aldridge] is a man of deep instinct, speaks slowly and with difficulty but with careful and correct choice of words; all his heart can be seen in his face and heard in his voice; the black eyes and the thick lips are, if possible, even more eloquent interpreters of his soul than Nielsen's tongue is of his; the high, somewhat reclining forehead gives Aldridge a noble, intelligent air, and one quickly learns that it does not lie.
>
> (*Snällposten*, 11 July 1857)

In this case, the reviewer explains the truthfulness of Aldridge's performances as a matter of pure 'instinct', transparently reflected in an almost forensically described physical appearance (although even in this case the reviewer is compelled to note Aldridge's 'careful' diction). A month before that, however, the reviewer of *Othello* in the same newspaper had specifically insisted on Aldridge's artistic integrity. The reviewer enthusiastically notes that Aldridge's displays of passion in the role 'produced sensations in the audience that they never previously experienced from attending our rather cold dramatic performances', but goes on to say that Aldridge 'is a great artist, among the greatest of the stage. He knows what he does and retains artistic control in the midst of raging; and he understands the poet whose eminent creation he is to represent' (*Snällposten*, 11 June 1857). The perception of Aldridge's passionate acting may be coloured by the fact that 'strong gestures and extreme emotions were believed to be traits of non-rational racial types';[28] however, the reviewer specifically emphasizes Aldridge's rational control of his instrument. In other words, Aldridge's acting is not 'nature' so much as a careful artistic expression based on an 'understanding' of Shakespeare. Race is not an integral part of such an argument: the implication is that Aldridge is a consummate artist regardless of his background. As we will see, even negative reviewers sometimes took a similar position.

It is true that, regardless of whether they are positive or negative, reviews rarely fail to mention race completely when discussing Aldridge's performances. This may have been because many people, not least Aldridge himself, considered it a selling point: as Krystyna Kujawinska Courtney suggests, race 'constituted a substantial part of [Aldridge's] carefully orchestrated theatrical event'.[29] Thus, even reviewers who make a point of Aldridge's abilities as an actor often lapse into racial categories when describing them. According to *Illustrerad Tidning*, the fact 'that he is an artist of the highest order, and not just a black artist, cannot be denied' – but even so, Aldridge shows 'more moderation in his acting than one could expect from someone of simmering Negro blood'.[30] Even less surprising are the negative assessments, such as a letter published some months after Aldridge's visit in *Örebro Tidning*, in which a member of the audience recalls seeing *Othello*: 'Ira Aldridge had the title role; he did not please me, and I cannot explain his great reputation in another way than him being measured against the yardstick of ordinary Negro education, in relation to which he is certainly a rather unusual phenomenon. In any other case, his stilted affectation is bound to provoke disgust instead of real aesthetic enjoyment' (*Örebro Tidning*, 29 September 1857).

Such reactions may bear witness to what Hazel Waters has termed 'a deepening polarisation over questions of black capacity' in nineteenth-century culture.[31] Beyond their overt racism, what the judgements on Aldridge reveal is, in fact, how complex was the relation between aesthetics and politics. Instead of a clear-cut conflict between the aesthetically and politically radical on the one hand and the aesthetically and politically conservative on the other, aesthetic judgement is entangled with discourses of race in sometimes unexpected ways. As we will see from the following discussion, those who were positive about Aldridge's performances and thought them innovative and original are sometimes more prone to lapse into racial categorization than those who condemn Aldridge's acting because it violated particular aesthetic standards. This is perhaps particularly evident from three of the longest and most elaborate discussions of Aldridge's performances, to which I now turn.

As noted, *Othello* was a huge success, although performances between 7 and 17 June had to be cancelled because several members of the cast had contracted smallpox. On 18 June, the Royal Theatre featured Aldridge as Shylock in the first four acts of *The Merchant of Venice*, as well as the fifth act of *Othello* – a performance that was repeated on 21 June. Accordingly, towards the end of Aldridge's visit, the reviews attempted a more comprehensive discussion of his qualities as an actor and these texts demonstrate, with particular clarity, the aesthetic categories by which performances were assessed, as well as how race is positioned in relation to those categories.

The first, published in *Aftonbladet* on 22 June, was (unlike the same newspaper's earlier review) largely negative about Aldridge's acting. As the reviewer hints, this could, of course, be taken as a violation of decorum and hospitality to the prominent guest, but the point is that one should not avoid passing judgement on Aldridge simply because of his background. Now that the requirements of curiosity and politeness are satisfied, it is time, the reviewer states, to judge Aldridge as an artist. Having clearly taken some trouble to analyse the performance, the reviewer reveals a lot of background assumptions about acting and theatrical convention. What particularly troubles the reviewer is Aldridge's style, which he considered mannered: 'We have seen a lot of mannerism on the stage, and of all kinds; but never this complete, this consistently adhered to'. From his examples, it is obvious that the reviewer has a particular problem with Aldridge's abrupt shifts between registers and moods – the actor is too quick to throw himself into fits of passion and the shifts even amount to inconsistencies of character, as in Shylock's farewell scene with Jessica, which Aldridge plays 'as if he were the père noble in a bourgeois tragedy' only to rage uncontrollably over his money and Jessica's escape shortly thereafter. *Aftonbladet*'s reviewer was certainly not alone in this perception, as we have seen. Indeed, the previously cited article in *Snällposten* notes how Aldridge is able, even in private conversation, to change from the serious to the comical so quickly that you seem to have 'another individuality' in front of you. While hugely impressed by Aldridge, the reviewer in the same newspaper had previously wondered at 'these transitions from one emotion to another; this transformation of the actor's face' (11 June 1857). However, while these reviewers express admiration, the one in *Aftonbladet* is hostile for exactly the same reason. Clearly, this was a style that made a deep impression yet also produced conflicting opinions.[32]

As previously noted, these observations on Aldridge's passionate style could, to some extent, be related to prejudice towards 'irrational' racial types, but the reviewer in *Aftonbladet* does not actually make such a connection. Instead, his unease seems more to relate to the notion that Aldridge's acting transgressed generic boundaries: it signalled 'bourgeois tragedy' in one scene only to reject that form in the next. This conservative understanding of dramatic convention is, in fact, evident from many other details in the review – for example, it informs the reviewer's ideals of diction. The reviewer criticizes Aldridge's tendency to emphasize 'insignificant' words and exemplifies with the 'if' in 'If you deny it, let the danger light' which Aldridge had evidently stressed. The implication is that of a clear-cut hierarchy between words in a sentence of which the emphasis on a preposition represented a clear violation. In a similar vein, the reviewer faults Aldridge for making unwarranted pauses, sometimes in the midst of sentences, implying a lack of adherence to classical rules of recitation. Aldridge's unorthodoxy also extended to a lack of faithfulness to the text: one of his devices, which the reviewer perceived as an irritating tic, was that of repeating words without any foundation for it in Shakespeare's text. What is more, at one point the character of Shylock sharpened his knife on the wooden floor, but the stage direction in 4.1 explicitly says that he sharpens it on his shoe.

While these underlying standards may seem largely dated from a twenty-first century perspective, the review is notable for its effort to make a balanced assessment and for its insistence that Aldridge be judged by his artistic effort, according to the same criteria as any other actor. Of course, this does not mean that the review is free from racial stereotyping: its description of Aldridge's facial features 'whose forms no one could deem shapely' is one glaring example. But on the whole, the review is suggestive of the European audiences who at this time, in Kujawinska Courtney's words, 'began to evaluate [Aldridge's] art, not the fact that he was "the Negro"', even if it meant negative reviews, as in this case.[33] Unity of character, orthodox recitation and faithfulness to the text are crucial categories to the reviewer in *Aftonbladet* and, while these are clearly of their time, they evidently made sense in their own context. In short, while hardly 'colour-blind' in the modern sense of the word, the review arguably reflects the classic humanist position that art should be judged on its own terms.

Among the subsequent responses, two articles in *Post- och Inrikes Tidningar* on 26 and 27 June, by the same individual who had reviewed *Othello*, merit most attention as they represent a step-by-step dismissal of the review in *Aftonbladet* and, more importantly, reveal a series of different assumptions on aesthetics and race. The *Aftonbladet* reviewer had dismissed the term 'Negro' as incorrect as Aldridge's skin was too light to merit the epithet. On 26 June, B-n replied in *Post- och Inrikes Tidningar* that this amounted to calling Aldridge an impostor and, furthermore, did not fail to bring up *Aftonbladet*'s mention of Aldridge's facial features. Such descriptions, B-n says, may belong in America but are unworthy of 'the cultivated and friendly Stockholm, where good manners are the condition of visits in decent company'. B-n concludes this salvo, 'To us, Mr. Aldridge's honest and intelligent face is far more beautiful and noble than a huge number of white ones'. The brash liberal positioning here is particularly interesting for the implicit links it establishes with aesthetics. B-n suggests that Aldridge's choice of roles is congenial with his temperament: 'Mr. Aldridge has had the good judgement to choose a repertoire which is best suited for the nature of his sensations: above all, Shakespeare's characters with strong personalities and great, violent passions'.[34] The assumption is that the 'nature' of actors determines which roles they should choose. In short, B-n's professedly anti-racist discussion of Aldridge seems based on an essentialist understanding of the actor's nature.

This position is clarified in B-n's next article, on 27 June, which continues the assault on *Aftonbladet*'s reviewer. Here, B-n rejects the emphasis on textual faithfulness as stuffy and pedantic. Had he been alive, Shakespeare 'would perhaps have been delighted at what he saw'. If any modification by the actor makes a deeper impression than in previous versions of the play, 'Shakespeare has been surpassed, which is good, notwithstanding all learned gentlemen'. What is interesting here is that B-n not only represents Aldridge's unorthodoxy as a deliberate artistic choice, he brings a moral dimension to it. Knowing what persecution means, Aldridge may not have the heart to represent Shylock as quite as abominable as Shakespeare depicts him, or as he has been played on the

German stage. As for Aldridge's shifts in tone and mood and the inability of *Aftonbladet*'s reviewer to understand them, B-n ascribes them to differences in temperament. Aldridge's shift from tenderness to cursing Jessica may look strange in the eyes of 'tranquil Northerners', B-n says – 'but let us imagine a Southerner, let us *see* Mr. Aldridge execute this scene, and there shall be no doubt'. These forays into climate theory recall B-n's previous review of *Othello*, which had stated that although Northern audiences may be alien to 'these violent extremes of the fiercest and beastliest rage alternating with the most profound and tender suffering and the most heartfelt joy', they are nonetheless able to sympathize with the character and feel that the depiction is true.[35] The reviewer for *Aftonbladet*, B-n says, is incapable of understanding any of this. He is a 'malevolent and narrow-minded reviewer' whose article 'has a put a blot on Swedish hospitality and will bear false witness abroad on the way in which people in this country perceive the great and noble in Mr. Aldridge's mission'. In other words, B-n continues to berate *Aftonbladet*'s reviewer for his lack of civilization and respect.

While the reviewer for *Aftonbladet* had thus insisted on the irrelevance of race in order to understand Aldridge's artistic achievement, B-n instead locates Aldridge's interpretation squarely in the context of difference between 'North' and 'South'. Aldridge's American birth is clearly less important in such a context than his African ancestry; what is more, the review obviously demonstrates the existence of a dichotomy of identities, where the 'Southern' is, above all, characterized by its passion and rapidly shifting humours. As we have seen, apart from drawing on humoural theory, B-n justifies Aldridge's performance on the basis of his having been the victim of persecution. From such a perspective, race is not irrelevant to an understanding of Aldridge's art, it is crucial to it. Indeed, B-n's reviews, while insisting on hospitality and politeness in the reception of Aldridge's performance, are far more reliant on discourses of difference between categories of people. They are not simply, as Fridén suggests, an anti-racist rebuttal of a racist critique. Rather, they represent a different plea for tolerance than the review in *Aftonbladet*: that Aldridge be judged specifically based on his background. In a sense, the ideas expressed in *Aftonbladet* and *Post- och Inrikes Tidningar* almost seem to anticipate the locked positions on twenty-first century identity politics: the right to be judged equally versus the right to be judged differently.

This was not the end of the debate, which, Lindfors suggests, deteriorated and 'no longer focused on Aldridge but instead had become an uncivil civil war between theater critics who exchanged angry insults and abusive *ad hominem* attacks'.[36] This characterization is certainly true in many ways – in fact, the arguments examined above tended to be repeated in various forms over the next couple of weeks.[37] The debate had more or less petered out by mid-July, when an editorial summary was published in *Post- och Inrikes Tidningar* which, of course, defended the newspaper's position vis-à-vis those of its attackers.[38] But there is more to the debate than just mudslinging. For one thing, the amount of space that the debate was given testifies to the interest that readers were thought to have in it. Notably, the discussion quickly reached a certain meta-level, with newspapers reporting on the reports[39] and the responses to Aldridge's visit were even echoed in the British press.[40] His visit left other traces in print: for example, his autobiography was quickly translated into Swedish and announced for sale in bookshops across the country.[41] The attention Aldridge received from the press was well reflected in real life: when he left for London via Hamburg on 2 July, an enthusiastic crowd followed him to the boat.

All in all, it is clear that Aldridge's visit had been a success in both commercial and artistic terms: he was handsomely paid for his work, attracted huge crowds to the theatre and his performances sparked a wide-ranging newspaper debate that demonstrates the complex configurations of race and aesthetics in mid-nineteenth-century Europe. This was, as Lindfors observes, nothing peculiar to Sweden: Aldridge's performances had also baffled and impressed audiences during his previous European tour and would continue to do so on his next, which followed shortly after his visit to Stockholm. What the reactions in the Swedish press demonstrate with particular clarity, however, is that many of the basic positions on race and aesthetics that are debated today were already, in some ways, in place in 1857. Whether Aldridge deserved to be judged independently of the background he so frequently drew attention to, or whether he deserved to be judged precisely because of it, is a question that echoes widely beyond his own lifetime and into our own.

Notes

1   Aldridge's visit to Stockholm and the reception of his performances there have been surveyed in some detail in Lindfors, *Ira Aldridge,* 47–66, an earlier version of which appeared as Lindfors, 'Ira Aldridge in Stockholm'. While rich and well-researched, Lindfors's account mostly remains true to the biographical format and, unlike the present chapter, does not discuss theatrical practice in any detail. For more general discussions of Aldridge's life and career, see also Lindfors, ed., *Ira Aldridge;* Waters, *Racism on the Victorian Stage,* 58–88 and the earlier Marshall and Stock, *Ira Aldridge.*

2   On 6 May, the Stockholm newspapers *Aftonbladet, Post- och Inrikes Tidningar* and *Stockholms Dagblad* all reported that Aldridge would visit the Royal Theatre on his journey to Petersburg, with *Riksbladet* following suit two days later. Local media all over the country evidently found this worth relaying; thus, *Calmarposten*, in the southeast of Sweden, announced, 'It is said that the famous actor Ira Aldridge, a negro, will, during his journey to Petersburg, where he is engaged over the summer, perform at the royal theatre as Othello in Shakespeare's masterpiece of that name' (*Calmarposten* 9 May). The same newspaper reports on Aldridge's expected arrival 'around the 16th' (13 May) and correctly states, on 27 May, that he did arrive 'last

Thursday', i.e. 21 May. Similar news was circulated in *Upsala* (8 May), *Norrlandsposten* (11 May), *Karlshamns Allehanda* (13 May), *Jönköpingsbladet* (14 May), *Vestmanlands Läns Tidning* (14 May), *Blekingsposten* (15 May), *Göteborgs Handels- och Sjöfartstidning* (15 May), *Umeåtidningen* (16 May), *Bohusläns Tidning* (20 May) and *Söderköpings Tidning* (20 May). The reports on Aldridge's imminent arrival are obviously derived from the Stockholm press but, taken together, these echoes in newspapers based throughout the whole of Sweden indicate how important the news was thought to be.

Translations of newspaper material are my own except otherwise noted; citations will be to name of newspaper followed by date and will appear parenthetically in the text.

3 Reported and dismissed in *Aftonbladet* and *Post- och Inrikes Tidningar*, both 5 May.

4 *Aftonbladet* and *Post- och Inrikes Tidningar*, both 22 May. The news of his arrival was echoed in *Upsala* (26 May), *Jönköpings Tidning* (27 May) and *Östgöta Correspondenten* (30 May), among others.

5 For the bookshops, see *Fäderneslandet*, 23 May. Aldridge retells his journey and arrival in a letter to his wife, reproduced in full in Marshall and Stock, *Ira Aldridge,* 207–9.

6 See Monié, who supplies the slightly misleading information that the Royal Theatre used Hagberg's translation 'nine times during the period June 1857 until March 1861 with the coloured actor Ira Aldridge in the role of Othello' (*Ord som himlen når,* 262; translation mine). Aldridge did not return to Stockholm and so was not, in fact, featured in the play after his visit in 1857.

7 For the latter, see *Blekingsposten*, 22 May; other examples are mentioned in Lindfors, *Ira Aldridge,* 51 and notes.

8 See Lindfors, *Ira Aldridge,* 51, who notes that a similar booklet was produced for *The Merchant of Venice.*

9 Fridén, '"Att vara eller inte vara"', 105.

10 In this desire for racial classification they obviously resembled other European critics at the time: see, for example, Jenkins, 'Ira Aldridge', 114–15.

11 For the French performance, see Molin, *Shakespeare och Sverige*, 14; the most detailed discussion of the 1827 production is in Bergman, *Regi och spelstil*, 163–93.

12 Productions at the Royal Theatre included *Hamlet* (1853), *The Merchant of Venice* (1854), *Macbeth* (1858), *Richard II* (1863), *Timon of Athens* (1866), *Coriolanus* (1866) and at the Mindre Teatern *All's Well that Ends Well* (1854, under the title *Konungens läkare* [*The King's Physician*], probably a Swedish version of Sille Beyer's Danish adaptation), *Romeo and Juliet* (1859), *The Taming of the Shrew* (1860) and *Henry IV* (1862, in a five-act version of both parts). With the exception of *Romeo and Juliet*, the productions at the Mindre Teatern were all Swedish premieres; for an overview of performances, see Derkert, *Repertoaren på Mindre Teatern*, 153. The jubilee year 1864 also saw a number of events related to Shakespeare, for which see Fridén, '"Att vara eller inte vara"', 106–9 and the Introduction to the present volume.

13 Indeed, the performance of *The Merchant of Venice* in which Aldridge starred recycled a translation by Nils Arfwidsson that had also been used for the 1854 production. Similarly, *All's Well That Ends Well* at the Mindre Teatern was performed using another translation than Hagberg's and, in some cases, a mixture of different translations, as in the Royal Theatre's production of *Macbeth* from 1858, which included material from both the versions of Hagberg and Geijer. See Monié, *Ord som himlen når*, 262; for *Macbeth*, Fridén, *Macbeth*, esp. 41–9 and Lindell and Hägglund's chapter in the present volume.

14 Fridén, '"Att vara eller inte vara"', 105.

15 As listed on the poster for *Othello*, 3 June 1857. Swartz replaced Dahlqvist as Iago in the performances from 18 June onwards; see Lindfors, *Ira Aldridge*, 55. Swartz's acting style was evidently not histrionic or classically inflected: one reviewer saw the 'profoundly romantic' as his main element, but also emphasised that 'Mr. Swartz is eminently capable of a certain genre in comedy or the so-called bourgeois drama' (*Aftonbladet*, 12 January 1856). For his interpretation of Hamlet, see Hedberg, *Svenska skådespelare*, 133–47; also, Lagerroth, 'Den djärve traditionsbrytaren', who notes that Swartz established a tradition of playing Hamlet as dreamy

and melancholy, with a 'muted voice and subdued movements' (264, translation mine).

16 Downer, 'Players and Painted Stage', 558. On acting styles and Shakespeare in the period see also, for example, Sillars, *Shakespeare and the Victorians*, 58–67.
17 Quoted in Marker and Marker, *A History*, 122–3.
18 Marker and Marker, *A History*, 123.
19 See *Aftonbladet* 4 June, also cited in Fridén, "'Att vara eller inte vara'", 105–6.
20 Marker and Marker, *A History*, 122.
21 Fridén, "'Att vara eller inte vara'", 106.
22 For example, Fridén suggests that in this production 'acting conventions, many of which had already gone stale, probably belonged to a classicist tradition typical of French tragedy' (Macbeth, 49).
23 See *Post- och Inrikes Tidningar*, 4 June. An illustration depicting the last scene of the play was published in *Illustrerad Tidning*, 20 June (reproduced in Lindfors, *Ira Aldridge*, 54).
24 The critic for *Söndagsbladet*, while enthusiastic about Aldridge's performance, was annoyed at the sound of rustling paper when the audience turned the pages in their Swedish-language booklets (Lindfors, *Ira Aldridge*, 52).
25 Bergman, *Regi och spelstil*, 184; translation mine.
26 *Fäderneslandet*, 19 December has an image of Aldridge as Othello, which, while evidently a racist caricature, may reveal something about the impression his acting made: leaning back, arms stretched out in front of him.
27 True, Aldridge has sometimes been seen as an originator of a more 'naturalistic' style of acting: see Waters, *Racism on the Victorian Stage*, 84–5. But as the Swedish reviews suggest, at the time Aldridge's acting was not always considered 'natural'.
28 Jenkins, 'Ira Aldridge', 116.
29 Kujawinska Courtney, 'Ira Aldridge', 108. Aldridge's own farewell address to the Swedish audiences, which was translated and published in *Post- och Inrikes Tidningar* on 30

June, explicitly draws attention to his own skin colour: 'A son of the South, with a face as black as the night / but with a soul delighting in the treasure of light, / I stand in front of you'.

30 In this quote, I am using the translation by Lindfors (*Ira Aldridge*, 52), who also discusses the review.

31 Waters, *Racism on the Victorian Stage*, 59.

32 Among those who sided with *Aftonbladet*'s assessment were two articles in *Svenska Tidningen*, which found Aldridge's mannerisms problematic and also commented on his seeming lack of attention to the text. For discussion, see Lindfors, *Ira Aldridge*, 57–8.

33 Kujawinska Courtney, 'Ira Aldridge', 108.

34 This passage is also translated by Lindfors, who uses 'quality' instead of 'nature' and renders the Swedish 'kraftmänniskorna' as 'Shakespeare's strong male characters' (*Ira Aldridge*, 58).

35 B-n frequently resorts to images of heat and temperament; he says of Aldridge's Shylock that 'the very manner, with its slow gestures and somewhat drawling recitation, here received … its veracity, and the strange impression of it evaporated in the heat that was transmitted from the actor's interior to that of the spectator' (*Post- och Inrikes Tidningar* 19 June).

36 Lindfors, *Ira Aldridge*, 62.

37 Such as the argument that it would be mistaken to praise Aldridge simply because of hospitality and the fact that he belonged to an oppressed race: see Ernst Ludvig, 'Bref till en vän i hufvudstaden', *Svenska Tidningen*, 13 July 1857. This was, in turn, a rebuttal of B-n's 'Slutord i den kritiska tvisten', which had appeared in *Post- och Inrikes Tidningar* on 6 July.

38 *Post- och Inrikes Tidningar*, 18 July. The editorial column only mentions Aldridge's name once, which suggests that the quarrel between the newspapers was no longer about him.

39 Attempts to summarize the debate were published in newspapers such as *Blekingsposten* 3 July and *Tomtebissen* 28 July, sometimes commenting sardonically on its level.

40 Most notably, a number of the positive Swedish reviews were picked up and summarized in the British *The Era* ('Swedish

Theatricals', 19 July). *Stockholms Dagblad* proudly published a translation of the article on 5 August, which was in turn copied in *Post- och Inrikes Tidningar* – whose review had been cited in *The Era* – on 8 August. Previously, on 7 June, *The Era* had reported on Aldridge's arrival in Stockholm in late May and, on 5 July, had included a brief note [citing *Post- och Inrikes Tidningar* slightly incorrectly as 'Post Tidning'] on Aldridge's success at the Royal Theatre.

41 The biography of Aldridge was announced as for sale in *Lunds Weckoblad* (16 July), *Snällposten* (30 July), *Vestmanlands Läns Tidning* (30 July), *Norrköpings Tidningar* (29 July and 1 August) and *Östgöta Correspondenten* (7 October).

Works cited

Digital archives, Royal Opera, Stockholm: www.arkiv.operan.se
The British Newspaper Archive: www.britishnewspaperarchive.co.uk
Digital newspaper archives, Royal Library, Stockholm: www.tidningar.kb.se
Bergman, Gösta M., *Regi och spelstil under Gustaf Lagerbjelkes tid vid Kungl. Teatern: Studier kring några av hans insceneringar* (Stockholm, 1946).
Derkert, Kerstin, *Repertoaren på Mindre Teatern under Edvard Stjernströms chefstid 1854–1863* (Stockholm, 1979).
Downer, Alan S., 'Players and Painted Stage: Nineteenth-Century Acting', *PMLA*, 61/2 (1946), 522–76.
Fridén, Ann, '"Att vara eller inte vara": Shakespeare på kunglig scen i 1800-talets Stockholm', in Claes Rosenqvist, ed., *Den svenska nationalscenen: Traditioner och reformer på Dramaten under 200 år* (Stockholm, 1988), 102–23.
Fridén, Ann, *Macbeth in the Swedish Theatre 1838–1986* (Malmö, 1986).
Hedberg, Frans. *Svenska skådespelare: Karakteristiker och porträtter* (Stockholm, 1884). Available at: http://runeberg.org/fhsvsk/0139.html.
Jenkins, Earnestine, 'Ira Aldridge as Othello in James Northcote's Manchester Portrait', in Adrienne L. Childs and Susan H.

Libby, eds, *Blacks and Blackness in European Art of the Long Nineteenth Century* (Farnham, 2014), 105–23.

Kujawinska Courtney, Krystyna, 'Ira Aldridge, Shakespeare, and Color-Conscious Performances in Nineteenth-Century Europe', in Ayanna Thompson, ed., *Colorblind Shakespeare: New Perspectives on Race and Performance* (New York, 2006), 103–22.

Lagerroth, Ulla-Britta, 'Den djärve traditionsbrytaren', in Ulla-Britta Lagerroth and Ingeborg Nordin Hennel, eds, *Ny svensk teaterhistoria*, ii: *1800-talets teater* (Hedemora, 2007), 261–76.

Lindfors, Bernth, 'Ira Aldridge in Stockholm', in Bernth Lindfors and Geoffrey V. Davis, eds, *African Literatures and Beyond: A Florilegium* (Amsterdam, 2013), 217–37.

Lindfors, Bernth, *Ira Aldridge*, iv: *The Last Years, 1855–1867* (Rochester, 2015).

Lindfors, Bernth, ed., *Ira Aldridge, the African Roscius* (Rochester, 2007).

Marker, Frederick J. and Lise-Lone Marker, *A History of Scandinavian Theatre* (Cambridge, 1996).

Marshall, Herbert and Mildred Stock, *Ira Aldridge: The Negro Tragedian* (London, 1958).

Molin, Nils, *Shakespeare och Sverige intill 1800-talets mitt: En översikt av hans inflytande* (Göteborg, 1931).

Monié, Karin. *Ord som himlen når: Carl August Hagberg – en levnadsteckning* (Stockholm, 2008).

Sillars, Stuart. *Shakespeare and the Victorians* (Cambridge, 2013).

Waters, Hazel, *Racism on the Victorian Stage: Representation of Slavery and the Black Character* (Cambridge, 2007).

7

Shakespeare's legacy and Aleksis Kivi: Rethinking Kivi's drama *Karkurit* [The Fugitives]

Riitta Pohjola-Skarp

Introduction

Finnish-language theatre was born on 19 May 1869 at the Nya Teatern (New Theatre) in Helsinki. The actor Oscar Gröneqvist came onstage in the role of Sakaio (Zacheus) and started counting his money: 'One thousand, two thousand, three thousand pence'.[1]

While this may sound familiar, it is not a Finnish adaptation of Shakespeare's *The Merchant of Venice*, but rather a new Finnish play by Aleksis Kivi (1834–1872). As the first Finnish-language play performed by professional actors, *Lea* is a landmark in Finnish theatre history, as well as an example of the enormous influence Shakespeare had on Kivi.[2] Indeed, Shakespeare was Kivi's dramaturgical teacher at a time when

Finnish was still being developed as a literary language. Kivi played a pivotal role in the development of Finnish literature and drama in mid-nineteenth century Finland.

Kivi, along with Mikael Agricola and Elias Lönnrot, is seen as the founder of written Finnish and was the first Finnish professional author to write in Finnish.[3] In the early nineteenth century Finland was part of a multilingual European theatre culture where theatre had been mainly performed in Swedish (or German or Russian) by travelling groups and actors. This internationalism gradually diminished during the nineteenth century as permanent theatre institutions were established and the emphasis shifted to dramatic art performed in the vernacular languages. It was thought theatre could play an important didactic role in creating national consensus and the importance of 'indigenous' or 'truly national' theatre was therefore emphasized. Due to its multilingual nature, in Finland drama was performed in three languages: the former imperial language, Swedish, still the language of élite culture; the new imperial language, Russian; and the vernacular language, Finnish. In 1827, the first theatre building was erected in the centre of Helsinki, staging some of the first attempts at a (Swedish-language) national dramatic repertoire.[4] In 1863, this was replaced by a classicist stone building, the *Nya Teatern* [New Theatre], which recruited its artists mainly from Sweden (from Stockholm and Gothenburg). From 1872 onwards, the same building also hosted the Finnish-language Finnish Theatre Company. While the New Theatre could continue to draw on the cultural life of Sweden, the Finnish-language theatre had to build its own repertoire and train its actors from scratch.

When these permanent theatre institutions were being established in the second half of the nineteenth century, there was a lack of Finnish-language drama. The problem for Finnish-language theatre was how to turn the language of manual labour, church and folklore into that of Shakespeare, Schiller and other classics. One of the first Finnish translations was J. F. Lagervall's (1787–1865) adaptation of *Macbeth*, *Ruunulinna* (1834), discussed elsewhere in this volume.[5] From the 1860s onwards, state and private initiatives (including literary prizes) supported the translations of European classics and inspired the first pieces of modern Finnish-language drama, including the plays of Aleksis Kivi.[6]

In this chapter, I analyse Shakespeare's influence on Kivi, focusing on *Karkurit* [The Fugitives], written in 1865, published in 1867, first performed in Swedish translation in 1872 and in its original Finnish in 1877. This play can be seen as Kivi's most 'Shakespearean' drama[7] and, as such, reveals the complex interaction between Shakespeare and Kivi as mediated at least partly by German Romanticism. In Europe, Romantic drama had, appealing to Shakespeare, challenged the rules of traditional classicistic dramaturgy and this influence could still be felt in the 1860s. For the Romantics, Shakespeare represented something new, open and universal, a contrast to neo-classical rules, genre boundaries and *Ständeklausel* [estates-clause], according to which tragedy represents the world of the nobility and comedy the world of the commoners. The Romantic influence is evident in the Schlegel-Tieck German translations of Shakespeare and these, in turn, influenced the Swedish translations by Carl August Hagberg, used by the bilingual (Finnish–Swedish) Kivi.

Karkurit can be seen as a 'hypertext', which is crafted upon *Romeo and Juliet* as 'hypotext'.[8] Kivi's play also includes elements of many of Shakespeare's late tragedies (*King Lear, Macbeth, Othello*) as well as comedies (*As You Like It, Twelfth Night*). My focus in this chapter is mainly on dramaturgy. First, I compare and contrast the plays, referring to the influential contemporary work *Die Technik des Dramas* by Gustav Freytag. In the next section, I extend the approach and examine the dramaturgy of *Romeo and Juliet* and *Karkurit* based on Robert Lanier Reid's *Shakespeare's Tragic Form* (2000), where he combines dramaturgical and psychological perspectives. In the fourth section, I analyse Kivi's use of dramatic and tragic irony in *Karkurit*, focusing on the new meaning of irony coined by the German Romantics. For A. W. Schlegel, Shakespeare is an outstanding example of the use of irony as a means of creating an ironic perspective in dramaturgy. In the fifth section, I examine the influence of German Romantic Shakespeare on Kivi's use of language and metre. Finally, in my conclusion, I consider the reception of Kivi's play, analysing how these Romantic elements were judged given that Finnish literature was already beginning to shift towards realism. What we find is that Kivi was an astute student of Shakespeare but at the same time quite original and independent, filtering national and European influences through his own artistic vision.

Romeo and Juliet and Kivi's most Shakespearean play *Karkurit*

Kivi wrote at a time when Finnish-language literature was explicitly seeking influence from foreign models. In 1849, the influential intellectual J. V. Snellman noted that 'less cultivated nations must always seek their literary models from those peoples who have reached a higher level of culture'. The next stage, then, consists of original native production which 'has turned the ideas borrowed-from-the-outside into a mere form of original spiritual development'. Snellman thought that 'Drama is the highest stage of poetry, and Shakespeare is the foremost playwright of all the dramatists in the world', which may have prompted Kivi to follow Shakespeare's example.[9]

From the beginning, critics noted the links between Kivi and Shakespeare; during his lifetime Kivi was praised for being 'the Finnish Shakespeare'.[10] The first detailed biography and study of Kivi, written some 40 years after his death, also points out the importance of Shakespeare, along with Cervantes, to Kivi[11] while scholars of Kivi have mainly studied his works in the frameworks of biography, literary scholarship and intellectual history.[12] While almost all these works include short references to the influence of Shakespeare, they do not examine in detail how deeply Kivi understood Shakespearean dramaturgy.

This is already evident in Kivi's first serious drama, *Kullervo* (1864).[13] His next serious drama *Karkurit* (1867) evokes *Romeo and Juliet* without mentioning it, demonstrating that literary influence could be quite subtle and did not need to call attention to itself.

The basic story of *Karkurit* and *Romeo and Juliet* is analogous: hatred between families leads to the deaths of young lovers and the repentance and reconciliation of the former enemies. In terms of plot structure, the biggest difference between *Romeo and Juliet* and *Karkurit* is the point of attack when 'the curtain goes up',[14] that is, at the very beginning of the action on stage.[15] Shakespeare uses an early point of attack, without a long prehistory, e.g. Romeo and Juliet meet at the end of Act 1. By contrast, the backstory in *Karkurit* is long, beginning 15 years before the start of the play and includes such elements as hatred between two fathers (Mauno and Markus), a debt which has come due and the secret engagement of Mauno's daughter Elma to Markus' son Tyko.

Karkurit: Plot analysis according to Freytag

At the time he was writing *Karkurit*, along with a one-act play called *Kihlaus* [The Engagement], there was a change in Kivi's dramaturgy towards the ideal type of closed form advocated by Gustav Freytag in *Die Technik des Dramas* (1863). This shift to an historical dramatic form has been attributed to conversations about drama theory between Kivi and his friend and mentor Kaarlo Bergbom in the summer of 1865: Bergbom actively followed the German literary and dramatic scene and may have been familiar with Freytag's work.[16] Freytag, who was trying to promote his conception of drama as a normative ideal,[17] presented his model with reference to Shakespeare's *Romeo and Juliet*.[18]

Freytag thought that the plot of drama is based on a pyramid-like structure. In his model, drama is divided into five parts or acts: exposition, rising action, climax, falling action and catastrophe.[19] Exposition presents the initial conflict, which is then intensified by the exciting force and rises towards the climax. A tragic force then initiates the protagonist's downfall or a decisive change in the direction of the plot which, after a delay induced by the force of the final suspense, culminates in the final catastrophe.[20] Since most readers are probably unfamiliar with *Karkurit*, this plot summary serves as a basic introduction to the play and afterwards I compare it to *Romeo and Juliet* in terms of use of time, *dramatis personae* and the tragedy of love.

First Act (exposition and inciting event)

At the beginning of the play Elma, the daughter of the Kuusela manor house, and her adopted sister Hanna reveal an alarming situation: Markus, the owner of the Viitala manor, is threatening to evict Mauno, the owner of Kuusela, who has not managed to pay back his debt. Niilo, the adopted son of Markus, wishes to marry Elma – and in return, he is willing to pay Mauno's debt. But Elma has already promised herself to Tyko, the biological son of Markus. If Elma were to marry Tyko, her father, Mauno, would be evicted from his home. If she were to marry Niilo, she would break the solemn oath she has sworn to Tyko. Thus, the play begins with a classic conflict between money and love. A romantic relationship is also set up between Hanna and Pauli, forming a happy contrast to Elma and Tyko's tragedy.

As in Kivi's other serious plays, there is a prophetic scene at the beginning of *Karkurit* where a soothsayer woman makes a vague oracle-like prophesy to the heroine by reading her palm, another dramaturgical tool Kivi may have adopted from Shakespeare. The forces of nature are also part of the exposition, in the form of a rising thunderstorm.

Tyko and Pauli, the son of Mauno, return from war and meet their old friend Yrjö. Tyko disguises himself as a travelling

Frenchman: he wants to spy on Elma, which is a mistake and a violation of their love (the inciting event).

Second Act (rising action)

Niilo, the villain of the play, comes onstage. He not only wants Elma, but also both of the manor houses, Viitala and Kuusela. As rising action, Niilo begins to woo Elma while blackmailing Mauno. At this point, the main antagonists of the family feud, Mauno and Markus, are introduced. Tyko is still pretending to a be a Frenchman. Niilo asks Tyko to woo Elma on his behalf and Tyko agrees (a device Shakespeare uses in *Much Ado About Nothing* and also in *Twelfth Night*, as discussed below).

Third Act (climax and tragic force)

On Niilo's behalf, Tyko proposes to Elma, which leads to the signing of a marriage accord. Elma regrets signing it and begins to castigate herself. I will return to the significance of this third act in more detail in my discussion of dramatic irony.

Fourth Act (falling action)

Mauno pays his debt to Markus in the Viitala manor park. Niilo provokes the two men and they agree to duel the following night. Hanna reveals that Elma only signed the marriage agreement to save Mauno, without intending to actually marry Niilo. Elma's deceit infuriates Tyko. Elma decides to kill herself, but Hanna takes the vial of poison which Yrjö swaps for a vial of harmless sleeping potion. Tyko secretly spies on Elma's preparations to die and becomes convinced of her love. Hanna, meanwhile, discovers the true identities of Tyko and Pauli. Pauli proposes to Hanna and the Act concludes happily.

Fifth Act (force of the final suspense and catastrophe)

It is night and Elma lies on a mound of stones in feigned death. Yrjö has hoped that seeing Elma seemingly dead would restrain Mauno and Markus and end their duel, but it does not. Their swordfight is interrupted by Tyko and Pauli. In the same scene, Martti, the steward of Kuusela, reveals Niilo's intrigues to Markus. This leads to a duel between Niilo and Tyko, which Niilo loses. He then shoots Tyko. Elma, lying on the mound of stones, is awakened by the gunshot and the two lovers have their last moment of happiness before they both die. Markus kills Niilo with his sword. There follows reconciliation: Markus and Mauno settle their differences, as do Pauli and Mauno. Hanna and Pauli inherit both estates.

The first thing to notice about Kivi's dramaturgical debt to Shakespeare is the use of time, which is similar in *Romeo and Juliet* and *Karkurit*, though Shakespeare's play, with its focus on the frantic haste of the rash lovers, is more compact, especially in contrast to Shakespeare's main source, Arthur Brooke`s *The Tragicall Historye of Romeo and Juliet* (1562). Events which in Brooke are spread out over at least nine months are compressed into four days and nights. Elsewhere, especially in Shakespeare`s histories and tragedies, more time passes between scenes. By contrast, while the time in *Karkurit* is similarly rather short, Kivi emphasizes the hesitancy of his characters through the use of elapsed time. Act 1 takes place in early evening, the time being mentioned by Pauli as he and Tyko arrive home. Act 2 takes place later that same night, with Act 3 the following day. Several days elapse between Acts 3 and 4, as Pauli mentions that he and Tyko have been home and wasting time in their disguises for almost a week. Acts 4 and 5 take place during the same 24-hour period, the fourth during the day and the fifth at night. The total time dimension of the play – five days – is a little longer than in *Romeo and Juliet*, but markedly concentrated compared to Kivi's previous play,

Kullervo. Another contrast I will not be exploring further here is connected to space: *Romeo and Juliet* is set in the urban city of Verona and, to a large extent, takes place indoors while *Karkurit* is set in the countryside and includes many powerful poetic descriptions of Finnish nature and landscape.

The *dramatis personae* in *Karkurit* differs considerably from Shakespeare's tragedy: *Karkurit* has two pairs of lovers, which is more typical of Shakespearean comedy. In terms of the structure of characters, *Karkurit* most resembles *As You Like It*: the relationship between Elma and Hanna is similar to the relationship between Rosalinda and Celia. These close female friends disguise themselves the same way as Tyko and Pauli, though for different reasons. In contrast to *Romeo and Juliet*, in *Karkurit* there is no character representing supreme secular power. Kivi's play also lacks a maternal character comparable to Lady Capulet and Juliet's Nurse; indeed *Karkurit* lacks an older female generation entirely. It does, however, include, a villain, Niilo, who does not exist in Shakespeare.[21] By contrast, one striking similarity is that of the young lovers, the more central figure is the female, Juliet and Elma. As René Weis argues, *Romeo and Juliet's* focus rests squarely on Juliet: 'The play may have started as "Romeo and Juliet" but it ends as "Juliet and Romeo", a hierarchy more truly reflective of the essence of drama'.[22] Kivi's play might well have been called *Elma and Tyko*.

Both in terms of style and theme, the plays begin in completely different ways: *Romeo and Juliet* starts with the comical frivolous witticisms of the servants, but is also concerned with the civic significance of the feud. By contrast, *Karkurit* begins with an elevated dialogue in blank verse between Hanna and Elma; I will return to Kivi's use of blank verse below. It has generally been remarked that *Romeo and Juliet* starts as a romantic comedy and only shifts into tragedy at the beginning of Act 3, when Romeo kills Tybalt, after Tybalt has killed Romeo's friend Mercutio and Romeo is expelled from Verona.[23] Such a shift from comedy to tragedy is missing in Kivi's play, which alternates comic and tragic scenes, providing a different kind of rhythm. All Shakespeare's tragedies include comic scenes (for instance, the gravediggers in *Hamlet* 5.1) and typical comic figures, such as the fool in *King Lear*. An analogous scene in *Karkurit* is the encounter of Martti and the shepherd Viitala between the elevated scene of Elma and Hanna and the scene of Tyko and Pauli in blank verse.

In terms of the tragedy, the love affair in *Karkurit* is fundamentally different from *Romeo and Juliet*. Contrary to Shakespeare's play, *Karkurit* is not dominated by a sudden infatuation and first love. Love in *Karkurit* is more about yearning, dreaming, waiting. While *Romeo and Juliet* meet and fall in love in Act 1, in Kivi's play Tyko and Elma fell in love eight years ago. Instead of the burning first love of Romeo and Juliet, Elma and Tyko see each other after a long separation and tension is built using the device of Tyko's disguise and whether the two will recognize each other before it is too late.

Another big difference between *Karkurit* and *Romeo and Juliet* is the approach to physical love, evidence of the influence of German Romanticism. *Romeo and Juliet* is full of vital sexuality both in the 'low' bawdy wordplay of the servants and the 'high' bawdy linguistic gaming of Mercutio and Benvolio. The love between Romeo and Juliet is physically fulfilled during the wedding night in the crucial Act 3. The German translation *Romeo und Julia* by A. W. Schlegel not only diminishes the bawdy jokes and vulgarities, he smooths the text throughout. Any overt sexuality between Romeo and Juliet was cut or concealed in the translations of the Romantic age which influenced Kivi. In other works, Kivi seems to shy away from sexuality: lovers merely embrace and sexual jokes are mainly treated in a comic light. When Kivi treats sexuality seriously, such as in *Kullervo*, where the protagonist seduces his sister (unbeknownst to him), it occurs offstage. *Kullervo* is based on a poem in the national epic *Kalevala*, where the seduction is portrayed as sexual intercourse (*Kullervo* 271–3).[24] By contrast, in *Karkurit*, the love between Elma and Tyko finds fulfilment on a spiritual, not a physical level.

Romeo and Juliet belongs to the early tragedies of Shakespeare where love is unconditional, with no trace of doubt. This is not the case in *Karkurit*. Tyko is possessed by a jealousy similar to that of Othello, a tragedy from Shakespeare's later period.[25] It is possible that Kivi could have seen *Othello* at a theatre in Helsinki in July 1865 while working on *Karkurit*. Hagberg's Swedish translation of *Othello* was published in the same volume as *Romeo and Juliet* and Kivi possessed a copy.

On a deeper level, in Shakespeare's love tragedies, as Catherine Bates points out, 'love sponsors all the forces of life, creating human families and social groups in the teeth of man's instinct for destruction – both self-destruction and the destruction of the Other. It is the perpetual struggle between these two forces which creates ... human civilization'.[26] In *Romeo and Juliet*, love is shown to be the agent of civilization. It promises to restore a whole system of values. It is all the more tragic that this redemptive move towards meaning and order should fail (188).

At the beginning of *Karkurit* Elma, the tragic heroine in the play, expresses her utopia of the ideal world where love can be a redemptive force:

> One day the overwhelming power of love,
> Will seize the dwellers of this earth; and they
> Who now mawl one another like wild beasts
> Will walk hand in hand, their joy resounding
> To the remotest corners of the earth.
>
> (1.1, p 140, ll 11–15)[27]

At the end of *Karkurit* the lovers Elma and Tyko are dead. Elma's father Mauno urges the living couple Hanna and Pauli:

> Go, live happily, and build peace and love
> In buildings where the fire of hatred raged.
>
> (5.5, p 233, ll 14–16)

Shakespearean dramaturgy and *Karkurit*

Gustav Freytag was attempting to turn the historically rather restricted method of composition, the ideal type of closed form, into something normatively absolute. Manfred Pfister states that Freytag applies his model to a selective corpus of texts, squeezing the tragedies of Shakespeare rather violently into the Procrustean bed of his dramatic categories.[28] I will extend the approach and further examine the dramaturgy of *Romeo and Juliet* and *Karkurit* on the basis of Robert Lanier Reid's analysis in *Shakespeare's Tragic Form* (2000). Reid compares the dramaturgical to the psychological structure of the plays. Reid argues that Shakespeare's five acts are arranged in three cycles to form a 2–1–2 pattern, with Acts 1–2 as *protasis,* Act 3 as *epitasis* and Acts 4–5 as *catastrophe* (24, 31). He also examines the role of multiple plots and centres of consciousness. For Reid, Shakespeare's most potent dramaturgical device is *epiphany*, a recognition that awakens faith in spiritual identity, arousing the spiritual body.[29]

Shakespeare's dramaturgical plan has three main structural features: a confrontational climax for each of the five acts, with arrangement of the acts in three cycles: the opening cycle (Acts 1 and 2), central cycle (Act 3) and the final catastrophe (Acts 4 and 5). Each cycle is accented by an intense, repetitive 'epiphanal encounter', a moment of intense recognition (111). This sequence of deepening disclosure is far more complicated than in Aristotelian tragedy and its most famous example *Oedipus Rex* (23).

Each cycle is centrally animated by an encounter with otherness, manifested in three figures who exemplify the three main types of human bonding and identification. Central to the first phase (Acts 1–2) is confrontation with a figure representing parental power and social authority, a persona greater-than-oneself (in Freudian terms, the superego). Central to the second phase (Act 3) is confrontation with a figure representing others seen as comparable to oneself, a universal siblinghood, an endless supply of mirroring selves, doubles, rivals – and insofar as this figure reflects repressed elements, the shadow self. Central to the final phase (Acts 4–5) is confrontation with a figure, usually female, which embodies the highest spiritual aspirations of the protagonist – one who inspires or gives love, fulfilling a craving for absolute love (16).

The psychic antithesis at the centre of Shakespearean tragedy is predominantly a male version of the polarity between an idealized self and an earthly double. But the love-tragedies disclose an alternative mode of psychic antithesis, based on sexual difference: male and female consummate their love. This central crisis is either a maimed public ceremony or a chaotic disruption of nature. Act 3 brings the most intense display of Fortune's twists, as the mind, working at top speed, tries to match the freakish turnings of the wheel (34–5).

Dramaturgy in *Romeo and Juliet*

Reid's main focus is on the sophisticated form of this dramaturgical pattern, as found in the late tragedies *King Lear* and *Macbeth*, but he also observes the pattern in the earlier tragedy of *Romeo and Juliet*. Acts 1–2 turn from feuding (1.1) to kisses (1.5). At the end of Act 1 an epiphanal encounter serves as axis for the two-act cycle, 'in the magic of Romeo and Juliet's initial communion of spirits' (32–3). While this climactic event provides partial closure, it also propels the lovers into Act 2. Romeo and Juliet surge toward communion and they are wed. 'Acts 1–2 as *protasis* introduce the main character's dilemma and initiate the action with a total cycle of development – a cycle that counterpoints ugly street-fighting with enraptured courtship' (37). The two-act cycle ends in hastily sanctioned marriage.

Act 3 illustrates the *epitasis*, crisis and turning point. In duels Romeo engages not one but two doubles, Tybalt and Mercutio. Romeo ensures his own doom. Reversing the arc, Juliet's angry grief converts to a deeper devotion and consummation of their love. Each lover meets and surmounts an antithetical self. The impulsive nurse serves as a female blocking double, shadowing Juliet. In the two halves of Act 3, Shakespeare provides a double *anagnorisis-and-peripety*, each lover undergoing a soul-crisis that divides and then reunites them. At the centre of Act 3 is the bedroom scene where Romeo and Juliet's union is sexually consummated, a love-epiphany intensified by guilt (his duels before, her family deceptions after) (37, 80).

Acts 4–5 are an equally perfect example of the complex two-act catastrophe with its double-ending – Juliet's feigned death, providing the epiphanic turning point. The lovers' fourth-act withdrawal (Romeo to exile, Juliet to the tomb) with the pathos resulting from this double severance, sets up the conclusive finale Act 5, the cycle ending in love-deaths and spiritual consummation of the marriage (37–8, 80).

As Reid states, many critics fault the lovers' superficiality of development and insist on the need for a more substantial, soul-awakening anagnorisis in the cycle of Act 3. As a dark double, brutish Tybalt cannot match the antagonists of Shakespeare's later love-tragedies. But Reid points out that this rash thoughtlessness is archetypal, epitomizing the horrific deviance in gang wars, clan feuds and ethnic genocide (38).

Dramaturgy in *Karkurit*

A dramaturgical analysis based on Reid's model emphasizes the differences between *Romeo and Juliet* and *Karkurit*. In the former, epiphanies vary the miracle of love whereas, in *Karkurit*, the epiphany of love appears only once, at the end prior to the lovers' death. In the dramaturgy of *Karkurit* we can also see links to other Shakespeare plays, not only tragedies but also comedies. The lovers in *Karkurit*, Elma and Tyko, are the two central characters. In the first cycle of the play (Acts 1 and 2) the central figure is Elma, confronting her father Mauno; in the second cycle (Act 3) the central figures are Elma and Tyko; in the third cycle (Acts 4 and 5) it is Tyko. In the first cycle, Elma is compelled to confront a figure of authority, i.e. her father, who forces her to marry Niilo. The beloved father is now 'the Other', an authority threatening Elma:

ELMA
> Sir, you are my dearest father.

MAUNO
> Right now I am not dearest – destruction
> Threatens to approach my house, and I must
> Harden my heart to be as sharp as steel.
>
> (2.1., p 166, ll 32–6)

Instead of Romeo and Juliet's epiphanal encounter and the magic of their initial communion of spirits, in *Karkurit*, Elma confronts her father as an uncanny figure. In the central second cycle (confronting mirror-images of the self), Elma meets the masked Tyko without recognizing him. The core of the cycle is the proposal episode and the signing of the marriage contract as a maimed public ceremony. The cycle ends in Elma's feelings of guilt and remorse and the revelation of evil:

> This wild bunch of flowers
> Conceals a wily, cold, insidious snake;
> I was just now that messenger of peace,
> Who under white robes hides a blood-red battle
> Banner. Oh, I am cursed, my quaking soul
> Is trembling at the gates of darkness.
>
> (3.5., p 193, ll 8–14)

Again, this differs from *Romeo and Juliet* as, in Shakespeare's play, at the centre of Act 3 is the scene where Romeo and Juliet's union is sexually consummated, a love-epiphany. In *Karkurit* both Elma and Tyko are evading this epiphany, Tyko by remaining masked and Elma by pretending.[30]

It is not until Act 5, in the third cycle, that Tyko meets Elma, the female character who finally fulfils the aspirations for unconditional love. This is the only scene, the second to last in the play, where Elma and Tyko recognize each other and have their love-epiphany. They confess their love to each other before death:

TYKO
Here as a bride you stand, and now – "Nature,
Bless this marriage!"
Who dies happier than he who falls into
The death of sleep in th'arms of his beloved?
(5.4. p 229, ll 1–8)

ELMA
Already shines the eye of day above
And o'er the heather heath, fresh morning winds
Do blow. Come death, and welcome! How lovely 'tis
To die in the bosom of your true love.
(5.4. p 231, ll 13–16)

The dramaturgy of *Karkurit* presents three plot threads of varying hues. There is a dark framing plot around the play, its key words being hatred and debt. The key characters in this plot are Markus, Mauno and Niilo. The central main plot centres around love, the key words here being oath, fidelity and betrayal. The main characters in this plot are Elma, Tyko and Niilo, whose sinister and deceitful thread intertwines these two separate plots. This main plot is a knotty fabric of many different shades. As a third plot, there is a brighter strand which at first is extremely thin but which becomes stronger towards the end. This is Hanna's and Pauli's falling in love, shaped as a mirror image of Elma's and Tyko's love story and is the most positive plot thread of the play. There is no corresponding subplot in *Romeo and Juliet*, so this is a dramaturgically significant difference between the two plays. Among Shakespeare's plays, the relationship between the subplot and main plot in *Karkurit* could best be compared to that of *King Lear*. In Shakespeare's tragedy, the subplot around Gloucester varies the theme of the main plot: fathers (Lear and Gloucester) are subject to abuse by their vile children (Lear by his two daughters, Gloucester by his son) having rebuked their righteous child (for Lear, Cordelia and for Gloucester, Edgar). In *Karkurit*, the love story of the subplot forms a counterpoint to the main plot. It does not long for the past or reach out for the hereafter, but is an earthly tapestry with faith in a better future and, at the end of the play, turns gloom to light. In his treatment of the subplot, Kivi displays an independent dramaturgical vision in relation to the dramaturgy of Shakespeare's tragedies.

Taking a central place in the dramaturgy of *Karkurit* is the marriage proposal scene in the third act, a scene some readers have considered strange and artificial. Tarkiainen compares it to Shakespeare's comedy *Twelfth Night*.[31] In this serious play, Kivi utilizes many elements typical of Shakespeare's comedies, such as identity mix-ups and dressing in disguise. At the same time, the marriage proposal scene is an excellent example of the use of dramatic irony, a topic I shall turn to next, showing how Kivi's engagement with Shakespeare was mediated by Romanticism.

Dramatic and tragic irony – Shakespeare, the Romantics and *Karkurit*

Aleksis Kivi wrote *Karkurit* in an idealist-romantic manner which was already considered outdated in the 1870s when the play was first performed in Finland. However, another aspect in *Karkurit* is more successful and less outdated: the use of dramatic (and tragic) irony. Once again, Shakespeare is Kivi's guide, while German Romantics, above all A. W. Schlegel, are intermediary figures. It was actually A. W. Schlegel's younger brother Friedrich Schlegel who coined the term 'Romantic irony'. Before Friedrich Schlegel, irony had retained its classical meaning as a figure of speech, where the intention of the speaker is opposed to what he actually says and we understand the opposite of what he expresses in his speech. Romantic irony is, as defined by the *OED*, 'an attitude of detached scepticism adopted by an author towards his or her work, typically manifesting in literary self-consciousness and self-reflection'.

Friedrich Schlegel refers to the structure of the whole in the works of Shakespeare and describes it as 'this artfully ordered confusion, this charming symmetry of contradictions, this wonderfully perennial alternation of enthusiasm and irony which lives even in the smallest parts of the whole'.[32] For A. W. Schlegel, Shakespeare is an outstanding example of the use of irony as a means of creating an ironic perspective in dramaturgy. The mixing of comic and tragic elements, typical of Shakespearean drama, illustrates this. In Shakespeare's ironic attitude, A. W. Schlegel found the combination of creative absorption and 'cool indifference', though its mood was disillusioned: Shakespeare had seen 'human nature through and through', yet 'soars freely above it'.[33]

Dramatic irony – comic and tragic irony

A. W. Schlegel declared that 'where the genuinely tragic begins, all irony certainly ceases'.[34] But Schlegel's contemporary, Adam Müller, defines tragicomic as the essence of dramatic irony. According to him, in *King Lear* there is both the comic irony of the fool and the tragic irony of Lear.[35] The concept of 'tragic irony' was later developed in an early nineteenth-century article, 'On the Irony of Sophocles' (1833), by the English scholar Bishop Connop Thirlwall. He writes of two kinds of irony, the first what he calls the irony of action. The decisive step of Thirlwall's argument is that the irony of action presupposes irony in a second sense, the poet's irony. Thus, the irony of an action is combined with the irony in view of the action. The poet and the audience see the action not from the hero's point of view but from outside and above.[36] In the Aristotelianism of the German eighteenth-century theory of tragedy, the audience had to try to identify with the tragic hero's point of view. Thirlwall's argument is directed against this: tragic necessity requires ironic freedom because insight into the irony of fate cannot arise from the internal point of view of the hero within the play, but can come only from ironic detachment, from an external point of view. Theatre is a device that produces a specific structure of viewing through the separation of spectators and performance. The theatre creates a detached external position form where the audience can watch the events on stage without being involved, themselves.[37]

Dramatic and tragic irony in *Romeo and Juliet*

Dramatic irony is a form of irony which is expressed in the structure of a work: the audience's awareness of the situation differs substantially from the awareness of the characters. The words and actions of the characters therefore take on a different – often contradictory – meaning for the audience, compared to the characters. *Romeo and Juliet* is often used as an example of both dramatic and tragic irony. For example, the audience knows that Juliet is already married to Romeo, but her family does not. In the crypt, most of the other characters think Juliet is dead but the audience knows she only took a sleeping potion. Romeo is also under the same misapprehension when he kills himself. Without any connection to Romantic irony, Robert Sharpe calls Shakespeare 'one of the world's great ironists' in his book *Irony in the Drama*.[38] *Romeo and Juliet* produces tragic irony through the familiar tragic conventions of fate, chorus, omen, prophecy, etc. so that the audience is thoroughly aware of the tragic doom of the protagonists. As Sharpe puts it, 'The central irony of *Romeo and* Juliet is that the "stars", the tragic bias of events, make the general impetuosity of the characters produce, by an eyelash, a tragic outcome to good and promising actions'.[39]

Dramatic and tragic irony in *Karkurit*

In *Karkurit*, Kivi skilfully uses dramatic irony, again with Shakespeare as his 'teacher'. The most multifaceted scene is placed in the climax of *Karkurit* (Act 3). In this scene, the disguised Tyko is acting as Niilo's proxy and courting his own beloved Elma on behalf of another man. The scene is both comic and tragic. The dialogue is artificial and rigid, underlining the unrealistic mode of the scene. At the same time, the scene is a good example of dramatic irony. In many ways, the scene alludes more to *Twelfth Night* than to *Romeo and Juliet* – to the scenes where the heroine Viola, disguised as Cesario, courts Olivia on behalf of Orsino. Viola herself is in love with the duke, and Olivia falls in love with Cesario/Viola. The audience knows the real identity of Cesario/Viola. Kivi uses a similar kind of multiple dramatic irony. Tyko does not know that Elma still loves him and only him (the audience knows). Elma does not recognize that the 'French' proxy, courting her on Niilo's behalf, is Tyko (but the audience does). The spectator understands the double meanings of Elma's speech; Tyko does not. Elma answers the questions of the proxy, while thinking of Tyko as her loved one. Tyko misunderstands everything, thinking Elma loves Niilo.

In addition to dramatic irony, we can question whether *Karkurit* contains elements of tragic irony (a person acting blindly, in good faith, to his or her own destruction). Elma signs the contract of marriage with Niilo to save her father. By doing so she betrays her oath to Tyko and, as a result, will kill herself. The suicide does not succeed, because her poison has been replaced by a sleeping potion. However, Elma dies at the end of the play, because she cannot continue to live after Tyko's death. The moment of truth for Elma is at the end of Act 3, where she bitterly repents her own actions. For his part, Tyko makes an error in judgment or action (*hamartia*) when he disguises himself to spy on Elma. He makes another mistake when he decides to act as Niilo's proxy. One can say that Tyko acts blindly and furthers his own annihilation. Tyko becomes aware of the real situation (Elma loves him), his *anagnorisis* occurs in a situation where their love could still be saved. But the feud leads to a fight between the fathers of the two families. During the fight, Niilo shoots Tyko who dies in Elma's arms. In this sense, Kivi complicates the tragic irony of *Romeo and Juliet* by deepening the characterization and conflicts of his young lovers. As we will see next, the influence of German Romanticism extended beyond dramaturgy and the use of irony and also shaped Kivi's approach to his dramatic verse.

Romantic translations of *Romeo and Juliet* and *Karkurit*

German Romantic Shakespeare and Schlegel's translation *Romeo und Julia*

Romeo und Julia was one of the first German translations of Shakespeare by August Wilhelm Schlegel in 1797. The metrical Shakespeare translations begun by Schlegel and completed under Ludwig Tieck's supervision in 1833 have usually been categorized as 'Romantic'. Indeed the inspiration, the theory and perhaps the intention behind the translation process can be shown to be rooted in or related to Romantic ideas, even though the style and tone of the finished result is in general harmony with the diction of 'classical' serious drama of the entire Goethe era, as Werner Habicht argues.[40] But, as Christian Dietrich Grabbe wrote in 'Über die Shakspearo-Manie' (1827), Schlegel's Shakespeare had provided the most solid foundation for the durability of the Romantic school in Germany, but this was due to its embellished and uncritical reflection of the original.[41]

Schlegel's view of Shakespearean drama as organic poetry, as exhibited, for instance, in his essay on *Romeo und Julia* (1797), later elaborated on in his Lectures, is no doubt central to his contribution to Romantic aesthetics.[42] What Schlegel tended to overlook is that many additional phenomena, including those dismissed by him as historically superseded, such as quibbles, indecencies, metrical irregularities, etc., might also have to be considered as integral parts of the organic work of art and its historicity.[43] One of the best known and most influential 'veils' drawn by the translator Schlegel was across the figure of Romeo. It is not only the ribald jokes and the puns that Schlegel reduces, but his interventions are also so extensive that they constitute a distortion in the character. For example, Schlegel omitted most of the duel of jokes and mockery that ensues between Mercutio and Romeo in Act 2. Here, however, is exactly where we encounter a sharp-tongued and even malicious Romeo who has nothing whatsoever in common with Schlegel's romantic, spiritualized figure. It is only this 'purification' which can justify Romeo's 'romantic tendency' referred to by Schlegel in his 1797 essay.[44]

Schlegel and Hagberg's translation *Romeo och Julia*

In Scandinavia, Georg Brandes praised Schlegel's translation of *Romeo and Juliet* as a re-birth of Shakespeare: It was as if Shakespeare had been born in the middle of the eighteenth century in Germany in addition to Goethe and Schiller. 'Shakespeare was born in 1564 in England; he was re-born in 1797 in his German translator. *Romeo and Juliet* was published in London in 1597. In 1797 the tragedy was published in Berlin as a newborn work'.[45] The reason why the Schlegel/Tieck translations of Shakespeare were historically pre-eminent is that they appeared at a time when German literature was at a crucial stage in its development. 'The Schlegel/Tieck translations, by demonstrating that German could achieve a range and expressiveness equal to Shakespeare's English, validated the advancement of German literature to European status'.[46] Kivi also did this, demonstrating what the Finnish language could achieve through his authorship.

Kivi was influenced by reading Shakespeare through the lens of the Romantic age. Kivi read Shakespeare in a Swedish translation by Carl August Hagberg. The German Romantic translations of Shakespeare by A. W. Schlegel and Tieck influenced both Hagberg's translations and, indirectly, Kivi's reception of Shakespeare. Hagberg, discussed in the Introduction and Chapters 2 and 3 of this volume, translated Shakespeare's plays in 12 volumes in 1847–1851 under the title *Shakspeares Dramatiska Arbeten*. He translated from English, but also used the Schlegel/Tieck German translation. In Hagberg's Swedish translation, as Inga-Stina Ewbank argues, one may now and then find a line that corresponds more to Schlegel's comments than to Shakespeare's original.[47] Schlegel also completely omits the prologue in the beginning of his *Romeo and Juliet* translation – as so does Hagberg.[48] But Hagberg, too, retains independence from his German influences. Anders Österling and Nils Molin have stated that Schlegel's translations were indeed important tools and models for Hagberg but they were not prevalent influences. Hagberg's approach to Shakespeare differed from Schlegel's. Hagberg's Swedish translations are not dominated by the same Romantic euphonious language as Schlegel's German.[49]

Friedrich Gundolf translated Shakespeare's plays into German at the beginning of the twentieth century. He praised Schlegel's translation as 'the re-birth of Shakespeare as a German language phenomenon'.[50] But he also criticized the Schlegel/Tieck translations for failing to do justice to Shakespeare's Renaissance vitality: 'The strained force and ... the glowing spirit of the Renaissance is reduced to education, mood and mentality by the Romanticists'.[51] In his desire to prove Shakespeare's artistry, Schlegel failed to translate one crucial aspect of the plays: their roughness. Schlegel's translations seem directed towards the image of Shakespeare as a harmonious writer whose language is designed never to offend the sensibilities of his audience.[52] As one later critic put it, the ruggedness of Shakespeare's language had been subjected to 'a general process of smoothing, tidying and levelling of the versification'.[53]

Language and blank verse in *Karkurit*

Romeo and Juliet is one of Shakespeare's most poetic plays, written predominantly in blank verse, beginning with a sonnet-speaking chorus and including sonnets, end rhyme and other poetic features.[54] Kivi, too, when writing *Karkurit*, used blank verse more than in his other works.[55] In *Romeo and Juliet* 'the sonnet idiom becomes a universal language, a subtle indicator of cultural values'.[56] Kivi did not adopt any sonnet forms for *Karkurit*, despite Hagberg's attempts to faithfully translate them into Swedish. In general, we do not find love lyrics squeezed into a sonnet-like rhyme pattern in Kivi's writing.[57]

When *Karkurit* was published in 1867, its language was widely praised. 'Both as to its dramatic action and its poetic writing style, *Karkurit* is more artistic and radiant than its older siblings ... The language is much more focused, noble and true than in *Kullervo*'. At the end of the review, the critic notes that reading this play makes the lack of Finnish theatre feel all the more bitter, 'since this dramatic play is perfectly adapted to the demands of theatre'.[58]

Karkurit begins with a dialogue between Hanna and Elma, set in blank verse.

HANNA
My sister! Over there I see a road!
ELMA
And there's our home, so never more to fear
We'll lose our way.

(1.1, p. 139, ll 7–12)

Of the dialogue in the play, a quarter is in blank verse, unrhymed iambic pentameter. This choice was likely influenced by holding Shakespeare as a model, as trochaic metre was much more favoured by Kivi than iambic. This is natural to Finnish, where all words are accented on the first syllable and descending meters are more common. For instance, Kivi uses trochaic meter in all of his long, epic (non-stanza) poems. Over 60 per cent of all of the iambic verses Kivi wrote can be found in *Karkurit*. Kivi had important Swedish-speaking exemplars for his choice of blank verse as the poetic form to use in *Karkurit*: the most important among these were, naturally, the recent Swedish Shakespeare translations by Hagberg. Most influential for him among domestic Swedish-language drama was J. J. Wecksell's *Daniel Hjort* (1862).

Kivi wrote about his struggles to find a poetic metre in Finnish that would work for *Karkurit*. After abandoning the idea of using the traditional Kalevala meter (trochaic tetrameter), it took him a lot of sweat and tears to create a workable Finnish language blank verse. Given the inherent trochaic rhythms of Finnish, writers have needed to invent their own rules for creating ascending metres. Another difficulty arises from the large number of three- and four-syllable words and the scarcity of single-syllable words in the language. In Swedish, the situation is practically the opposite. Thus, Kivi got little help from Hagberg's translation for his issues with poetic rhythm.

Another issue is Shakespeare's variation between verse and prose. In *Karkurit*, the use of verse or prose is partially linked to social status: Martti, the shepherd and the old woman speak prose exclusively, as do, mainly, Yrjö and Niilo, the play's villain. The language used by the common folk in Kivi's play is considerably less rowdy than in Shakespeare: *Romeo and Juliet* is full of sexual innuendo and double meanings which we do not find in Kivi's play. When Kivi brings comical scenes into his serious play, as Shakespeare often does, the characters tend to speak prose. Most central in this is the estate manager Martti, who speaks in Kivi's first language, his Nurmijärvi dialect, in contrast to the generally poetic expression used in the play.

The experimentation of writers with new verse forms adopted from foreign models was often met with scepticism, or worse, at home. In the introduction to this volume, there is a quotation from August Ahlqvist, a university professor of Finnish, denigrating Slöör's 1864 translation of *Macbeth*. Ahlqvist was no great fan of Kivi either, and his assessment of *Karkurit* is full of vitriol especially connected to the metre. In the history of Finnish literature, Ahlqvist is best remembered for his shooting down of Kivi's novel *The Seven Brothers*, the first novel in Finnish, now considered a classic of Finnish literature. Ahlqvist's comments shed further light on the resistance to the transition from Romanticism to realism in Finland at the time, especially in terms of rough language, also associated with Shakespeare. Ahlqvist wrote that Kivi's novel expresses unprecedented cruelty, that it is 'not only devoid of beauty, but is, in crudely depicting what is crude and cruel, also factually ugly. ... Never in the history of the world has there been published a book containing so many swear words, curses, insults and cruel and crude depictions as in this book'.[59] Although the writing of *Karkurit* and *Seven Brothers* partly overlapped, there are only a few such insults and abuses in the play, for example in the speeches of the estate manager Martti, which are written in prose. In the concluding section, I consider in more detail what the reception of *Karkurit* reveals about the layers of influence and resistance towards Shakespeare and German Romanticism in Finland.[60]

Conclusion

The influence of Romantic Shakespeare on Kivi can be perceived as a mixed bag: at a time when Finnish was only beginning to be established as a literary language, writers were being encouraged to emulate canonical authors such as Shakespeare but, at the same time, the outdated Romantic influence could be damaging to later success on the stage. *Karkurit* was the first play of Kivi's to be performed – in Swedish under the title of *Flyktingarne*. There were two performances, two weeks before Kivi's death, at the *Nya Teatern* on 13 and 15 December 1872. *Karkurit* is not one of Kivi's outstanding works, although its initial reception was favourable. The new play was even considered better than his previous, now canonical plays, *Nummisuutarit* [The Heath Cobblers] or *Kullervo*. These two earlier works, however, are still among the most frequently performed of Kivi's plays, while *Karkurit* has been one of the least performed.

It is difficult to explain the later negative response to the play. It may have been partly due to the Finnish theatrical tradition, with its realistic aesthetics based on identification in terms of both acting and reception, an aesthetic adopted in Finnish performances of Shakespeare a decade later. In this sense, perhaps the use of dramatic (and tragic) irony in *Karkurit*, however artfully done, proved an impediment. In the play, the irony of action is combined with irony in viewing the action. The audience sees the action not from the hero's point of view but from outside and above. Kivi creates a detached external position from which the audience can watch the events on stage without being involved. The spectator's relationship to the events on the stage is the opposite of identification and 'Einfühlung'. *Karkurit* requires a spectator who is also an observer of human behaviour and its patterns. In addition to dramatic irony, the use of blank verse may also get in the way of audience identification, especially since the verse form and ascending rhythms are not natural to Finnish. As we saw earlier, the play was praised but also criticized for its language.

In thinking about the influence of Shakespeare on Kivi, we see that he was open to foreign models but selective and innovative in how he developed them. Kivi's dramaturgy absorbs elements from Shakespeare's *Romeo and Juliet* as well as from Shakespearean comedy, though he combines them in creative ways and brings in original elements, much as Shakespeare did with his sources. In terms of language and verse, while Kivi struggled to adapt Finnish to the metrical demands of blank verse, his efforts proved remarkably influential for the reception of Shakespeare in Finland, especially the subsequent development of a tradition of iambic pentameter translations into Finnish. The impact of Kivi's language on early translations of Shakespeare into Finnish is obvious, beginning from Paavo Cajander's first complete works translation project (1879–1912). *Romeo and Juliet* was Cajander's second Shakespeare translation and the first to be performed in Helsinki, in May 1881. In *Karkurit*, Kivi developed the blank verse which Cajander could rely on in his Finnish translations and which was so important in the development of literary Finnish, even if later translators rejected iambic metre in favour of those more natural to Finnish.

I will close by comparing the influence of Shakespeare and Kivi in their own cultures. As I mentioned at the outset, even during his lifetime, Kivi was already being compared to Shakespeare: indeed Fredrik Cygnaeus, an important cultural figure in his own right, predicted in 1865 that Kivi would become Finland's national writer. Just as Shakespeare's birthday is celebrated in Britain, in Finland Kivi's birthday has become a celebration of Finnish literature. If we think about the centres and peripheries of cultural influence in Europe, however, we do see that to some extent influence is a one-way street: a writer in a smaller language can be influenced by writers from more dominant ones, but at least in Kivi's day, it was much more difficult for a writer like himself to become a living part of world literature.

Notes

1 Kivi, *Lea*, 185.
2 A one-act play on a Biblical theme, alluding to the story of Jacob, Leah and Rachel (Gen., 29–31) and Zacchaeus [Sakaio], Lk, 19, 1–10. On the exotic setting, see Pikkanen, *Casting the Ideal Past*, 128–9. Kivi's first biographer, Viljo Tarkiainen,

believes *The Merchant of Venice* was an even greater influence than the Bible, though Tarkiainen also emphasizes Kivi's originality (*Alexis Kivi*, 343–4).

3   See the biography of Aleksis Kivi in the National Biography of Finland. Available at: https://kansallisbiografia.fi/english/person/2826.
4   Pikkanen, 'Theatrical Societies'.
5   See the chapter by Nummi, Bastman and Laamanen.
6   Pikkanen, 'Theatrical Societies'.
7   Pohjola-Skarp, 'Romantiikan draama', 93.
8   For these concepts, see Genette, *Palimpsests*, 5.
9   Citations are to Snellman, 'Svensk litteratur', 553.
10 Cygnaeus, 'Om Alexis Kivis komedi'.
11 See Tarkiainen, *Aleksis Kivi*, 119–22 and *passim*.
12 See Koskenniemi, *Aleksis Kivi*; Kinnunen, *Aleksis Kiven näytelmät*; Koskimies, *Aleksis Kivi*.
13 See Nummi, 'Kullervo', 161–3.
14 Levitt, *Structural Approach*, 24.
15 Pfister, *Theory and Analysis*, 283.
16 Pohjola-Skarp, 'Karkurit', 82–3.
17 Pfister, *Theory and Analysis*, 241.
18 Freytag, *Technik*, 88–9, 108–9, 111–12.
19 Freytag, *Technik*, 102–22; Pfister, *Theory and Analysis*, 241.
20 Pfister, *Theory and Analysis*, 241.
21 The character Niilo resembles the character Franz Moor in Schiller's *The Robbers*, a play which also influenced Kivi's *The Fugitives*, beginning with the name of the play.
22 Weis, Introduction, 7.
23 Shapiro, 'Romeo and Juliet', 498; Snyder, *The Comic Matrix*, 59.
24 Lönnrot, *Kalevala*, 35: 69–188.
25 *Romeo and Juliet* was likely written in 1596–1597 and *Othello* in 1603–1604; see Weis, *Shakespeare Revealed*, 201–2 and 283–5.
26 Bates, 'Shakespeare's Tragedies', 183.

27 Translations from *Karkurit* are by Nely Keinänen and Kimmo Absetz. Kivi did not number his scenes, but the references here are to the critical edition, which added Act and Scene divisions, plus line numbers starting afresh on each page, so page numbers here are also included.
28 Pfister, *Theory and Analysis*, 239–40.
29 Reid, *Shakespeare's Tragic Form*, 69. Subsequent references to Reid are given parenthetically in the text.
30 Cf. Reid's idea of Hamlet's evading epiphany, 76–7.
31 Tarkiainen, *Aleksis Kivi*, 229.
32 F. Schlegel, '[Athenäums-Fragmente]', 208; trans. in Behler, *German Romantic Literary Theory*, 149.
33 A. W. Schlegel, *Vorlesungen*, 136.
34 A. W. Schlegel, *Vorlesungen*, 137.
35 Müller, Über die dramatische Kunst', 242–3.
36 Thirlwall, 'Irony', 500, Menke, 'Ästhetik', 183.
37 Menke, 'Ästhetik', 184–5. Compare Brecht's Non-Aristotelian drama and 'Verfremdung'.
38 Sharpe, *Irony*, 52. For Sharpe, 'in the ironic mood one is conscious of contradictions but is above being frustrated by them', *Irony in the Drama*, viii.
39 Sharpe, *Irony*, 65.
40 Habicht, 'Romanticism', 45.
41 Habicht, 'Romanticism', 45.
42 A. W. Schlegel, *Vorlesungen*, 164–6.
43 Habicht, 'Romanticism', 47.
44 Greiner, 'The Comic Matrix', 211.
45 Quoted, in translation, in Ewbank, 'Shakespeare Translation', 3.
46 Ewbank, 'Shakespeare Translation', 3.
47 Ewbank, 'Shakespeare Translation', 4.
48 The Folio edition of Shakespeare's plays also omits the prologue.
49 Österling, *Minnesteckning*, 138; Molin, *Shakespeare och Sverige*, 190.

50 Gundolf, *Shakespeare*, 354.
51 Gundolf, 'Vorwort', 6.
52 Williams, *Shakespeare*, 151–2.
53 Atkinson, *August Wilhelm Schlegel*, 152.
54 Halio, *Romeo and Juliet*, 51.
55 Laitinen, 'Karkurien silosäkeistä', 98.
56 Levenson, 'Introduction', 56.
57 The first Finnish-language sonnet was written by August Ahlqvist in 1854.
58 Bergbom, review in *Kirjoitukset*, 292–5.
59 Ahlqvist, 'Seitsemän Veljestä', 3.
60 Kivi's next full-length play, *Canzio*, was also influenced by Shakespeare. Of Kivi's plays, *Canzio* is the most Romantic, this time via the influence of French Romanticism, à la Victor Hugo (Pohjola-Skarp, 'Romantiikan draama', 83–7). It is also the least performed of his plays.

Works cited

Ahlqvist, August, 'Seitsemän Veljestä. Kertomus, tehnyt A. Kivi', review of Alexis Kivi, *Seitsemän Veljestä*, in *Finlands Allmänna Tidning* (20–21 May 1870), 115–16.

Atkinson, Margaret E, *August Wilhelm Schlegel as a Translator of Shakespeare* (Oxford, 1952).

Bates, Catherine, 'Shakespeare's Tragedies of Love', in Claire McEachern, ed., *The Cambridge Companion to Shakespearean Tragedy* (Cambridge, 2002), 182–203.

Behler, Ernst, *German Romantic Literary Theory* (Cambridge, 1993).

Bergbom, Kaarlo, review of *Karkurit*, in *Kirjoitukset*, ii: *Tutkimukset ja arvostelut* (Helsinki, 1908), 291–5. Original review in *Kirjallinen kuukauslehti* (4 April 1867), 110–13.

Brandes, Georg, *Hovedstrømninger i det nittende aarhunderedes literatur II. Forelæsninger holdte ved Kjøbenhavns universitet i foraarshalvaaret 1873. Den romantiske skole i Tyskland*, (1873; 5th edn, Copenhagen, 1923).

Cygnaeus, Fredrik, 'Om Alexis Kivis komedi "Nummisuutarit"', in *Samlade Arbeten*, vi: *Literaturhistoriska och blandade arbeten IV* (1865; Helsingfors, 1889), 339–62.

Cygnaeus, Fredrik, 'Företal till Alexis Kivis roman "Seitsemän veljestä" äfven som historien om detta företals uppkomst' in *Samlade Arbeten*, vi: *Literaturhistoriska och blandade arbeten IV* (1873; Helsingfors 1889), 375–85.

Delabastita, Dirk, and Lieven D'hulst, eds, *European Shakespeares: Translating Shakespeare in the Romantic Age* (Amsterdam, 1993).

Ewbank, Inga-Stina, 'Shakespeare Translation as Cultural Exchange', *Shakespeare Survey*, 48 (1995), 1–12.

Freytag, Gustav, *Die Technik des Dramas* (1863; 13th edn, Leipzig, 1922).

Furst, Lillian R., 'Shakespeare and the Formation of Romantic Drama in Germany and France', in Gerald Gillespie, ed., *Romantic Drama* (Amsterdam, 1994), 3–15.

Genette, Gérard, *Palimpsests: Literature in the Second Degree*, trans. Channa Newman and Claude Doubinsky (Lincoln, 1997).

Grabbe, Christian Dietrich, 'Über die Shakspearo-Manie' [1827]. Available at: www.zeno.org/Literatur/M/Grabbe,+Christian+Dietrich/Theoretische+Schriften/%C3%9Cber+die+Shakspearo-Manie.

Greiner, Norbert, 'The Comic Matrix of Early German Shakespeare Translation', in Delabastita and D'hulst, eds, *European Shakespeares* 203–17.

Gundolf, Friedrich, *Shakespeare und der deutsche Geist* (Berlin, 1914).

Gundolf, Friedrich, 'Vorwort', in *Shakespeare in deutscher Sprache*, i (Berlin, 1925), 5–9.

Halio, Jay L., *Romeo and Juliet: A Guide to the Play* (Westport, 1998).

Habicht, Werner, 'The Romanticism of the Schlegel-Tieck Shakespeare and the History of Nineteenth-Century German Shakespeare Translation', in Delabastita and D'hulst, eds, *European Shakespeares*, 45–53.

Kinnunen, Aarne, *Aleksis Kiven näytelmät: Analyysi ja tarkastelua ajan aatevirtausten valossa* (Helsinki, 1967).

Kivi, Aleksis, *Kullervo* [*Kullervo: A Play in Five Acts*], ed. Jyrki Nummi et al (1864; Helsinki, 2014).

Kivi, Aleksis, *Karkurit* [*The Fugitives: A Play in Five Acts*], ed. Riitta Pohjola-Skarp et al (1867; Helsinki, 2017).

Kivi, Aleksis, *Lea*, in *Yö ja päivä. Lea. Alma. Margareta*, ed. Pentti Paavolainen et al (1869; Helsinki, 2019).

Kivi, Aleksis *Kirjeet* [Letters: Critical Edition], ed. Juhani Niemi et al (Helsinki, 2012).

Koskenniemi, V. A., *Aleksis Kivi* (1934; Helsinki, 1954).

Koskimies, Rafael, *Aleksis Kivi: Henkilö ja runous* (Helsinki, 1974).

Laitinen, Heikki, 'Karkurien silosäkeistä', in Aleksis Kivi, *Karkurit*, ed. Riitta Pohjola-Skarp et al (Helsinki, 2017), 98–124.

Levenson, Jill L., 'Introduction', in William Shakespeare, *Romeo and Juliet*, ed. Jill L. Levenson (Oxford, 2000), 1–125.

Levitt, Paul M., *A Structural Approach to the Analysis of Drama*, De probrietatisbus litterarum, Series maior, 15 (The Hague, 1971).

Lönnrot, Elias *Kalevala* [1949]. Available at: http://nebu.finlit.fi/kalevala/index.php?m=1&l=1.

Menke, Christoph, 'Ästhetik der Tragödie. Romantische Perspektiven' in Bettine Menke and Christoph Menke, eds, *Tragödie – Trauerspiel – Spektakel* (Berlin, 2007), 179–198.

Molin, Nils, *Shakespeare och Sverige intill 1800-talets mitt: En översikt över hans inflytande* (Gothenburg; 1931).

Muir, Kenneth, *The Singularity of Shakespeare and Other Essays* (Liverpool, 1977).

Müller, Adam, 'Über die dramatische Kunst. Vorlesungen gehalten zu Dresden 1806', in *Kritische ästhetische und philosophische Schriften*, ed. Walter Schroeder and Werner Siebert, i (1806; Neuwied, 1967), 141–291.

Nummi, Jyrki, 'Kullervo – viisinäytöksinen tragedia', in Aleksis Kivi, *Kullervo*, ed. Jyrki Nummi et al. (1864; Helsinki, 2014), 60–163.

Österling, Anders, *Minnesteckning över C. A. Hagberg* (Stockholm, 1921).

Pfister, Manfred, *The Theory and Analysis of Drama*, trans. John Halliday (Cambridge, 1988).

Pikkanen, Ilona, *Casting the Ideal Past: A Narratological Close Reading of Eliel Aspelin-Haapkylä's History of the Finnish Theatre Company (1906–1910)* (Tampere, 2012).

Pikkanen, Ilona, 'Theatrical Societies: Finland', in Joep Leersen, ed., *Encyclopedia of Romantic Nationalism in Europe* (2019). Available at: https://ernie.uva.nl/, article version 1.1.1.2/a, last accessed 27 May 2020.

Pohjola-Skarp, Riitta, 'Karkurit – viisinäytöksinen murhenäytelmä' in Aleksis Kivi, *Karkurit*, ed. Riitta Pohjola-Skarp et al (1867; Helsinki, 2017), 53–97.

Pohjola-Skarp, Riitta, 'Romantiikan draama, Shakespeare ja Canzio', in Aleksis Kivi, *Canzio: Näytelmä viidessä näytöksessä*, ed. Toim. Juhani Niemi et al (Helsinki, 2019), 75–94.

Reid, Robert Lanier, *Shakespeare's Tragic Form: Spirit in the Wheel* (Newark, 2000).

Schlegel, August Wilhelm, 'Über Shakespeare's Romeo und Julia' [1797]. Available at: www.friedrich-schiller-archiv.de/die-horen/die-horen-1797-stueck-6/ii-ueber-shakespeares-romeo-und-julia/.

Schlegel, August Wilhelm, *Vorlesungen über dramatische Kunst und Literatur I–II*, in Edgar Lohner, ed., *Kritische Schriften und Briefe V–VI* (1809; Stuttgart, 1966–7).

Schlegel, Friedrich, '[Athenäums-Fragmente]', in Ernst Behler, ed. *Kritische Friedrich-Schlegel- Ausgabe*, pt. 1, ii: *Charakteristiken und Kritiken 1 (1796–1801)*, ed. Hans Eichner (1798; Paderborn, 1967), 165–256.

Shakespeare, William, *Romeo and Juliet / Romeo und Julia – Shakespeare's Works*, trans. August Wilhelm Schlegel and Ludwig Tieck, in L. L. Schücking, ed., *Shakespeares Werke*, iii (Wiesbaden, nd)

Shakespeare, William, *Shakspeares Dramatiska arbeten*, trans. Carl August Hagberg, x (Lund, 1861). Available at: http://runeberg.org/hagberg/j/.

Shakespeare, William, *Romeo and Juliet*, ed. René Weis, The Arden Shakespeare (London, 2012).

Shapiro, Stephen A., 'Romeo and Juliet: Reversals, Contraries, Transformations, and Ambivalence', *College English*, 25/7 (1964), 498–501.

Sharpe, Robert Boies, *Irony in the Drama: An Essay on Impersonation, Shock, and Catharsis* (Westport, 1975).

Smidt, Kristian, 'The Discovery of Shakespeare in Scandinavia', in Delabastita and D'hulst, eds, *European Shakespeares*, 91–103.

Snellman, J. V., 'Svensk litteratur', in *Samlade arbeten*, vi: *1847–1849* (1849; Helsinki, 1996), 550–67.

Snyder, Susan, *The Comic Matrix of Shakespeare's Tragedies: Romeo and Juliet, Hamlet, Othello, and King Lear* (Princeton, 1979).

Tarkiainen, Viljo, *Aleksis Kivi: Elämä ja teokset* (1915; Helsinki, 1984).

Thirlwall, Connop, 'On the Irony of Sophocles', *The Philological Museum II* (np, 1833), 483–537.
Weis, René, *Shakespeare Revealed: A Biography* (London, 2007).
Weis, René, Introduction to William Shakespeare, *Romeo and Juliet*, ed. René Weis (London, 2012), 1–117.
Williams, Simon, *Shakespeare on the German Stage*, i: *1586–1914* (Cambridge, 1990).
Wolffheim, Hans, *Die Entdeckung Shakespeares: Deutsche Zeugnisse des 18. Jahrhunderts* (Hamburg, 1959).

8

Anne Charlotte Leffler's Shakespeare: The perils of stardom and everyday life

Lynn R. Wilkinson

In 1873, Anne Charlotte Leffler's play, *Skådespelerskan* [The Actress], was accepted at Dramatiska Teatern (the Dramatic Theatre) in Stockholm. Premiering in December of that year, it was a success, thanks in part to the performance of the star actress, Elise Hwasser, as the protagonist, a young actress by the name of Ester Larson, who would herself like to become a star. She hopes to do so by performing tragic roles like Shakespeare's Juliet, and the opening of Act 2 of this two-act play shows her rehearsing a scene from *Romeo and Juliet* in front of a mirror. A performance within a performance, this scene raises questions about Ester Larson's ambitions and the significance of *Romeo and Juliet* for the enactment of everyday life in mid-nineteenth-century Sweden and Europe and stardom itself.

Skådespelerskan was the first of Anne Charlotte Leffler's plays to be performed. She went on to have a distinguished career as a writer and playwright. Fourteen of her plays were published or performed in Stockholm and elsewhere and she also published two novels and many novellas, as well as articles in journals and newspapers. She herself noted, however, that her ambition to become a playwright was somewhat paradoxical; at the time she wrote *Skådespelerskan,* she had only rarely been to the theatre because her parents disapproved of it. However, the money she earned from the first successful run of *Skådespelerskan* allowed her to travel and see plays both at home and abroad. Her letters and reviews note the kinds of performances she attended and the names of playwrights she deemed important. Ibsen figures most prominently among these names, Shakespeare only rarely, partly, it seems, because for Leffler, Shakespeare increasingly represented a more old-fashioned and constricting view of women at a time when the struggle for women's rights was taking hold in Sweden and beyond. As I discuss in the first section of this chapter, Leffler's earliest references to Shakespeare (from the early 1870s) are mainly positive: as a canonical author, Shakespeare's works could confer stardom on actors who performed certain roles successfully, as Ester Larson hopes to achieve by performing Juliet and, indeed, as Leffler herself hoped to achieve by writing plays. An early letter describes a visit to Dramatiska Teatern in Stockholm, where Leffler saw the actor Edvard Swartz perform Hamlet, an experience she describes as transformational. The theatre became for her a transcendent world juxtaposed with ordinary life, a world in which women, too, could play significant roles.

At the same time, however, Leffler was concerned about the kind of role model a character like Juliet represented. Thus, in the second section, I consider in more detail the implications of Ester Larson's wish to play Juliet as seen in two plays, *Skådespelerskan* (1873) and *En räddande engel* [A Saving Angel] (1883), where Shakespeare's *Romeo and Juliet* figures as a model for misguided notions of romantic love, where women are expected to sacrifice themselves for their husbands. Similar themes emerge in a final set of Shakespearean references in a series of articles Leffler published about her stay in London in spring 1884, *Londonlif* [London Life] and *Lösa blad från det moderna London* [Pages from Modern London]. Here, Leffler contemplates the limits and possibilities of tragic versus comedic roles for female actors, especially in contrast with Ibsen, whose plays were presenting very different models. And, as an aside, we can also see Leffler's frustration with melodramatic Victorian acting styles, in contrast to the more realist and naturalist styles which accompanied the rise of Ibsen. By the mid-1880s, Leffler had come to see Shakespeare as merely a good English playwright, whereas Ibsen represented new directions in world, as well as Nordic, drama.

Edvard Swartz's otherworldly Hamlet and the aura of the theatre

At the time Leffler saw Edvard Swartz perform Hamlet, he had been playing the role for decades. Swartz had debuted in the role on 7 November 1853 and continued to perform it until he retired from Stockholm's Dramatic theatre in 1881. He was the fifth Swedish actor to play the role at that theatre.[1] The first was Gustaf Fredrik Åbergsson, who debuted in 1817; he was followed by Olof Ulrik Torsslow, Nils Wilhelm Almlöf and Georg Dahlqvist. In the words of Ulla-Britta Lagerroth, their performances were characterized by 'the grand gestures typical of the time and melodic recitation of the text, thus scarcely any noticeably new interpretation of the role'.[2] In contrast to his predecessors, Swartz played Hamlet as a melancholy young man riven with doubt. His performances were also the first to use the new translation of Shakespeare by Carl August Hagberg.

Leffler describes her reactions to Swartz's performance in a letter to her cousin Amanda Leffler dated 25 April 1870. Amanda Leffler was a pietist Christian whose religion led her to reject most worldly entertainments; thus Leffler's evocation of Swartz's performance as utterly convincing, true and idealistic aims, in part, to persuade her cousin that the theatre is a noble art and that playwrighting can be a Christian calling. In the letter, the theatre is an ideal world and the actor a saintly presence surrounded by an aura. Both, however, provoke ecstasy.

> You have of course read *Hamlet*. Imagine this superhumanly difficult role played by Schwarz so that no one remembered in the course of the evening that it was a play one was looking at; it seemed one was looking at life itself, not an artistic representation. Words can't express the overpowering impression this evening made upon me, I grow ecstatic just thinking about our great Schwarz's brilliant performance. It was as if Shakespeare was illuminated for me with a new light; as if I now first understood him correctly and as though a new light, the bright halo of genius now illuminated even the smallest detail in this consummate masterpiece.[3]

If, however, Leffler's remarks are permeated by the idealism of the early and mid-nineteenth century, her depiction of Edvard Swartz as the inhabitant of a transcendent world who provokes the spectator's ecstasy also evokes his stardom, as well as the possibility that Anne Charlotte Leffler intended to imitate him by following him into the theatre, but as a playwright, not an actor. The 'bright halo of genius' that surrounds him evokes the aura of art; Swartz is consecrated by his association with Shakespeare's *Hamlet*, a 'consummate work of genius'.

Interestingly, the same letter contains an account of another kind of performance, this time outside the conventional theatre. Leffler tells her cousin that she had attended a masquerade ball, where she enjoyed the anonymity and role-playing, which took her out of her identity as a middle-class woman who rarely attended such events:

> I had more fun than I ever expected, hardly danced at all, but instead walked around in the large, magnificently decorated apartment, which consisted of 24 rooms, arm in arm now

with one mask, now with another. Unlike everyone else, I didn't have the courage to address anyone, but remained passive, but as soon as I was alone an instant a gentleman came up and offered me his arm. In that way, I made a whole lot of acquaintances, who then invited me to meet them in a certain room after the unmasking, so that we could find out with whom we had been talking. You can't imagine what a colourful and bizarre spectacle the festive rooms offered: costumes from every period and every nationality, pierrots, harlequins, fortune-tellers, peasant girls, wild women, noble ladies from the time of the Louis in France or Gustav III in Sweden, knights of the middle ages, yes, everything imaginable combined in a colourful confusion.
(Leffler, letter to Amanda Leffler, 25 April 1870).

Thus, the letter juxtaposes performances in the theatre, portrayed as an ideal world, with those of everyday life. It was a relationship that preoccupied Leffler in some of her later works, including the two plays that feature the character Ester Larson.

Performing Juliet onstage and off: Leffler's *Skådespelerskan* and *En räddande engel*

The scene in which Ester Larson rehearses the role of Juliet in front of a mirror comes at the beginning of the second act of a two-act play. It is central to the play, as are the choices its protagonist faces between marriage or a life in the theatre. The character, an actress and orphan who grew up in a circus, has become engaged to a middle-class man by the name of Helge and is visiting his family in the countryside for the first time. The visit is not going well; Ester Larson's behaviour scandalizes most of the family and her fiancé reveals himself to be a prudish young man with fixed ideas about the role she will play after she marries him, which will entail her leaving the theatre and devoting herself to him and their home. Although she has promised him to leave the theatre, Ester has not broken off her engagement; moreover, her rehearsal of Juliet suggests that she is in the process of resolving to return to the theatre despite her promise. Interestingly, as we learn later in the play, she has no immediate prospects of playing this role.

Ester is rehearsing Juliet's speech as the character contemplates taking Friar Laurence's potion. She quotes from the play:

> How if, when I am laid into the tomb,
> I wake before the time that Romeo
> Come to redeem me? There's a fearful point.
> Shall I not then be stifled in the vault[?]
> (RJ 4.3.30–3; Skådespelerskan, 45)[4]

Ester's rehearsal suggests her increasing awareness that the theatre may provide her with a refuge from the stifling world of her fiancé and his family. But it also indicates that she has ambitions to become an artist and star, much like Edvard Swartz. As she puts it a little later in the same scene, before she is interrupted by her fiancé:

> I am an artist. I have the divine spark of genius. Despite all of the flaws that still mark my performances, I will one day show all my detractors that the coquettish and unnatural Ester Larson is one of the fortunate who are able to conquer a world with their genius.
>
> (Skådespelerskan, 46)

In the meantime, she tries to persuade Helge that her dreams of stardom are not at odds with their marriage plans: 'I will be your Julia and I will force you to be my Romeo, despite your protests and your very rational words about a sensible love' (Skådespelerskan, 46).

Despite her words, it becomes increasingly clear after this scene that Ester cannot leave the theatre and has no future in the world of Helge and his family. However, the visit has galvanized her ambitions. Ester's decision to rehearse a scene from *Romeo and Juliet*, as well as her articulation of her desire to be an artist, are very probably in response to a conversation she had in Act One with her fiancé's younger sister, Agda, about the theatre. Agda had seen Ester Larson perform in Karlstad and had found the experience as compelling as Leffler had found that of Edvard Swartz in 1870. It had been difficult for the child to think about anything else afterwards: 'I was so taken by her that I couldn't think about anything else for a long time afterwards', Agda recounts (*Skådespelerskan*, 15–16). Moreover, as Ester later tells Agda, she remembers her, a 13- or 14-year-old girl in the audience, whose clear gaze suggested an alternative to the glances from the young men, who saw only an attractive young woman, not an actress (*Skådespelerskan*, 24–5).

In another conversation with Agda, which takes place just before she leaves Helge and his family, however, Ester also articulates her awareness that realizing her ambitions will require hard work and study:

> Yes, let me travel to Paris and study. You probably won't be able to accompany me, but several years from now, I will return and make my debut as Juliet and then you'll sit among the spectators and smile at me through your tears as you did back then.
>
> (*Skådespelerskan*, 72)

Trying on the role of Juliet, then, helps Ester Larson to choose her vocation in the theatre, instead of marriage. However, she is also beginning to question the model of romantic love that led her to become engaged to an inappropriate man. Should she, like Juliet, continue to honour a love pact that may prove lethal? The kind of marriage her fiancé offers her may be a different version of the burial vault Juliet is contemplating.

Premiering six years before Ibsen's *A Doll's House*, Leffler's *Skådespelerskan* also depicts a young woman who walks away from a middle-class marriage and its conventions. Unlike Ibsen's Nora, however, Leffler's Ester Larson has somewhere to go and earn a living: the theatre. Like Leffler, moreover, Ester Larson is familiar with role-playing and its pleasures. Indeed, since she grew up performing, she sees herself as a conglomeration of roles, as Helge learns when he tells her to just be herself around his family. Ester retorts: 'Myself? Who is that? Is it Ester Larson? I have never played Ester Larson and I don't know any such person' (*Skådespelerskan*, 39). Ester's ability to shift roles at will sets her at odds with Helge's family. It also enables her to return to the theatre, which appreciates and rewards such skills, and it may also enable her to resist too close an identification with Shakespeare's Juliet and the notions of romantic love she has come to embody, at least for some spectators and readers.

In Leffler's highly successful one-act play, *En räddande engel*, which premiered in 1883, the same year that *Skådespelerskan* was published, we learn that Ester Larson has indeed performed the role of Juliet very successfully, thus emphasizing the idea that theatre itself could provide women with some degree of independence. The news crops up in a conversation between Arla, a naïve young woman who has not yet learned to make conversation, and one of her dancing partners. Arla, however, asks an interesting question:

CHAMBERLAIN
(twisting his moustache in a distinguished manner)
> Yes, it's true that there's no arguing about taste, but it is still generally accepted that Ester Larson's debut as Juliet was absolutely brilliant.

ARLA
> But surely the chamberlain doesn't think that she was Shakespeare's Juliet.

(En räddande engel)[5]

Unlike Leffler in her 1870 letter to her cousin, Arla distinguishes between text and performance. She goes on to say that Ester Larson does not correspond to the way she had imagined Juliet when she read the text – as 'young and pure' (*En räddande engel*). Her words also raise the question of the actor's part in creating a role or, in other words, her status as a creative artist, a status to which Ester Larson clearly aspires and which she aims to attain by playing tragic roles such as Shakespeare's Juliet. Ester Larson's aspirations and success in one tragic role at least situate her among actual actresses such as Johanne Luise Heiberg in Denmark, Rachel in France, or, closer to home, Elise Hwasser, who played Ester Larson in the 1873 staging of *Skådespelerskan*. All were from humble backgrounds but rose to prominence by playing such roles.[6] Leffler's character, however, also harks back to a fictional character in Zacharias Topelius's, *Fältskärns berättelser* [Tales of a Barber Surgeon] (1853–1867), a popular series by the Swedish-speaking Finnish author. There, a wild young woman by the name of Ester Larsson (with two s's) eventually settles down and marries an aristocrat. That might also have been a desirable fate for Leffler's Ester Larson; as Ingeborg Nordin Hennel has shown, working conditions for Swedish actresses in the nineteenth century were very demanding and made marriage to a prosperous man a desirable prospect.[7] Since there are no further references to Ester Larson in Leffler's works, however, we never learn whether the character marries. Interestingly, however, Elise Hwasser's career may suggest the character's development beyond Leffler's texts and their performances. During her long career, Hwasser played Desdemona, Ophelia and Lady Macbeth, as well as Juliet. In 1858, she married Daniel Hwasser, secretary at Dramatiska Teatern, although that did not put an end to her acting career. Like Leffler, however, she came to see Ibsen as a dramatist who was far more important than Shakespeare, ultimately retiring to an estate she named Østråt, after Ibsen's *Lady Inger of Østråt*.[8] Perhaps Ester Larson was also able to combine marriage and the performance of serious dramatic roles in works by Ibsen and other Scandinavian playwrights, including Leffler.

Nor do we learn whether the types of roles Ester Larson covets rob her of the energy and spontaneity she displayed as a young woman who grew up in a circus. In their previously cited biographies of Rachel and Johanne Luise Heiberg, Rachel M. Brownstein and Vibeke Schrøder emphasize the painful conflicts these women experienced as they remade themselves according to the models offered by the culture of elite European theatres in the early and mid-nineteenth century.

What we do understand, especially in *En räddande engel*, is that *Romeo and Juliet* itself serves as a model for notions of romantic love that some young women follow. In the play, Arla falls prey to the attentions of Captain Lagerskjöld, a notorious rake who has also courted her very young sister Gurli. He compares her to Juliet and persuades her to lean in to him as they waltz, later kissing her bare arm. Arla then asks Gurli whether her arm is as hot or her heartbeat as fast as she imagines them to be. Her sister provides a fanciful explanation: 'Real love strikes like lightning. It hasn't been many days since you told me about Romeo and Juliet – they also saw each other for the first time at a ball' (Leffler, *En räddande engel*). This is also the explanation Arla later offers her mother, who criticizes the way she has behaved with Captain Lagerskjöld.

Here the story of *Romeo and Juliet* functions as a ploy for male predators such as Lagerskjöld and a mystification for naïve young women like Arla and her sister. But it may also be that the character of Juliet is an even more sinister model, especially for those such as Ester Larson, with artistic or professional ambitions. Not for nothing does Anne Charlotte Leffler choose to show her in the earlier play reciting words in which Juliet contemplates death and her role as a woman who makes the ultimate sacrifice. Shakespeare's *Romeo and Juliet* stands for a notion of love that is death-bound and destructive, especially for women.

Leffler's decision in 1883 to publish *Skådespelerskan* together with another early play, *Under toffeln*, may well have reminded her of Ester Larson, as *En räddande engel* is an adaptation of a novella she published in 1882 in her highly successful collection, *Ur lifvet* [From Life]. The novella also includes a scene between Arla and the chamberlain, who discuss a recent performance of *Romeo and Juliet*. But in the novella, it is a certain Miss Berg who has performed the role of Juliet, to the satisfaction of spectators and critics alike. We do learn, however, that *Romeo and Juliet* is one of the two plays that Arla has seen and that her father has questioned her judgement because she has seen so little of the theatre (Leffler, 'En bal i "societeten"', 32–3).

By 1883, many women, at least those in the middle classes, had come to question not only marriage, but also notions of romantic love. Ibsen's *A Doll's House* (1879) had certainly cast the former in a critical light, while the passage of laws granting married women some property rights had also given women new choices even within marriage. These choices form the crux of the other play by Leffler, *Sanna kvinnor* [True Women], which premiered on 15 October 1883, as part of the same programme as *En räddande engel*. In that play, a daughter attempts to persuade her mother not to give her profligate husband the small inheritance she has received from her sister, as he has run through the rest of his wife's money and now lays claim to this small sum, which is all she has left. The daughter, Berta, explains to her mother that notions of truth change over time and that since married women have gained some property rights, they – and women in general – no longer need to act like dogs. In the end, however, the wife gives in to her husband, who then celebrates her as a 'true woman' (*sann kvinna*), by which he means a wife who sacrifices everything for the man she loves. Significantly the name of the wife and mother in *True Women* is Julie. A descendent of Shakespeare's tragic heroine, she continues to play a role that no longer makes sense in western Europe in the 1880s.

Englishness and the resources of comedy: Leffler on the theatre in London and Ellen Terry in Henry Irving's *Much Ado About Nothing*

In the spring of 1884, the year after *Sanna kvinnor* and *En räddande engel* premiered, Anne Charlotte Leffler travelled to Denmark, Germany, England and France, spending almost three months in London. She wrote about her experiences in the English capital in a series of articles that appeared in periodicals and newspapers in Sweden and Denmark. A playwright herself, she was, of course, curious about the theatre in London and she discusses it extensively in three articles published in the newspaper *Stockholms Dagblad* in 1884 and 1885. By this time, however, Shakespeare has lost some of his lustre. He now takes second place to Ibsen and other Scandinavian dramatists.

Almost half of 'Londonlif', which appeared in the issue of Saturday 10 May 1884, is devoted to Leffler's impressions of the theatre, mostly revealing Leffler's disapproval of London stage practices, including an overly melodramatic performance of Ibsen's *A Doll's House*, although she does express admiration for the performance of *Othello* given by a travelling Italian troupe. She notes that it is often more enjoyable to look at the elegant clothing of spectators than the stage, because the quality of the plays, as well as the performances, is quite bad:

> The plays, as well as the way they are performed, all belong to a time that has long passed for us. These are sensation pieces with splendid sets, a lot of shrieking, weeping, love, hatred, betrayal, jealousy – all of the traditional theatrical passions rendered with the traditional theatrical mimicry, and the public is entranced.
>
> ('Londonlif')

Similarly, the only version of *A Doll's House* that has been performed in London is an adaptation by two Englishmen which transforms Ibsen's 'modern social drama' into a clichéd melodrama. Perhaps because the actors are foreigners, she is most positive in this piece about the performance at Covent Garden Theatre of *Othello* by an Italian troupe, especially the actor, Salvini, who played the title role. She praises his beautiful voice and his ability to convey different moods and passions, but finds his gestures awkward, even inappropriate. Leffler also criticizes the representation of the death of Desdemona behind a curtain because she thinks it weakened the effect.

A reference to the American actress Mary Anderson is particularly interesting in connection to the themes raised by *Romeo and Juliet* discussed above. Leffler finds Mary Anderson – all the rage in London, at the time she writes – to be a bad actress, although she is attractive. Like Sarah Bernhardt, Mary Anderson cultivates her offstage image, although in the case of the American actress, it is an image that emphasizes her virtue. Mary Anderson is said to be preparing to perform the role of Juliet by travelling to Verona; Leffler hopes that Juliet will whisper the correct interpretation of her role to the virtuous American. The implication is that Mary Anderson will have to abandon her virtuous pose to portray Juliet and her passion, but one wonders how likely it is that a fictional character will succeed in persuading Mary Anderson to do anything.

The two articles published a year later in *Stockholms Dagblad*, as part of the series, *Lösa blad från det moderna London*, are more mixed in their judgement. One finds both good and bad theatre in London, Leffler writes at the beginning of the first, published on 29 April 1885. There are excellent performances, whose actors are the equal of their finest colleagues in other European cities. Mr and Mrs Kendal (W. H. and Madge Kendal) are very fine character actors; they and the other members of their troupe match the achievements of the French national theatre. But the good drowns in the bad. Leffler notes the kitschy publicity for a play called *Claudian*, which she had seen and found to be very childish, its greatest interest being Wilson Barret, the actor playing the protagonist, who was also famous for his performance as Hamlet.

Here, as well, Leffler argues that the surroundings of London performances are often more compelling than the plays themselves. The spectacle of young girls prostituting themselves in the streets of the theatre district, she writes, often made her forget what she had seen in the theatre. In contrast, the auditorium of St James Theatre had more in common with the home of a wealthy and elegant young woman than a theatre itself.

The third article, published on 3 May 1885, opens with two positive discussions. The first turns to a performance of Sheridan's *The Rivals* by another pair of star actors, Mr and Mrs Bancroft, a performance that Leffler finds excellent in every way. The second discusses an adaptation of George Eliot's *Adam Bede*, which reminds Leffler of why she prefers adaptations to many conventional plays: like novels, these plays follow the slow development of a human life, with its many details. However, over half of the text is devoted to a discussion of Henry Irving and Ellen Terry.

Like the Kendals, Irving and Terry were a pair of star actors who performed Shakespeare, with Irving also serving as stage manager and director. Leffler's evaluation of their work is ambivalent. Are Henry Irving and Ellen Terry good actors? Opinions are divided, she writes. Many spectators find Irving's accent and declamation off-putting, but they may also be the key to his popularity among the uneducated. Like Shakespeare, Irving appeals to many segments of London society. Leffler compares him to August Lindberg. Both are excellent directors and actors. She finds Irving's gestures particularly compelling.

Most people, Leffler writes, agree that Ellen Terry is charming, but is she more? The English actress seems the incarnation of the ideal Englishwoman, but she lacks the virtuosity of Sarah Bernhardt or the elevated style of Adelaide Ristori. Leffler notes that Ellen Terry seemed to glide across the stage like a female character in a novel from the first half of the nineteenth century:

> But to describe Ellen Terry's gait, I must turn back to the Romantic era. I don't know how to explain it realistically, but she unquestionably floated across the stage. There was something catlike, leaping, unexpected in her movements that I have never seen elsewhere.
> ('Teatrar', in Leffler, *Lösa blad*, 3 May 1885)

Leffler thus explicitly ties Ellen Terry's acting style to that of the generation of the Danish actress Johanne Luise Heiberg, making it seem old-fashioned and out of sync with the kind of acting demanded by, say, Ibsen's social dramas. But characterizing Ellen Terry's movements as cat-like suggests that something more is at stake here.

The image of Ellen Terry that has been handed down to us is dominated by her depiction in John Singer Sargent's portrait of 1889, which shows Terry as Lady Macbeth, clad in a green dress covered with insect wings and holding a crown over her head. Performances in such tragedies, Nina Auerbach argues, made Ellen Terry a star and lent her respectability, at the same time as they imprisoned her in a narrow range of roles that blotted out the energy and unconventionality of her youth.[9]

Leffler, however, discusses her performance in Shakespeare's comedy *Much Ado About Nothing*. Here we see a very different version of Ellen Terry. Playful and aggressive, her catlike movements allow her to hold her own:

> When she teased Benedict, it was a moving and enchanting provocation. And how she managed to glide away and make herself inaccessible after she said something mean! And then her lovely caressing tenderness when she finally allowed herself to be conquered! Nothing of Sarah Bernhardt's sensuous passion, but instead the somewhat shy and reserved, but still fervent devotion of the young Englishwoman.
> ('Teatrar', in Leffler, *Lösa blad*, 3 May 1885)

Comedy quite clearly gave Ellen Terry more room for manoeuvre than the tragedies in which she and so many other actresses became and remained famous.

The cost of stardom?

At the beginning of her discussion of Henry Irving and Ellen Terry, Anne Charlotte Leffler poses the question: Was Ellen Terry a good or even a great actress? Her verdict is ambiguous. Leffler concludes that she is a good English actress. Such also seems to be Leffler's evaluation of Shakespeare. He is an English genius whose works are less important to an educated Scandinavian in the late nineteenth century than many of Leffler's contemporaries, especially Ibsen. Her references to Shakespeare's work, however, also bring into focus its market value. He emerges as a star playwright whose works are able to make or break actors, transforming some into stars themselves, but often at the cost of their having to perform tragic roles, not always exclusively onstage.

As previously mentioned, we never learn what happens to Ester Larson after her first success as Juliet. Does she come to experience a conflict between the energy and resourcefulness of her youth and the conventions of tragic roles? Does she discover, perhaps like Ellen Terry, that comedy gives a woman performer more room to manoeuvre?

Leffler never addresses this question explicitly in relation to Shakespeare and his works. However, she does portray the cost of stardom in one of her late novellas. In 'Gamla jungfrun' [The Old Servant], Olga, the daughter of a baroness, dreams of becoming a great opera star in London, another Kristina Nilsson. Her mother supports her dreams by selling off parcels of the family estate. In the meantime, Olga squanders the baroness's money to help a young English artist, with whom she is in love, but who throws her over when it becomes clear that she will never get the lucrative engagement at the opera they both covet. During a rare visit to her mother in the country, Olga visits an old servant of the family, a 90-year-old woman who devoted her entire life to serving Olga's family and who is now retired and living in a small cottage. The old servant has looked forward to the family's visit for months. But when she and Olga come face to face, the young woman is horrified by what she sees: a woman who has lived an uneventful life, with no worldly passions, only deprivation. The sight makes her resolve to return to London and the theatre, even though it may bankrupt her mother and the family:

> She had hung her burning hopes on the old woman's blessing, but not in the sense that the latter had understood; no, on this blessing from a ninety-year-old whose whole life had been one long deprivation, she built up once again her enchanting dreams of the happiness her whole being longed for; she refused again with disgust the resignation that once had seemed possible for her, and when the wagon drove up to the farm, she had already made such progress in her dreams that she believed that a letter would meet her with the notification that she had gotten the engagement after all and that *his* betrayal had only been apparent, a letter that once again opened the doors to the world of strong and lovely emotions which for her were life itself.
> ('Gamla jungfrun', 115–16)

For Olga and, perhaps, Leffler herself, by the late 1880s, the ideal world of Edvard Swartz's Hamlet had turned into a mirage.

Unlike Ester Larson and Leffler herself, Olga fails to distinguish between on- and offstage performances: she wants to transform her life into an exciting drama or opera in which she plays the starring role. Nor does she seem to realize how much work it takes to become an artist. Her illusions come at a very high cost, especially for others. For Ester Larson, in contrast, Shakespeare offers tragic roles that may allow her to establish herself as a serious artist in a world in which actresses are often viewed as attractive objects of the sexualized gaze. As we have seen, Ester also realizes that she is capable of performing a wide variety of roles onstage and off. One hopes that, like Ellen Terry, she managed to find roles that counteract the fixation on death, especially the death of female characters in Shakespeare's tragedies. The scene at the beginning of Act Two of *Skådespelerskan* certainly implies that she does not want to play the role of Juliet offstage, to immure herself in a marriage to a man with very fixed ideas about how his future wife should behave. Although in some respects *Skådespelerskan* anticipates the plot of Ibsen's *A Doll's House*, the latter play and *Ghosts* changed Leffler's view of contemporary drama and what it could and should do. Whereas in her 1870 letter to her cousin Amanda, she seems to believe that Shakespeare and *Hamlet* represent the pinnacle of western drama, after 1879 that place came to be occupied by Ibsen. Instead, Shakespeare came to represent the summit of English drama, an author whose work had the power to confer stardom on some actors. In her piece on theatre in London published on 3 May 1885, Leffler notes how Ellen Terry was able to reconcile stardom, Shakespeare and performance, appearing in *Much Ado About Nothing* as an agile, articulate and autonomous female character, the opposite, perhaps, of Juliet, who drinks her potion despite her doubts. Other writing from the early 1880s, most notably *Sanna kvinnor* and *En räddande engel*, suggest that a fixation on Juliet and the kind of ill-fated and irresistible passion she has come to represent in Western tradition, play into the hands of paedophiles and greedy and reckless husbands who have convinced their wives that 'true women' give all, especially their financial all, to their mates. By the end of the decade, Leffler had also become critical of the notion of stardom itself. If some performers – Leffler mentions Kristina Nilsson, but she might also have named Jenny Lind – are able to attain fame and fortune performing throughout the western world, others wreak havoc at home and abroad through their pursuit of unfounded dreams of stardom. Such dreams are as tragic as the fate of Juliet, but offstage rather than in the theatre. They represent a confusion of life and art that Ester Larson, Leffler and, one hopes, many of Leffler's readers, have learned to reject.

Notes

1. My discussion of Edvard Swartz and his predecessors follows Lagerroth, 'Den djärve traditionsbrytaren', 264–5.
2. Lagerroth, 'Den djärve traditionsbrytaren', 264. Unless otherwise noted, translations are my own.
3. Letter from Anne Charlotte Leffler to Amanda Leffler, dated 25 April 1870; all subsequent references to Leffler's writings within parentheses in the text. Spellings of Swartz's name vary. I have preserved Leffler's spelling in this letter, but otherwise used the spelling which appears in Lagerroth's account of Shakespeare performances in Lagerroth, 'Den djärve traditionsbrytaren'.
4. Leffler's wording follows Carl August Hagberg's translation (although she omits the line divisions): 'Men tänk, då jag är graflagd, om jag skulle uppvakna förrän Romeo har kommit att mig befria, hvilken gruflig tanke? Skall jag ej kväfvas då i detta hvalf!'
5. References to *En räddande engel* are to the unpaginated manuscript stored at the Royal Library, Stockholm.
6. On Rachel and Johanne Luise Heiberg, see Brownstein, *Tragic Muse*; Schrøder, *Dæmoni*. On Elise Hwasser, see Hennel, 'En stjärnskådespelerska' and 'Elise Hwasser'; also Ohlsson, 'Ebba Charlotte Elisa (Elise) Hwasser' and Hedberg, 'Elise Hvasser', especially 153.
7. See Hennel, *Mod och försakelse*.
8. Hélène Ohlsson notes that Hwasser played Desdemona in 1853, Ophelia in 1857 and Lady Macbeth in 1886. She does not provide dates for her performance or performances of Juliet.

9   In her biography of Ellen Terry, Nina Auerbach emphasizes the loss of freedom that the new respectability entailed. She comments on Ellen Terry's appearance at Drury Lane in 1906, on the fiftieth anniversary of her theatre career:

> The capering daughter of strolling players had grown into 'this uncrowned Queen of England'; once she had flung herself about in scanty costumes, but now she stood stiff and grand, swathed in heavy satin; long pointed sleeves pulled down her arms, a heavy train curled around her legs and enclosed them. White lace covered her bodice modestly. Like the jubilee itself, her regal dress embraced and enclosed her. As a child, she had played acrobatic boys; as a hoydenish young woman she had courted ostracism by becoming the mistress of the aesthetic architect, Edward William Godwin. Godwin had faded out of her life, leaving two brilliant, difficult children and a memory that became more perfect as it grew less clear. The wayward girl was herself a memory to the 59-year-old darling who had turned into a beloved epitome of British womanhood, smiling through a jubilee that commemorated a good woman more fulsomely than it applauded an actress. (Auerbach, *Ellen Terry*, 3–4).

Works cited

Auerbach, Nina, *Ellen Terry: A Player in Her Time* (New York, 1987).

Brownstein, Rachel M., *Tragic Muse: Rachel of the Comédie Française* (New York, 1993).

Hedberg, Frans, 'Elise Hvasser' [sic], in *Svenska skådespelare: karakteristiker och porträtter* (Stockholm, 1884), 148–61.

Hennel, Ingeborg Nordin, *Mod och försakelse: Livs- och yrkesbetingelser för Konglig Theaterns skådespelerskor 1813–1863* (Stockholm, 1997).

Hennel, Ingeborg Nordin, 'En stjärnskådespelerska', in Tomas Forser, ed., *Ny Svensk teaterhistoria*, ii: *1800-talets teater*, ed. Ulla-Britta Lagerroth and Ingeborg Nordin Hennel (Möklinta, 2007), 218–39.

Hennel, Ingeborg Nordin, 'Elise Hwasser – Ibsens första svenska favoritskådespelerska', in Roland Lysell, ed., *Ibsens kvinnor – tolkade av scenens kvinnor: Skådespelerskor och regissörer i möte med Ibsens kvinnoroller* (Lund, 2011), 17–75.

Lagerroth, Ulla-Britta. 'Den djärve traditionsbrytaren', in Tomas Forser, ed., *Ny Svensk teaterhistoria*, ii: *1800-talets teater*, ed. Ulla-Britta Lagerroth and Ingeborg Nordin Hennel (Möklinta, 2007), 261–76.

Leffler, Anne Charlotte, *Skådespelerskan: Dramatisk teckning i två akter*. In *Skådespelerskan; Dramatisk teckning i två akter; Under toffeln: komedi i två akter* (Stockholm, 1883), 1–77.

Leffler, Anne Charlotte, 'En bal i "societeten"', *Ur lifvet* [i] (Stockholm, 1882), 1–88.

Leffler, Anne Charlotte, *Sanna kvinnor: Skådespel i tre akter* (Stockholm, 1883).

Leffler, Anne Charlotte, *True Women: A Play in Three Acts* (London, 1890).

Leffler, Anne Charlotte, 'En räddande engel. Proverb i 1 akt', Royal Library, Stockholm, Mittag-Leffler collection.

Leffler, Anne Charlotte. 'Londonlif. Bref till Stockholms Dagblad af A. Ch. E-n', in *Stockholms Dagblad* (10 May 1884).

Leffler, Anne Charlotte, *Lösa blad från det moderna London*, in *Stockholms Dagblad* (25 January 1885–3 May 1885).

Leffler, Anne Charlotte, 'Gamla jungfrun', in *Ur lifvet*, iii, pt. 2 (Stockholm, 1889), 85–116.

Leffler Edgren, Anne Charlotte, *True Women*, trans. Anne Charlotte Hanes Harvey, in Katherine E. Kelly, ed., *Modern Drama by Women, 1880s–1930s: An International Anthology* (London, 1996), 17–43.

Ohlsson, Hélène, 'Ebba Charlotte Elisa (Elise) Hwasser', in *Svenskt kvinnobiografiskt lexikon*. Available at: www.skbl.se/sv/artikel/EliseHwasser, accessed 28 March 2021.

Schrøder, Vibeke, *Dæmoni og dannelse: Johanne Luise Heiberg* (2nd edn, Copenhagen, 2001).

Shakespeare, William, *Romeo and Juliet*, ed. René Weis, The Arden Shakespeare (London, 2015).

9

Knut Hamsun's criticism of Shakespeare

Martin Humpál

Knut Hamsun (1859–1952) is often regarded as Norway's greatest prose writer and many have claimed that, after Henrik Ibsen, no other Norwegian writer has had a greater influence on world literature. It might therefore be of interest to know what a writer of such stature has to say about other authors of high international recognition, including Shakespeare. Those who expect Hamsun to have appreciated the qualities of Shakespeare's plays might easily be disappointed. Hamsun's pronouncements about Shakespeare are mostly critical and it is a criticism of a relatively crude, perhaps even primitive, kind:

> Look at literature to date!
> An endless rigmarole of how boy meets girl! Over and over again. But all worked out in whole numbers! Dear God, we know these things in general terms. Shakespeare has them

---

Work on this chapter was supported by the European Regional Development Fund project 'Creativity and Adaptability as Conditions of the Success of Europe in an Interrelated World' (reg no: CZ.02.1.01/0.0/0.0/16_019/0000734).

all collected, but in big bold numbers which even every cobbler and his wife can accept and respond to. The play of his emotions is all exaggeration and sheer obviousness, all as plain as a pikestaff.[1]

However, this is certainly neither the first nor the last time that a writer of enormous literary talent uses strong words to attack Shakespeare's prominence. In fact, Hamsun is in 'good company' in this regard: literary giants such as Tolstoy and George Bernard Shaw – roughly Hamsun's contemporaries – are among those who employed very harsh vocabulary to reject Shakespeare's works, as I will discuss below.

Despite their crudeness and superficiality, Hamsun's statements constitute an interesting case of Shakespeare reception from around the year 1890 when a significant number of Scandinavian writers turned against the then dominant realist and naturalist literature and began to look for radically new ways of representing the world. Hamsun was one of the very first – and one of the most innovative – of these authors who were more interested in literature that focused on the inner life of individual human beings rather than on society as a whole. This type of literature, which flourished in the 1890s, has acquired various names in literary scholarship, for example Symbolism, Neo-Romanticism and Modernism. For the purposes of this chapter it is not important to discuss which of such terms best fits that literary bent. It is sufficient to state that Hamsun's novels from the early 1890s, especially *Sult* (1890, *Hunger*) and *Mysterier* (1892, *Mysteries*), are nowadays often regarded as examples of early Modernism.[2] The majority of Hamsun's statements on Shakespeare that we know of come from about the same time: they are to be found in the essays and lectures he wrote around 1890. I will attempt to show that, despite their problematic value as arguments, most of these statements about Shakespeare are in accord with the view of literature's function that Hamsun held at that time and can therefore be understood in direct relation to his early modernist literary programme and to his novels of the 1890s.

Hamsun's first statements on Shakespeare

Hamsun spent almost four years in the United States in the 1880s, and on his return to Europe wrote a book of essays called *Fra det moderne Amerikas Aandsliv* (1889, *The Cultural Life of Modern America*). This book is permeated with anti-American sentiment, although Hamsun does have several positive things to say about the United States. Nonetheless, later the author himself came to dislike this text to such an extent that he refused to allow it to be reprinted in his lifetime, not even including it in his *Samlede verker* [Collected Works].[3] In any event, it is in this book that one finds Hamsun's first discussions of Shakespeare. In the chapter 'Dramatic Art' Hamsun expresses, among other things, his opinion as to why Shakespeare is staged so frequently in the United States. The three reasons he gives quite clearly reveal that he does not consider Shakespeare to be as great a playwright as many others do: '[F]irst, because he is the grand old master who is performed everywhere under the sun; second, because he is an antique, since his writings originated prior to 1700; and, third, because in America he is considered half-American, that is, a national possession.'[4] Thus, it seems that Hamsun excludes the possibility that the ubiquitous presence of Shakespeare's plays on American stages has to do with the quality of the dramatist's works. Hamsun devotes a whole paragraph to explaining why Shakespeare is outdated:

> Shakespeare is the only dramatist whose works ... the Americans attempt to produce in toto. The reason the Yankees make this exception for Shakespeare can be explained in a few words. Shakespeare is the universal genius, the grand old master. There is a brutal simplification in Shakespeare's depiction of human emotions that makes them quite different from our own: his portrayals of love, wrath, desperation, and merriment fail to come off from sheer violence. We

recognize these uncompromising emotions without shading or nuance as belonging to a bygone age when men still frothed at the mouth – consequently Shakespeare is not a modern psychologist. ... There is too little complexity in his depiction of the emotions which, without pause for accident or contradiction, head straight for the abyss of extremes. Hamlet's psychology is an oasis, but there are desolate spots in that oasis. Shakespeare's plays are again just as simple, just as uncomplicated as the emotions he portrays; they are very often naive in comparison with the work of modern dramatists. The most marvellous things happen in *Othello*, for example, simply because a handkerchief falls on the floor. Shakespeare is not a modern dramatist, but a dramatist he will remain until the end of time.[5]

In this assessment Hamsun anticipates what he will develop in greater detail in what one must consider the main repository of his statements on Shakespeare: his lectures from 1891. Therefore I will not yet comment on the passage that I have just quoted. I will return to it in my discussion of Hamsun's literary programme and its relation to his negative views of Shakespeare.

Hamsun's lectures on literature from 1891

In 1890 Hamsun published his novel *Hunger*, which some consider to be the author's best work and which is certainly Hamsun's most influential work internationally. This essentially plotless text portrays the life of a young starving writer in Christiania (today's Oslo) who struggles to survive and make a literary breakthrough. By completely disregarding contemporary social issues, the novel radically challenged the realist and naturalist Norwegian literature of its time and, by employing innovative narrative techniques to focus intensively on the subjective workings of the protagonist's mind, the text anticipated many later modernist works. Despite its rather unconventional nature, *Hunger* was received quite well. Nonetheless, the author was not completely satisfied, because he felt that his novel was misunderstood by some critics and he was still overshadowed by some of the more established and internationally known Norwegian authors. Hamsun craved greater recognition of what he was trying to achieve in literature; therefore he set out on a lecture tour in 1891. He visited 12 Norwegian towns in which he gave three lectures called 'Norsk Literatur' [Norwegian Literature], 'Psykologisk Literatur' [Psychological Literature] and 'Modeliteratur' [Fashionable Literature]. Today these lectures – although they were not published until 1960 – can be read as a proto-modernist manifesto because, at the time, they promoted several new literary ideas and approaches that much later came to be called modernist. They constitute Hamsun's literary programme, as it materialized in the author's early novels such as *Hunger* (1890), *Mysteries* (1892) and *Pan* (1894).

In view of these lectures, Hamsun seems to have two goals which are, in fact, two sides of the same coin. First, he wants to convince the audience that current Norwegian literature is of poor quality; it is behind the times, it is not modern enough. His harsh criticism is directed at some of the most revered contemporary Norwegian writers of his time, mainly those that are sometimes called 'the Four Great' ('de fire store'): Henrik Ibsen, Bjørnstjerne Bjørnson, Alexander Kielland and Jonas Lie. Second, Hamsun wants to promote a new type of literature he calls 'psychological literature' which, according to his criteria, no contemporary Norwegian author writes. The underlying message of the lectures is obvious: it is only Hamsun (and perhaps some younger writers) who will be capable of writing genuine psychological literature

One of Hamsun's main arguments concerns the concept of a literary character and this is where Shakespeare enters the picture. Hamsun complains that contemporary Norwegian literature only produces one-dimensional characters; he sees one of the reasons in the naturalist theories of 'dominant disposition' ['den herskende Evne'].⁶ However, he also finds characters of single dimension in Shakespeare's works, among others:

> This conception of the human being as 'stock character' has to a great extent and throughout the ages dominated theatre. Molière's miser is nothing but a miser. Othello in Shakespeare is nothing but jealous, Iago is nothing but a villain. ... A play must always be lucid and easy to follow both from the front and the rear stalls; thus, a personage which does not have the necessary clarity and lucidity will simply fall through. But a personage which has clarity is, once more, a stock character and a type.⁷

Hamsun has nothing but words of contempt for those contemporary writers who give each of their characters a certain distinctive feature or a set of features which all point in one direction, i.e, they contribute to illuminate one single trait that the character is supposed to represent:

> Now, this is and will continue to be nothing but an external distinctive mark and has nothing to do with psychology. As far as the use of such naive instruments is concerned, we have not progressed much beyond Molière and Shakespeare. There is no doubt that in Shakespeare's time people were less complex and less intricate than they are nowadays; modern life has *influenced*, *changed* and *refined* the human being, our brains work feverishly and our nerves are in a bleeding state, so to speak. And if people have become more complicated, literature should become so, as well. Shakespeare's people are people from the days of yore, they do not speak with contemporary voices, their emotions have no middle tones; as for strength, they are either strong or weak, as for the heart, they are either black or white, there are no nuances, they rage. In our days there appear phenomena of all sorts that were unknown in Shakespeare's time; suicides are on the rise, and even in a country such as England the cases

of mental diseases more than doubled during the last twenty years; the use of stimulants is increasing, electricity rushes feverishly through all our actions. The general nervousness has permeated our innermost being and coloured our entire mental life. It manifests itself in the current French spiritism and the mystical novel, it manifests itself in the new English theosophy, it leaves its imprint even on such absurd phenomena as philatelism, peculiar insane motions in the heart and mind, delicate, disharmonious stirrings, the soul in a vague and indefinite distress. Metaphysics, politics and morality have changed since Shakespeare's time, man has entered the pace of modern nerve life and thinks and feels and imagines differently than back then.[8]

It seems that, for Hamsun, only literature that reflects modernity in the present moment is of any value.[9] He cannot, however, dismiss the fact that a great majority of contemporary people do enjoy Shakespeare, so he has a few words to say about this as well. First, he repeats his claim from *The Cultural Life of Modern America* that Shakespeare's popularity is, to a great degree, based on the fact that he has become an authority, he then admits that there is, after all, something enjoyable about Shakespeare, but he drives the point home regarding the idea of stock characters:

> But now one might ask: if contemporary people are really different from Shakespeare's, how can it be, then, that people who live today still enjoy Shakespeare's works, how can they understand it and be moved by it? … The main reason is that Shakespeare's personages are types and stock characters, and as such each of them is set in motion by one dominant disposition, one essential human emotion which will never become too old, but will always be known to humans; *those common thoughts, ideas and emotions will never fall out of use*: love, anger, fear, astonishment are everlasting forces that are always in the game. And therefore *we* enjoy Shakespeare – especially when he is being interpreted by an

actor who is a modern human being. However, this does not make Shakespeare a modern psychologist.[10]

Hamsun thus admits that Shakespeare has, in some sense, written timeless texts. However, this does not seem to be a mark of high quality for the Norwegian writer, because his view of literature has an elitist foundation: he puts Shakespeare together with every other author who write texts with typified characters; he admits that they are popular with a large audience, whereas real psychological literature can only reach a limited number of individuals. 'But,' adds Hamsun, 'such literature can have a greater value as revelation than many typified literary works taken together'.[11]

I would now like to consider all these quotations within the entire context of Hamsun's literary programme and in relation to his novelistic production of the 1890s. I certainly do not agree with Hamsun that Shakespeare is a bad psychologist, but some of Hamsun's statements about the English playwright become more understandable within his – admittedly narrow – definition of psychological literature. All Hamsun's statements from around 1890 indicate that he regarded the human being as an inexplicable mystery governed by the irrational forces of the unconscious. But how can one portray such a human being without creating just another character type? Both Hamsun's lectures and his early novels offer several possible answers. I will narrow them down to two general aspects of his aesthetics. I will call the first extensive, the other intensive.

The extensive aspect of Hamsun's aesthetics

According to the young Hamsun the human being is a plurality, a multiplicity of concrete details, all of which make the individual unique and all of which must therefore be depicted. In effect, Hamsun's early novels often become an endless stream of details, even what one might call 'streams of consciousness'. Here, it is difficult or impossible to distinguish between thematically relevant and irrelevant information.[12] Thus, the essential part of Hamsun's concept of psychological literature is redundancy, digression and superfluity. Characteristically, Hamsun's lectures are full of expressions such as 'delicate trifles' and 'the delicate secondary qualities'.[13]

However, such a concept of literature requires plenty of textual space. In other words, the novel may be an appropriate medium for this. Is drama just as appropriate? Hamsun's answer is a categorical no: 'It is my secret opinion that there has not yet lived a dramatist on this earth who has been a fine psychologist. Not as a dramatist';[14] 'a play is and will remain too narrow a framework in order to be able to contain more than only souls in contours'.[15] One might not agree with the categorical formulation of this view, yet obviously a play in some sense does have to be more economical than a novel, so there is, after all, something to Hamsun's arguments, especially if one tries to understand them in connection with what I have just described as the extensive aspect of his aesthetics. Nevertheless, Hamsun is deeply unfair to Shakespeare and drama, because he does not (want to) realize that other people may have other criteria for what 'good psychology' in a play is than those he himself uses.

Hamsun is unfair to Shakespeare in yet another sense. When judging the aesthetic quality of Shakespeare's works he more or less disregards some crucial genre differences between novel and drama, ignoring the fact that plays are usually meant to be performed. He is unable or unwilling to consider a theatre performance as something separate; he looks for (and does not find) quality exclusively in Shakespeare's texts.[16] In those few cases he does mention the difference between text and performance, he uses it only to disparage the English dramatist's plays in their written form: 'The effect of Shakespeare's plays is not as great when one reads them as when one sees them staged'.[17] In other words, Shakespeare's texts or, as Hamsun also puts it, 'Shakespeare books'[18] are not good *literature*.

At this point it is necessary to mention that Hamsun himself wrote both novels, novellas, short stories, poetry and drama. Perhaps significantly enough, both his international fame and his critical success mainly rest on his novels and novellas. In addition, Hamsun scholars tend to agree that, while his prose ranks highest and his poetry comes second, his plays are certainly the weakest part of his literary output: they have rarely been staged in Norway and even less so abroad, with the exception of Germany and Russia.[19] Evidently, Hamsun was not a gifted playwright. In contrast, the strength of his talent came to thrive naturally in longer prose, where he was faced with fewer formal hindrances: in prose he was able to give free rein to his penchant for streams of 'delicate trifles', digressions and multiple contradictions.[20]

The intensive aspect of Hamsun's aesthetics

By the intensive aspect I mean the fact that Hamsun clearly conceives of the human mind as something full of internal contradictions and as something that is constantly changing. In his lectures he says: 'I want "contradictions" within the human soul to be seen as downright natural, and I dream of a literature filled with people in whom inconsistency is literally the main characteristic – not the only characteristic, not the dominant characteristic, but a very prominent and a very decisive one.'[21] Hamsun succeeds quite well in implementing this intention, especially in his novels *Hunger* and *Mysteries*. Can one see any of Shakespeare's characters in the same way? It may be a matter of dispute, but I think one can safely say that Shakespeare never goes so far in the internal make-up of his characters. Some of Shakespeare's characters *are* certainly inconsistent and internally contradictory, but hardly to the same degree as some of the characters of Hamsun's early novels. If I should choose one word to describe the main element of Hamsun's programme of psychological literature, it would be the word 'irrationality'. Perhaps, then, the main source of Hamsun's criticism of Shakespeare might become even clearer: Shakespeare does portray irrationality in human behaviour, but it does not seem to play such an excessive role as in Hamsun's aesthetic world. Once again, then, Hamsun may be unjust to Shakespeare, but within the specific sphere of what I call the 'intensive' aspect of his aesthetics, his objections to Shakespeare are somewhat understandable.

Hamsun almost never gives concrete examples from Shakespeare's plays when he criticizes them, he usually only speaks of the English playwright's works and characters in general terms. Yet one of the exceptions is quite telling: Hamsun admits that the character of Hamlet is much better than other characters in Shakespeare's plays. As I have already quoted above, the Norwegian writer claims: 'There is too little complexity in [Shakespeare's] depiction of the emotions which, without pause for accident or contradiction, head straight for the abyss of extremes. Hamlet's psychology is an oasis'. The strong image of an oasis within what otherwise is a desert clearly reveals that Hamlet is quite to Hamsun's liking. This is not surprising, since Hamlet is certainly one of the most, if not *the* most, inconsistent and self-contradictory, of Shakespeare's characters. In other words, Hamsun likes the psychology of Hamlet because, to some degree, it corresponds with his own idea of what good psychology in literature means.

For the very same reasons, Shakespeare's *Hamlet* has been criticized by many writers, critics and other intellectuals over the centuries. In this regard I will mention Leo Tolstoy as one of the more recent and obvious examples. Tolstoy is one of the best-known detractors of Shakespeare. He even went so far as to write an entire book to condemn the English playwright: *On Shakespeare and on Drama* (1909). His statements are very harsh, to the point that one can indeed speak of his 'hatred' or 'extreme' dislike of Shakespeare.[22] Tolstoy openly called the English dramatist 'my enemy'[23] and he explained why he wrote a book about him as follows: 'I want to prove that Shakespeare is not only not a great writer, but a terrible fraud and poor stuff.'[24] Tolstoy had several reasons for his hostility to Shakespeare and it is not necessary to mention all of them here. I will, however, point out one that is relevant for his discussion of Shakespeare's characters: 'a truly naive demand for literal verisimilitude and realism',[25] which was, among other things, related to Tolstoy's reliance on the aesthetic criteria of French neo-classicist art and literature. Gibian gives the following summary of Tolstoy's statements on Hamlet, including some quotes from the Russian writer's text:

> Hamlet ... is utterly inexplicable. His actions and words are entirely inconsistent and unmotivated; there is 'therefore no possibility of attributing any character to him'. Critics who praise the character of Hamlet merely show their eagerness by hook or by crook to find beauties in an 'obvious crying failure ... [I]t is clear as day that Shakespeare did not succeed and did not wish to give any character to Hamlet, did not even understand that this was necessary'.[26]

In a similar way, Tolstoy complains in January 1896 in a letter to N. N. Strachov:

> What [a] coarse, immoral, mean, and senseless work *Hamlet* is. ... The author was so occupied with effects that he didn't take the trouble to give the main character any character, and all thought that this is a brilliant portrayal of a characterless man. Never had I understood with such clarity all the inability of the mob to judge, and how it can deceive itself.[27]

Thus, what Tolstoy considers to be unforgivable flaws, Hamsun sees as a mark of quality in *Hamlet*. 'Inconsistent and unmotivated' actions and words? 'No possibility of attributing any character' to the protagonist? Yes, indeed, that is exactly what the Norwegian writer tries to achieve when he creates the main characters in novels such as *Hunger*, *Mysteries* and *Pan*.

However, one must not forget that the 'oasis' Hamsun finds in *Hamlet*, is still an exception in his general view of the English playwright. Otherwise he regards the psychology of Shakespeare's characters as without contradictions and inconsistencies. Many critics have nonetheless found these phenomena in Shakespeare's plays and, unlike Tolstoy and similarly minded critics, have also regarded them as marks of quality. For example, Robert Bridges does not consider contradictions in Shakespeare as flaws[28] and claims that, 'in order to attain the surprising, [Shakespeare] will risk, or even sacrifice, the logical and consistent'.[29] Similarly, John Palmer claims the following:

> Shakespeare can ... exhibit [his characters], if he chooses, behaving as men and women do, at odds with themselves, betraying inconsistencies and contradictions which no other dramatist has dared to permit in an equal degree. ... Commentators on Shakespeare are puzzled by such inconsistencies and some critics have egregiously discovered them to be faults. But in no respect is Shakespeare's genius more manifest than in allowing his characters to act in ways which, at first sight and to the strictly logical mind, seem at variance with their essential qualities.[30]

Since this view is far from uncommon, one may once more conclude that Hamsun is being unfair to Shakespeare. Yet if other readers, being either detractors such as Tolstoy, or defenders such as Palmer, have noticed the inconsistencies and contradictions in Shakespeare's works, why is it that Hamsun has not? Perhaps the answer is easier than one may think: there is no evidence that Hamsun was an avid Shakespeare reader or theatregoer in the years before he began to mention the English dramatist in his texts; one may therefore wonder how much Shakespeare Hamsun had actually read or seen performed.[31]

Conclusion

To conclude, I would like to answer a question that might naturally occur to a reader of this chapter: if Hamsun's main concern was prose and if he was convinced that the genre of drama was inferior to the genre of the novel, why did he devote so many paragraphs to Shakespeare in his literary programme? Would it not be enough just to defame other novelists or prose writers? Could he not leave playwrights out of his criticism?

I can provide two possible answers. First, at the time when Hamsun wrote his depreciatory remarks on Shakespeare, people were much more prone to consider plays as *literature* than they are nowadays. Even Ibsen's realist dramas of contemporary life were often seen as 'literary dramas'.[32] In this regard Hamsun might relatively naturally have considered the English playwright as part of the same 'field' that he was attacking.

The second possible answer is not unrelated to the first, but is, in a way, even more relevant. The young Hamsun was a very conceited writer who considered himself to be a genius and who, in my opinion, consciously employed various strategies to convince the reading public of this fact.[33] In his struggle for recognition Hamsun seems to have felt the need to publicly attack geniuses who might otherwise overshadow him, be it Ibsen or Shakespeare.[34]

In this particular regard, Hamsun reminds us of another writer of his generation, George Bernard Shaw. The latter is famous for his many outrageous claims about the low quality of Shakespeare's plays; indeed, a number of critics have pointed out that Shaw's shocking dismissals of the Bard of Avon were, to a large degree, a conscious strategy by which Shaw wanted to create space for his own plays (and for Ibsen) in Britain: 'Shaw had fierce competition. English theaters neglected him but produced "Shakespear," as Shaw spelled it. To gain a name for himself, Shaw attacked Shakespeare.'[35] Here is one of the well-known examples of Shaw's extreme statements: 'With the single exception of Homer, there is no eminent writer, not even

Sir Walter Scott, whom I can despise so entirely as I despise Shakespear [sic] when I measure my mind against his.'[36] This and similar pronouncements by Shaw were so scandalous in some circles that Silverman pointed out in 1957 that '[a]s a critic of Shakespeare, Bernard Shaw has been practically ignored by the summaries and surveys of Shakespeare criticism'.[37] Not all of Shaw's remarks on Shakespeare are dismissive, though: several scholars have pointed out that Shaw also has a number of good things to say about the playwright. However, on the whole, 'Shaw's appraisal of Shakespeare, though it includes much praise, strikes the reader as being primarily negative'.[38]

Hamsun and Shaw are dissimilar in many ways and so are their reasons for denigrating Shakespeare. In Shaw's opinion, art and literature must have a moral purpose: works of art are supposed to improve people and society; accordingly, Shaw complains that, in his works, Shakespeare allegedly accepted the morality of his times, rather than criticizing it.[39] Nothing could be further from Hamsun's view of literature, at least at the time when he wrote his remarks on Shakespeare: around 1890, the Norwegian writer criticized all moralist literature. Yet, while Hamsun's and Shaw's views of Shakespeare are based on different assumptions about the role of art and literature in society, the two writers share the same strategy: to use scandalous statements about Shakespeare to shake contemporary readers and gain their own place in the sun. In this regard, the following statement about Shaw can easily be applied to Hamsun: 'Shaw's criticism tells less about Shakespeare and Ibsen than about Shaw. ... The criticism is less "Shakespeare as seen by Shaw" than "Shaw about Shaw via Shakespeare"'.[40] Similarly, Hamsun's iconoclastic statements on Shakespeare reveal more about Hamsun and his view of art and literature than about Shakespeare's plays. In spite of, or perhaps because of that, Hamsun's criticism constitutes an intriguing view of Shakespeare's reception in Scandinavia. After all, Lutz may be right when he states: 'Great writers are worth listening to even when their criticism is erratic, for it shows something about themselves.'[41]

Notes

1. From a letter to Yngvar Laws, written probably in August–November 1888, in Hamsun, *Selected Letters*, 88.
2. See, e.g., Humpál, *The Roots of Modernist Narrative*; Kittang, *Luft, vind, ingenting*; and Vassenden, 'En Ildebrand i en Boglade'.
3. See, e.g., Ferguson, *Enigma*, 105, 239 and Morgridge, 'Editor's Introduction', xxiv, xxx. In a letter to Albert Langen from 25 April 1914, Hamsun called the book 'too juvenile' and 'very childish' (Letter 1258, in *Knut Hamsuns brev 1908–1914*, 520, my translation). Besides such general words of dismissal, however, he did not reveal any concrete reasons, so one can only speculate about them. At a general level, it seems quite likely that he was aware of the fact that the text contains too many exaggerated anti-American claims, including one of the book's concluding statements that Americans simply have no culture.
4. Hamsun, *The Cultural Life of Modern America*, 100.
5. Hamsun, *The Cultural Life of Modern America*, 99.
6. Hamsun, *Paa Turné*, 31. Hamsun's lectures from 1891 were published in Norwegian as *Paa Turné* for the first time in 1960. To my knowledge, they have never been officially translated into English. All translations of passages from *Paa Turné* in this chapter are therefore mine.
7. Hamsun, *Paa Turné*, 31.
8. Hamsun, *Paa Turné*, 46–7, emphasis in original.
9. In this Hamsun fits perfectly into the modernist paradigm. Many theorists of modernism have described the eminent focus on the present as a characteristic modernist idea and they usually trace it back to Charles Baudelaire and his famous essay 'The Painter of Modern Life' (1863). For example, in his book *Five Faces of Modernity*, Matei Calinescu defines Modernism as 'an aesthetics of transitoriness' (3) and points out that Baudelaire, in his essay, conceives of an aesthetic modernity as 'the present in its 'presentness,' in its purely instantaneous quality' (49). Similarly, in *Modernisms: A*

Literary Guide, Peter Nicholls finds in Baudelaire's essay a paramount emphasis on 'the flux and movement of life in the present' (5).

10 Hamsun, *Paa Turné*, 47–8, emphasis in original.
11 Hamsun, *Paa Turné*, 48.
12 For the phenomenon of stream of consciousness in Hamsun's novels, see, e.g., Humpál, *The Roots of Modernist Narrative*, and Jörg Pottbeckers, *Stumme Sprache*.
13 Hamsun, *Paa Turné*, 67, 83.
14 Hamsun, *Paa Turné*, 34.
15 Hamsun, *Paa Turné*, 32.
16 Notwithstanding the fact that Hamsun and Tolstoy criticized Shakespeare for quite different reasons, it is interesting that Tolstoy, too, sometimes judged Shakespeare's plays as literary texts per se, rather than texts to be performed. See, e.g., Gibian, *Tolstoj and Shakespeare*, 33–7.
17 Hamsun, *Paa Turné*, 47.
18 Hamsun, *Paa Turné*, 47.
19 For an assessment of Hamsun's dramas and their reception history, see, e.g., Baumgartner, *Den modernistiske Hamsun*, 78–9, Ferguson, *Enigma*, 165–6 and Johannessen, 'Dramatisk raptus'.
20 A letter to his friends Bolette and Ole Johan Larsen from 9 July 1895 illustrates this very well. In this letter Hamsun bemoans the fact that he had to omit a great deal of 'nice' material that should have been included in his latest play. He then complains in general terms: 'And that's what drama is about: to leave out all the nice things.' Letter 382, in *Knut Hamsuns brev 1879–1895*, 473, my translation. Hamsun uses similar formulations in his 1899 lecture '[Digterliv]' where he mentions Shakespeare in his discussion of Ibsen: 'Even as a literary form, the dramatic literary form is deficient, inasmuch as one has to express oneself in it only through direct speech, one deprives oneself of description, one deprives oneself of the adjective. Am I of the opinion, then, that Shakespeare, too, was deficient? My answer is an absolute yes.' Hamsun, '[Digterliv]', 106, my translation.
21 Hamsun, *Paa Turné*, 63.

22　Gibian, *Tolstoj and Shakespeare*, 9–10.
23　Gibian, *Tolstoj and Shakespeare*, 21.
24　Qtd. in Gibian, *Tolstoj and Shakespeare*, 29.
25　Gibian, *Tolstoj and Shakespeare*, 43–4.
26　Gibian, *Tolstoj and Shakespeare*, 36.
27　Qtd. in Gibian, *Tolstoj and Shakespeare*, 22.
28　Bridges, 'On the Influence of the Audience', 72.
29　Bridges, 'On the Influence of the Audience', 69.
30　Palmer, *Political Characters of Shakespeare*, 34–5.
31　The important Norwegian writer Arne Garborg (1851–1924) was one of Hamsun's contemporaries who implied that Hamsun's knowledge of Shakespeare was poor. In an article published on 2 April 1893 in the newspaper *Dagbladet*, Garborg criticizes Hamsun's public lectures and suggests that he 'would do much better to set about humbly *studying* Shakespeare, Goethe etc., rather than to run around like a hell of a guy and get people to laugh at them'. Garborg, 'Svært til kar', 55, orig emphasis, my translation.
32　In fact, in countries such as Germany, France and Britain Ibsen's realist plays led to a revival of the literary drama and contributed to the increased commercial viability of selling printed plays. See Fulsås and Rem, *Ibsen, Scandinavia and the Making of a World Drama*, 148–59, 229–36.
33　The following statement, made by the Norwegian critic Kristofer Randers in 1892, can serve as an example of how some of Hamsun's contemporaries saw him: 'Hamsun takes up a singular position in our literature. Oppositional to the point of fanaticism, with a morbid need for independence and an urge to contradict which often takes him into the wildest paradoxes, he stands alone and independent from the ruling tastes and fashions of literature and politics here at home. As a human he is a radical aristocrat, as an artist, temperamental and individualistic in the extreme. What he hates is authority in whichever character – received truths, bourgeois decency, schoolmasters' doctrinarism and the judgement of the masses.' Translated and quoted by Peter Sjølyst-Jackson in *Troubling Legacies*, 37.

34 The fact that Hamsun's lectures were meant to advertise his own writing is indirectly revealed in the following passage from his lecture 'Psykologisk Literatur': 'There is a writer here at home who recently published a book which was different from all other Norwegian books, among other reasons because it was about a temperamental person. The book was not good, it did not sell. However, two months after it had come out the writer had received half a hundred thank-you letters from various Norwegian women and men, unknown people that he had never met before, as well as from well-known people, including a couple of celebrities. I have this from the writer himself.' Hamsun, *Paa Turné*, 64–5. It is easy to agree with the editor of *Paa Turné*, Tore Hamsun, who added the following footnote to the passage I have just cited: 'This quite certainly concerns Hamsun's own book, *Hunger*' (*Paa Turné*, 64).

35 Lutz, *Pitchman's Melody*, 13. See, e.g., P. A. W. Collins who in his article 'Shaw on Shakespeare' speaks of Shaw's 'calculated blasphemies about Shakespeare' (1), and Robert B. Pierce who writes in 'Bernard Shaw as Shakespeare Critic' that Shaw's 'attack on Shakespeare is a rhetorical extravagance justified by a strategic purpose' (118).

36 Qtd in Lutz, *Pitchman's Melody*, 101.

37 Silverman, 'Bernard Shaw's Shakespeare Criticism', 734.

38 Silverman, 'Bernard Shaw's Shakespeare Criticism', 735.

39 See, e.g., Lutz, *Pitchman's Melody*, 39, 43, 46, 59, 76–7, 85.

40 Lutz, *Pitchman's Melody*, 137.

41 Lutz, *Pitchman's Melody*, 139.

Works cited

Baumgartner, Walter, *Den modernistiske Hamsun: Medrivende og frastøtende*, trans. Helge Vold (Oslo, 1998).

Bridges, Robert, 'On the Influence of the Audience' [1907], in A. M. Eastman and G. B. Harrison, eds, *Shakespeare's Critics from Jonson to Auden: A Medley of Judgments* (Ann Arbor, 1964), 69–72.

Calinescu, Matei, *Five Faces of Modernity: Modernism, Avant-Garde, Decadence, Kitsch, Postmodernism* (Durham, NC, 1987).
Collins, P. A. W., 'Shaw on Shakespeare', *Shakespeare Quarterly*, 8/1 (1957), 1–13.
Ferguson, Robert, *Enigma: The Life of Knut Hamsun* (New York, 1987).
Fulsås, Narve and Tore Rem, *Ibsen, Scandinavia and the Making of a World Drama* (Cambridge, 2018).
Garborg, Arne, 'Svært til kar' [1893] in *Artiklar og essay 1891–1923* (Oslo, 2001), 53–5.
Gibian, George, *Tolstoj and Shakespeare* (The Hague, 1957).
Hamsun, Knut, *The Cultural Life of Modern America*, ed. and trans. Barbara Gordon Morgridge (Cambridge, MA, 1969).
Hamsun, Knut, '[Digterliv]', *Edda*, 90/2 (1990), 102–13.
Hamsun, Knut, *Knut Hamsuns brev 1879–1895*, ed. Harald S. Næss (Oslo, 1994).
Hamsun, Knut, *Knut Hamsuns brev 1908–1914*, ed. Harald S. Næss (Oslo, 1996).
Hamsun, Knut, *Paa Turné: Tre foredrag om litteratur av Knut Hamsun*, ed. Tore Hamsun (2nd edn, Oslo, 1971).
Hamsun, Knut, *Selected Letters*, i, 1879–1898, eds, Harald Næss and James McFarlane (Norwich, 1990).
Humpál, Martin, *The Roots of Modernist Narrative: Knut Hamsun's Novels* Hunger, Mysteries, *and* Pan (Oslo, 1998).
Johannessen, Oddbjørn, 'Dramatisk raptus', in Ståle Dingstad, ed., *Den litterære Hamsun* (Bergen, 2005), 55–75.
Kittang, Atle, *Luft, vind, ingenting: Hamsuns desillusjonsromanar frå* Sult *til* Ringen sluttet (2nd edn, Oslo, 1996).
Lutz, Jerry, *Pitchman's Melody: Shaw about 'Shakespear'* (Lewisburg, 1974).
Morgridge, Barbara Gordon, 'Editor's Introduction', in Knut Hamsun, *The Cultural Life of Modern America* (Cambridge, MA, 1969), ix–xxxiv.
Nicholls, Peter, *Modernisms: A Literary Guide* (Berkeley, 1995).
Palmer, John, *Political Characters of Shakespeare* (London, 1945).
Pierce, Robert B., 'Bernard Shaw as Shakespeare Critic', *SHAW: The Annual of Bernard Shaw Studies*, 31 (2011), 118–32.
Pottbeckers, Jörg, *Stumme Sprache: Innerer Monolog und erzählerischer Diskurs in Knut Hamsuns frühen Romanen im Kontext von Dostojewski, Schnitzler und Joyce* (Frankfurt am Main, 2008).

Silverman, Albert H., 'Bernard Shaw's Shakespeare Criticism', *PMLA*, 72/4 (1957), 722–36.
Sjølyst-Jackson, Peter, *Troubling Legacies: Migration, Modernism and Fascism in the Case of Knut Hamsun* (London, 2010).
Vassenden, Eirik, 'En Ildebrand i en Boglade: Modernisme og vitalisme i Hamsuns *Sult* og i *Sult*-resepsjonen', *Norsk litteraturvitenskapelig Tidsskrift*, 13/2 (2010), 101–15.

Afterword: Towards a regional methodology of culture

Alexa Alice Joubin

Working with German and French versions, eighteenth-century Nordic translators brought Shakespeare's texts and broader European contexts to bear on each other. While they privileged the tragedies, such as early Finnish versions of *Macbeth* and the first Danish translation of *Hamlet* by Johannes Boye in 1777, Englishness was but one of several components, alongside those from continental Europe, of these cultural transactions. Instead of reinforcing cultural hierarchy and the idea of unilinear transmission of cultures, the early translations created a web of inter-connections that empowered readers and audiences for whom English was a second language.

Since its first staging in Copenhagen in the early nineteenth century, *Hamlet* has both visceral and dramaturgical connections with Denmark thanks, in part, to the famed 'Hamlet's castle' (Kronborg) in Helsingør and to the Scandinavian legend *Amleth*. Nordic Shakespeares are also found in unexpected places. Finnish, Norwegian, Polish and English actors perform together in *Songs of Lear* (directed by Grzegorz Bral, 2016), a work by the Polish company Teatr Pieśń Kozła (meaning Song of the Goat). Nordic performances have also engaged with world events. Hundreds of balloons in *Lér Konungur* (directed by Benedict Andrews, 2010), the National Theatre of Iceland in Reykjavik's adaptation of *King Lear,* are reminiscent of those at American political conventions. With its characters milling around in conservative contemporary business attires, the production critiques neoliberal, free-market capitalism driven by corporate interests.

Nineteenth-century Nordic Shakespeare, the focus of this book, is defined by its rich diversity and has been recognized for its lasting influence on our understanding of Shakespeare. The nineteenth century was an era when Denmark, Finland, Iceland, Norway and Sweden redefined themselves as sovereign nation-states with distinct national literatures. It was also an era when these cultures negotiated their relationships to other European cultures, especially French classicism and German Romanticism. Nineteenth-century Swedish actor Hedvig Charlotte Raa-Winterhjelm, for example, astonishingly performed in three languages in four Nordic countries. The chapters in this volume invert the concept of 'global' Shakespeare by showing the interactions between forces from multiple centres of cultural production both within and beyond the Nordic countries. Nordic Shakespeares are neither part of the world Englishes cultural sphere nor cultures that are diametrically opposed to the Anglophone world.

The case studies in this volume share a penumbra even though they bear different cultural coordinates. When light is shed over an opaque object, it casts a shadow with a partially shaded outer region. Nineteenth-century Nordic Shakespeares form a penumbra of multiple cultural texts as they evoke discrete plot elements of Shakespeare and culturally-specific themes. Judith Buchanan theorizes that, in this manner, adaptations contain a 'textual penumbra', a body of extra-textual information closely associated with the adaptations that enrich their meaning.[1] An innocuous penumbra could be an awareness by the audience or reader of previous works by the artist. A more intrusive penumbra could be directors' statements on record or the significance of the venue.

We gain new insights on cultural history through the study of the intra-regional influence of Shakespeare across a geocultural area, such as the Nordic countries, rather than siloed, 'national' Shakespeares in individual countries. In this model of regional studies, there are no singular, unitary centres and peripheries in the cultural exchange, because the diffuse nature of disseminating ideas on varied but connected cultural terrains enables us to have a more comprehensive vision of claimed affinity with, indifference to, and resistance of, Shakespeare. Along with the Romantics, Søren Kierkegaard is well known for his admiration of Shakespeare. As James Newlin's chapter shows, the Danish philosopher ends up appropriating and using *King Lear* as a guiding force in his books *Either/Or* and *Stages on Life's Way*. Finnish writer Aleksis Kivi used Shakespeare as a model for vernacular theatre. In contrast, the 1920 Norwegian Nobel laureate for literature Knut Hamsun, like his contemporaries George Bernard Shaw and Leo Tolstoy, used harsh words to reject Shakespeare's aesthetic merits – an author (in Hamsun's view) who creates only typified characters that may be popular with the masses but are of little value. All these positivist and antithetical strands co-exist in Nordic reception histories of Shakespeare. Relational, cultural meanings emerge through negation of and negotiation with Shakespeare.

The first phase of the sustained study of Shakespeare and globalization unfolded over the past few decades, where national politics have been brought to bear on Shakespeare's afterlife.[2] The rise of global Shakespeares as a field was concomitant with the emergence of polity-driven historiography, both of which facilitated linear, synchronic narratives about cultures. The global and the national became politically expedient categories of difference. There is an historical reason why the global is imagined to be whatever the United States and the UK are not.[3] Since 1949, the United States and UK have been close military allies as NATO (North Atlantic Treaty Organization) partners, though their governments diverge on foreign policy and worldviews. Their political and cultural differences notwithstanding (which is captured aptly by Oscar Wilde: 'we have really everything in common with America nowadays, except, of course, language'), these two countries – with a combined population of 400 million – have collectively maintained the dominant role of Anglophone cultural production in the modern world.[4] This phenomenon has contributed to the tendency, in English-language scholarship, to assume that the global refers to the cultural realms beyond the United States and the UK.

The current, second phase of global studies is challenging fixed notions of cultural authenticity, drawing more attention to 'regional' Shakespeares.[5] Our current phase of the study of cultures is informed by non-linear, rhizomatic networks that blur the lines between central and peripheral locations of cultural production. The 'inescapable plurality' of centres and peripheries, as Nely Keinänen and Per Sivefors call it, moves the field beyond narrowly defined national Shakespeares. Nordic Shakespeares, as this volume reveals, developed within a history of mediated influences and Shakespeare has served as a foil for artists in media beyond theatre. In other words, this book enriches our understanding of Nordic cultures and Shakespeare by offering layered meanings of cultural dissemination, carefully dissecting the idea of Shakespeare's singularity.

This book, along with other recent works, examines the transnational cultural flows that go beyond the scope of geopolitical divisions of nation-states and cultural profiling. The multiplicity of the plural term global Shakespeares helps us push back against deceivingly harmonious images of Shakespeare's ubiquitous presence. This book has risen to meet the challenge of collation of empirical data across a geocultural sphere. Globalization is difficult to study empirically when 'evidence is far better organized on a national rather than cross-border basis'.[6] Focusing on incongruent layers of influence and difference, including Nordic, French, German and English sources, in the early dissemination of Shakespeare, this book contends that, in some cases, national boundaries were significant factors in the dissemination of Shakespeare and evolution of local cultures and, in other cases, the nation-state was not as useful as an organizing principle through which to understand Nordic Shakespeares and their cultural meanings. While at times the Nordic cultures had antithetical relations with one another, there was also significant cooperation that went beyond the nation-state.

A regional methodology with a transnational framework can identify shared and conflicting patterns of cultural dissemination. Regional data is widely available but difficult to classify; this book has organized and synthesized important sectors of Nordic histories to serve as a key method 'for disrupting nationalist and globalist paradigms', according to Aaron Nyerges and Thomas Adams.[7] From literary history to social sciences, including American studies, scholars have recently been calling for renewed attention to the region as a unit of knowledge. A regional methodology attends to intra-regional idiosyncrasies and connections by breaking down perceived, clear cultural boundaries between nation-states.

Notes

1   Buchanan, *Shakespeare on Film*, 10.
2   Kennedy, ed., *Foreign Shakespeare*.
3   Deb, 'The Rise of the Global Novelist'.
4   Wilde, *The Canterville Ghost*, 7.
5   Desmet, Iyengar and Jacobson, eds, *The Routledge Handbook*; Joubin, *Shakespeare and East Asia*; Della Gatta, *Latinx Shakespeares*.
6   Turner and Holton, 'Theories of Globalization', 5.
7   Nyerges and Adams, 'Introduction', 6. See also Pryse, 'Afterword'.

Works cited

Buchanan, Judith, *Shakespeare on Film* (Harlow, 2005).

Deb, Siddharta, 'The Rise of the Global Novelist', *New Republic*, 25 April, 2017. Available at: https://newrepublic.com/article/141676/rise-global-novelist-adam-kirsch-review, accessed 10 September, 2019.

Della Gatta, Carla, *Latinx Shakespeares: Staging U.S. Intracultural Theater* (Ann Arbor, 2022).

Desmet, Christy, Sujata Iyengar and Miriam Jacobson, eds, *The Routledge Handbook of Shakespeare and Global Appropriation* (New York, 2019).

Joubin, Alexa Alice, *Shakespeare and East Asia* (Oxford, 2021).

Kennedy, Dennis, ed., *Foreign Shakespeare: Contemporary Performance* (Cambridge, 1993).

Nyerges, Aaron and Thomas Adams, 'Introduction: Regionalizing American Studies Within and Beyond the Nation', *Australasian Journal of American Studies*, 36/2 (2017), 3–10.

Pryse, Marjorie, 'Afterword: Regional Modernism and Transnational Regionalism', *Modern Fiction Studies* 55/1 (2009), 189–92.

Turner, Bryan S. and Robert J. Holton, 'Theories of Globalization: Issues and Origins', in Bryan S. Turner and Robert J. Holton, eds, *The Routledge International Handbook of Globalization Studies* (2nd edn, New York, 2016).

Wilde, Oscar, *The Canterville Ghost* (Prime Classics, 2005).

APPENDIX:

A timeline of significant Shakespeare-related events in the Nordic countries before 1900

As the heading suggests, this timeline does not claim to be a complete register of all relevant events, but the editors hope it gives a picture of just how complex and dynamic the history of Shakespeare was during the period.

The editors are grateful to Leena Vahvelainen, who prepared the initial version of this timeline and to Kent Hägglund for his invaluable expertise on the Swedish context.

1696	In Sweden, first known owner of a Shakespeare play: Ambassador Peter Julius Coyet is said to have acquired the second folio while visiting England on a mission during the 1650s–1660s.
1735	In Sweden, a selection of Addison's essays appears in Swedish in *Den Engelske Spectator*, discussing Falstaff and Othello.
1742–1743	In Denmark, selections from Addison's *Spectator* published, with extracts from *Ham* and *MND* (in rhymed alexandrines), possibly the first words of Shakespeare in Danish.

1763	In Sweden, C. C. Gjörwell responds to Voltaire's 'Appel à toutes les nations' (1761), writing that the 'English nation's enthusiastic idea of Shakespeare resembles too much their otherwise violent nature'.
1762–1766	C. M. Wieland translates 22 plays from Shakespeare into German prose; Copenhagen resident Heinrich Wilhelm von Gerstenberg attacks the translation and defends Shakespeare.
1768	Christian VII of Denmark travels to London, meets David Garrick and sees *Richard III*.
1769	The Swedish clergyman, poet and travel writer Jacob Wallenberg sees *Ham* in London and reports in his *Sanfärdig resebeskrifning*.
1769	Johannes Ewald, a Danish poet, inspired by Shakespeare and Ossian, both of whom he probably read in Wieland's translations; in 1775, writes a historical drama in 11-syllable unrhymed iambic verse.
1775	In Denmark, J. J. Eschenburg's revision of Wieland's German translation makes a strong impression; Swedish clergyman Jacob Wallenberg, who in 1769 saw Garrick play Hamlet in London, finishes *Susanna*, a Biblical play influenced by *Oth*.
1776	In Sweden, *RJ* is performed by Seuerling's travelling company in Norrköping, likely the first Shakespeare performance in the Nordic countries; translated by Peter Lindahl, possibly from English, but may also have been influenced by Ducis's melodramatic version or, more likely, C. F. Weisse's German prose translation of 1768. This production travels widely, e.g. in Oulu, Finland in 1780, with Margaret Seuerling as Juliet, seen by Frans Michael Franzén.
1777	First Danish (prose) translation of Shakespeare appears, *Hamlet*, by Johannes Boye, a 21-year-old student. A review by Claus Fasting calls Shakespeare 'the most original genius, next to Homer and Ossian, that the world has known'.
1778	Jacob Wallenberg publishes his Biblical play *Susanna*, considered to be influenced by *Oth*.

1782	In Norway, first extract of Shakespeare published, from *AC* (3.2), in a student publication with a nationalist agenda.
1785	The Swede Peter Moberg sees *Mac* in Edinburgh.
1786	Swedish King Gustav III writes an opera libretto with Johan Henrik Kellgren (1757–1795), borrowing the plot and several scenes from *R3*, making him among the first writers to be influenced by Shakespeare in Sweden.
1787	In Sweden, first performance of *Ham*, in Gothenburg, for Gustav III's birthday, directed by Andreas Widerberg who also plays Hamlet.
early 1790s	In Denmark, prose translations of *Mac*, *Oth*, *AW*, *KL*, *Cym* and *MV* by Nils Rosenfeldt, a young lawyer; in Sweden, Carl Gustaf af Leopold, Shakespeare's 'greatest adversary', 'intentionally mistranslates' a scene from *R3*, perhaps inspired by Voltaire. Inspired by Shakespeare, Swedish-Finn Frans Michael Franzén writes on historical/mythological themes and experiments with iambic pentameter verse in Swedish.
1791	In Sweden, King's French troupe performs *Mac* (in Ducis's version).
1792	In Sweden, Eric Skjöldebrandt translates one of Hamlet's soliloquies into Swedish, part of an essay on the sublime in literature; German-language *Ham* in Odense, Denmark.
1794	Hans Wilhelm Riber translates Nahum Tate's stage version of *KL* for the Danish Royal Theatre.
1795	Frans Michael Franzén travels to London, sees Kemble's *Ham* and *Mac* the latter he finds disappointing.
1797	August Wilhelm Schlegel's writings on Shakespeare, e.g. essay on *RJ*, influential in the Nordic countries.
early 1800s	Arrival of Romanticism to Denmark and Sweden, inspired by Shakespeare and Ossian, looking back to Nordic history for inspiration.

1801	First Battle of Copenhagen: Danish-Norwegian fleet defeated by Admiral Nelson, in order to prevent a Franco-Danish alliance. Levin Christian Sander and Knud Lyhne Rahbek translate *Mac* into Danish; in Sweden, Peter Moberg includes a translation of Hamlet's 'To be' speech in a primer.
1802	*Oth* performed in Stockholm by a French company.
1803	Peter Foersom, a Danish actor and linguist, translates *JC* and offers it to theatres, but is declined.
1805	In Denmark, the early Romanticist Adam Oehlenschläger writes *Aladdin*, a play influenced by *Tem* and *MND* and called 'the most lifelike Shakespeare imitation which Danish literature possesses'.
1807–1818	Foersom continues to translate Shakespeare, producing Danish translations of *Ham, KL, RJ, R2, 1 and 2H4, H5,* and *1H6 and 2H6*, and a Schiller-influenced *Mac*. The emphasis on tragedies and histories reflects the influence of Romanticism. Foersom's translations are based on English editions by George Steevens and Edmond Malone and use blank verse.
1807	Second Battle of Copenhagen, British bombardment of Copenhagen creates strong anti-English feelings, leading Denmark-Norway to side with Napoleon, albeit with much reduced forces; Oehlenschläger in his *Nordiske Digte* [Nordic Poems] hails Shakespeare as 'a model for the new Danish poetry'.
1808	Quoting from *R2*, Foersom attacks the English: 'That England that was wont to conquer others/ Hath made a shameful conquest of itself' (2.1.65–6).

1808–1809	The Finnish war, fought between Sweden and the Russian Empire, results in the loss of Finnish territories for Sweden and Finland's becoming an autonomous Grand Duchy in the Russian Empire; Swedish king Gustav IV Adolf ousted, replaced by Jean-Baptiste (Karl Johan) Bernadotte, a French officer in the Napoleonic wars.
1809–1810	The Swede Erik Gustaf Geijer spends almost a year in England, sees John Philip Kemble's *Ham*, will later translate *Mac*.
1811	Foersom publishes an essay, *Læsning for Dyrkere og Yndere af Skuespilkunsten* [Reading for Worshippers and Lovers of the Art of Acting] which contains an account of theatrical practice on the English stage.
1813	First performance of Shakespeare in Denmark-Norway, *Ham* starring Foersom, directed by Frederik Schwarz, at the Royal Danish Theatre in Copenhagen, cuts all references to Norway; first complete published translation of a Shakespeare play appears in Swedish, *Mac* by Erik Gustaf Geijer, translated from English, later becomes a source for the Finnish Fredrik Lagervall's *Ruunulinna* (1834).
1814	As part of the Treaty of Kiel, Denmark surrenders Norway to the king of Sweden, in exchange for Swedish Pomerania and Rügen, new Norwegian constitution one of the most democratic in Europe.
1815	In Sweden, a musical version of *RJ* is produced in Stockholm, translated from French by Carl Gustaf Nordforss, not well received.
1816	Oehlenschläger translates *MND* into Danish, some of the Falstaff scenes in Foersom's translation are performed in a recital in Copenhagen, Foersom adapts Schiller's stage version of *Mac* into Danish; *KL* proves a box-office disaster at the Royal Theatre, Copenhagen; Georg Scheutz translates *JC* into Swedish.

1817	*Mac* performed, unsuccessfully, for the first time in Denmark; a German translation of *Ham* is advertised in a bookstore in the Finnish city of Turku, demonstrating the beginnings of a reading public for Shakespeare; first known reference to Shakespeare in Iceland, a letter by the poet Bjarni Thorarensen to Grímur Jónsson Thorkelin, who writes (in English): 'There is something rotten in the state of Southern Amt'; *Ham* is performed in the Swedish provinces by touring company under the direction of Fredrik Wilhelm Ståhlberg.
1818–1825	P. F. Wulff, a captain in the navy, continues Foersom's work on a Danish Shakespeare, completing Foersom's *2H6* and producing translations of *3H6*, *R3*, *Oth*, *Cor*, *KJ*, *H8*, *Cym* and *AYL*.
1818	First performance of *Ham* in Finland, in the city of Turku, in Swedish with the Swedish actor Fredrik Julius Widerberg (son of Andreas Widerberg, first to play Hamlet in Sweden in 1787) playing the title role and leading a company based in Gothenburg, where *Ham* is also performed; first translation of Shakespeare into *bokmål*, one of two standard varieties of Norwegian, an anonymous *Cor*; a Swedish grammar school teacher, Sven Lundblad, translates *KL* into Swedish; one of Lundblad's students is Carl August Hagberg, who will later be responsible for the first complete works translation project into Swedish.
1819	Oehlenschläger publishes Danish translation of seventy-two stanzas from *VA*; in Sweden, first extant translation of *Ham*, a prose translation by P. A. Granberg, cuts all mentions of Norway, framed as a nationalist exercise in overcoming French literary influence; *Ham* performed in Sweden in the industrial town of Norrköping.

1820	An early nationalist magazine in Finland publishes a travelogue by archdukes Johan and Ludwig of Austria visiting England, which includes a half-page description of visiting Shakespeare's house in Stratford-upon-Avon; the library catalogue of F. A. Meyer in Turku (Finland) includes a copy of Johannes Falk's German translation of *Cor* (1811), as well as Nicholas Rowe's edition of Shakespeare's complete works in eight volumes, showing rise of reading public; in Sweden, *MV* translated into Swedish by Georg Scheutz, *Ham* translated into Swedish by Bishop Olof Bjurbäck, also includes a nationalist essay on the need to elevate Swedish literary culture.
1820	21 *Ham* performed in Gothenburg using Granberg's translation.
1824	In Finland, *Ham* performed in Turku in Swedish; the Swedish-Finn Axel Gabriel Sjöström submits a poem to the Swedish Academy called 'Juliets uppvaknande och död' [Juliet's Awakening and Death].
1825	*AC*, *R2*, *MW*, *AYL* and *TN* translated into Swedish by J. H. Thomander; *Ham* performed in Gothenburg starring Fredrik Julius Widerberg.
1826	*Ham* revived in Denmark, first Shakespeare performed after a nine-year gap; Icelandic poet Bjarni Thorarensen asks his friend Bjarni Thorsteinsson if he can borrow his copy of the complete works (the father of Steingrímur Thorsteinsson, who later becomes one of Iceland's prominent early Shakespeare translators); *Oth* translated into Swedish by Karl August Nicander; performances of *Ham* in Gothenburg by the Widerberg company.

1827	The first playhouse opens in Christiania, Norway; the first Swedish-language production of *Oth* in Stockholm is cancelled after eight performances; the periodical *Kometen* publishes anonymous Swedish translations (actually by Thomander) of some scenes from *Tim*.
1828	A poem on Shakespeare is published in Norway and Denmark; *RJ* performed at the Royal Theatre, Copenhagen, using an edited version of Foersom's translation; *MV* staged in Copenhagen, also at the Royal Theatre, using a new translation by A. E. Boye and K. L. Rahbek.
1829	The Norwegian poet Henrik Wergeland, inspired by Shakespeare, publishes a nationalist poem 'Ode to the Freedom of Norway'; *Ham* performed in Gothenburg, using Granberg's translation.
1830	*MW* performed, unsuccessfully, at the Royal Theatre, Copenhagen; in Turku, Finland, Swedish translation by Lars Arnell of the farewell scene from *RJ* is published in the local paper *Åbo Underrättelser*; first known performance of Shakespeare in Norway, actors from Copenhagen play the balcony scene from *RJ* and scenes from *Ham* in Christiania in Danish; *RJ* performed in Gothenburg in Ducis's eighteenth-century version, which has also been used for tours in 1826–1827 in the towns of Norrköping, Örebro, Malmö and Jönköping.
1833	H. C. Wosemose publishes his Danish translation of Shakespeare's *Udvalgte sørgespil* [Select Tragedies], comprising *Ham*, *JC* and *KL*; first Shakespearean comedy performed in Sweden, in Gothenburg, by a German touring company, *Liebe kann alles oder Die bezähnte Widerspänstige*, an eighteenth-century adaptation of *TS*.
1834	In Finland, first adaptation of a Shakespeare play, J. F. Lagervall's *Ruunulinna*, an adaptation of *Mac* with a strongly nationalist agenda, never performed; a Swedish translation by Carl N. Keckman written on the interleaves of a first edition of Lagervall's play, never published.

1835	The Swede Erik Gustaf Geijer publishes a revised version of his poem 'Shakespeare', originally written in 1814; *Ham* performed in Gothenburg and Norrköping.
1836	The Swedish publisher Norstedts issues *The Tempest, an Outline Sketch of the Play: With Introductory Remarks and an Analysis of the Characters*, in English, by George Steevens.
1839	*RJ* performed by troupe led by C. A. F. Berggren in Eskilstuna, Sweden.
1838	*Mac* performed at the Djurgårdsteatern, then just outside the city of Stockholm, using a Swedish version by Hinrik Jakob Sandström modelled on Schiller's German version.
1839	*Mac* performed in Gothenburg, by the same troupe as at the Djurgårdsteatern the year before; P. Westerstrand publishes *Sammansvärjningen emot Julius Caesar* [The Conspiracy Against Julius Caesar], a free translation 'suited for the Stage'; in Gävle, Sweden, foundation of the grammar school Atheneum, which has plays by Shakespeare on its English curriculum for the higher levels.
1840–1848	Carl August Hagberg lectures regularly on Shakespeare as part of his work as a professor at Lund University.
1842	In Stockholm, royal theatre monopoly abolished; founding of the private Mindre Teatern, which came to host several premieres of Shakespeare plays in the 1850s but was later sold to the Royal Theatre for more small-scale productions under the name of the Royal Dramatic Theatre.
1843–1845	In Denmark, Søren Kierkegaard publishes reflections on *KL*.
1843	In Finland, *Ham* at the Swedish Theatre in Helsinki, using Granberg's 1819 Swedish translation, provokes heated discussion about the quality of the translation; after years of silence, a brief article on Shakespeare's life in a Norwegian periodical, *Skilling Magazinet*.

1844	In Norway, the first complete Shakespeare production, *Mac* at the Christiania Theatre, using Foersom's Danish translation and Danish actors; *Ham* performed in Gothenburg.
1845–1850	New edition of Foersom's and Wulff's Danish translations, edited by Offe Høyer, who also contributes a translation of *MM*.
1845	Grímur Thomsen, an Icelander studying in Copenhagen, writes about Shakespeare in a doctoral dissertation on Byron, refers to German Shakespeare scholars but not English; first *Oth* in Norway, at the Christiania Theatre in a Danish translation by Peter Frederik Wulff; in Sweden, *RJ* at the Royal Theatre, Stockholm, in a translation by F. A. Dahlgren that leaves out passages thought to be obscene, played only four times.
1846	In Sweden, *Lady Macbeth*, an 'essay towards a revision of Macbeth', by future member of the Swedish Academy, Carl David Skogman, only 20 copies printed.
1847–1851	Hagberg publishes translations of 36 Shakespeare plays into Swedish, inspired in part by the German translator Ludwig Tieck. The standard Swedish translations throughout the rest of the nineteenth century and into the twentieth.
1847	In Denmark, Johanne Luise Heiberg's performance of Juliet (at age 35) is celebrated by Kierkegaard in *Crisis in the Life of an Actress*; *Viola*, the first of Sille Beyer's many adaptations of Shakespeare, in Copenhagen, possibly the first Shakespeare adaptation by a woman performed in the Nordic countries; premiere of *KL* in Stockholm at the Mindre Teatern, using an unpublished translation by Georg Scheutz; *Ham* performed in Gothenburg.
1849	Denmark becomes a constitutional monarchy; *AYL* at the Royal Theatre, Copenhagen, in Sille Beyer's adaptation *Livet i skoven* [Life in the Woods]; *Ham* performed in Gothenburg.

1850	*AW* at the Royal Theatre, Copenhagen, in Sille Beyer's adaption, *Kongens læge* [The King's Physician].
1851	At the Royal Theatre, Copenhagen, revival of *KL* in a successful production and *Ham* performed by Fredrik Høedt to widespread acclaim; the Lambs' *Tales from Shakespeare* published in Swedish translation.
1852	At the Royal Theatre, Copenhagen, Johan Ludvig Heiberg refuses to take on *R3*, since 'the gloomy atmosphere of the play is distinctly foreign to the temperament and character of the Danish people'; *RJ* at the Christiania Theatre, Norway, in Foersom and Boye's translation, Beyer's *Livet i skoven* (in Danish) at the Christiania Theatre.
1853	*LLL* at the Royal Theatre, Copenhagen, in Beyer's adaption; in Norway, Ivar Aasen publishes the first excerpts of Shakespeare in Landsmaal, a Norwegian dialect; in Sweden, *Ham* is performed in Stockholm using Hagberg's translation, with Edvard Swartz in the title role; *AW* is performed in a version entitled *Konungens läkare* [The King's Physician; presumably a Swedish translation of Beyer's Danish adaptation]. Directed by Edvard Stjernström, this is the first Shakespearean comedy performed in Swedish.
1854–1869	The Danish author and critic Carsten Hauch writes a series of essays on *Mac*, *KL*, *RJ* and *MND*.
1854	In Norway, Beyer's Danish adaptation of *AW*, *Kongens læge* [The King's Physician] and *Blind alarm*, an adaptation of *MA*, performed at the Christiania Theatre; in Sweden, *MV* at the Royal Theatre with Georg Dahlqvist as Shylock, using a measured and psychologically realistic acting style; *Konungens läkare* at the Mindre Teatern, Stockholm.

1855	First translations of two of Shakespeare's sonnets into Danish (*Son* 27 and 30); in Norway, Sille Beyer's adaptation of *AYL* performed in Bergen, directed by Henrik Ibsen, who also gives a public lecture on Shakespeare, *Mac* translated by Nils Hauge into Dano-Norwegian, first complete translation by a Norwegian writer.
1856	*TS* at the Casino theatre, Copenhagen, in a translation by Anton Smith and Erik Bøgh; in Sweden, English becomes a mandatory subject for most secondary grammar school students.
1857	The African-American actor Ira Aldridge visits Stockholm, performing Othello and Shylock at the Royal Theatre in English, with rest of cast speaking Swedish; premiere in Stockholm of Otto Nicolai's opera based on *MW*, with the libretto translated from German by CVA Strandberg.
1858	In Norway, *Hon maa tæmmes* [She Must Be Tamed], an adaptation of *TS*, at the Christiania Theatre; in Sweden, first production at the Royal Theatre of *Mac*, translation by Carl August Hagberg, performance criticized for using outdated classical conventions.
1859, 1864	In Finland, Fredrik Cygnaeus lectures on drama, including Shakespeare, at the Imperial Alexander University in Helsinki (now University of Helsinki).
1859	*MA* in Copenhagen at the Royal Theatre, in Sille Beyer's adaptation *Kjærlighet paa vildspor* [Love on the Wrong Track]; *RJ* at the Mindre Teatern, Stockholm.
1860	In Norway, Sille Beyer's adaptation of *TN* at the Christiania Theatre, focuses on Viola; in Sweden, *MND* staged at the Royal Theatre, a royal gala performance in connection with the coronation of King Karl XV, *TS* at the Mindre Teatern, Stockholm under the title *Så tuktas en argbigga*; *Ham* in Gothenburg, using Hagberg's translation.

1861	In Norway, *MV* at the Christiania Theatre, adapted from KL Rahbek's Danish translation.
1861–1873	In Denmark, Edvard Lembcke working on his complete works translation project into Danish, the standard Danish translation at the end of the nineteenth century.
1862	Swedish premiere of *1H4* and *2H4*, in a conflated five-act version at the Mindre Teatern, Stockholm, directed by Stjernström who also plays Falstaff, first performance of history play in Sweden.
1863	In Finland, Swedish-language *MV* at the Swedish Theatre; *R2* is performed for the first time in Sweden at the Royal Theatre, starring Edward Swartz in the title role.
1864	In Denmark, Lembcke's *Ham* published, largely based on Foersom's translation; tercentenary of Shakespeare's birth, celebrated in Sweden with theatre performances including a premiere of *TN* and, in Finland, with a gala celebration including recitations of excerpts translated into Finnish for the event, tercentenary commented upon in the press in Norway but barely mentioned in Denmark, which is at war with Germany; Steingrímur Thorsteinsson translates *KL* into Icelandic, not published until 1878.
1865	In Finland, Aleksis Kivi writes *Karkurit* [The Fugitives] based on *RJ* (published 1867, performed in Swedish in 1872, in Finnish in 1877); in Norway, Bjørnstjerne Bjørnson's controversial production of *MND* at Christiana Theatre, using Oehlenschläger's Danish translation, with actors performing with Norwegian pronunciation.
1866	In Finland, Swedish-language *TS* and *Ham* at the Swedish Theatre; in Norway, *WT* at the Christiania Theatre in a version drawing on Shakespeare's play and Dinglestedt's *Ein Wintermärchen*; two Swedish premieres, both at the Royal Theatre: *Tim* and *Cor*.

1867	In Denmark, *MV* performed at the Royal Theatre, Copenhagen, in Lembcke's translation; in Finland, Swedish-language *RJ* and *KL* at the Swedish Theatre; in Norway, Bjørnson's conflation of *1H4* and *2H4* at the Christiania Theatre; *RJ* at the Royal Theatre, Stockholm; Georg Scheutz publishes an annotated English version of *Mac* 'for the use of schoolchildren'.
1868	In Denmark, *WT* is performed using an adaptation by HP Holst, based on a German acting version by Franz von Dingelstedt; in Finland, Swedish-language *Oth* at the Swedish Theatre.
1869	Caspara Preetzman ('Caralis') publishes Danish translations of five sonnets; in Finland, Aleksis Kivi writes *Canzio*, a tragedy influenced by Shakespeare, not performed until 1901, *MA* at the Swedish Theatre in Helsinki and in Gothenburg, Sweden; in Iceland, Matthías Jochumsson finishes his first translation of *Mac* into Icelandic, not published until 1874 and starts working on *RJ* and *Oth*, using the English and Hagberg's Swedish translations as source texts.
1870	In Denmark, literary historian Georg Brandes publishes *Kritiker og portraiter*, which includes essays on several plays by Shakespeare and is read by, among others, the aspiring playwright August Strindberg; in Norway, *Ham* at the Christiania Theatre, using the Danish translation by Foersom and Lembcke; first Swedish performance of *MW*, at the Mindre Teatern in Gothenburg, directed by Ludvig Josephson, who in all directs seven of the nineteen Swedish Shakespeare premieres from the 1850s to the 1880s; Swedish author Anne Charlotte Leffler sees Edvard Swartz perform Hamlet; Swedish actress Charlotte Raa-Winterhjelm on tour in Sweden and Finland, playing Lady Macbeth (in Swedish).

1871	First Danish production of *Cym*, at the Royal Theatre, performed 43 times until 1888; in Finland, Swedish-language *MND* at the Swedish Theatre in Helsinki; first Swedish performance of *WT*, at the Royal Theatre, Stockholm; first performance in Stockholm of *MW*, at the Södra Teatern; first complete Swedish translation of *Son*, by the academic and poet, Carl Rupert Nyblom.
1872	In Finland, Kaarlo and Emilie Bergbom found the Finnish Theatre, which will later be instrumental in bringing Finnish-language Shakespeare to Finland; Swedish-language *Mac* at the Swedish Theatre in Helsinki; *R3*, in a revised Swedish version by Frans Hedberg, performed for the first time at the Royal Theatre, Stockholm; *RJ* at the Royal Dramatic Theatre, Stockholm; August Strindberg borrows from *JC* for his play *Mäster Olof*.
1873	In Finland, Charlotte Raa-Winterhjelm performs first scenes of Shakespeare in Finnish, Ophelia's mad scene (trans. Antti Törneroos (Tuokko) and Lady Macbeth's sleepwalking scene (trans. Kaarlo Slöör-Santala), Swedish-language *WT* at the Swedish Theatre in Helsinki; in Norway, *MW* at the Christiania Theatre; in Sweden, Anne Charlotte Leffler publishes *The Actress*, which includes a scene where the title character rehearses a scene from *RJ*; first performance of *MA* in Stockholm at the Royal Dramatic Theatre.
1874	In Denmark, *RJ* at the Royal Theatre, using Lembcke's translation; in Iceland, Matthías Jochumsson's translation of *Mac* published, first in Icelandic; in Norway, *Cor* at the Christiania Theatre in a version by Hartvig Lassen.
1876	First Swedish translation of *Luc*, under the title *Lucretia*, by Adolf Lindgren.
1877	In Iceland, Steingrímur Thorsteinsson translates four lyrics from Shakespeare plays (*Cym*, *AYL* and *LLL*); *MA* revived at the Royal Dramatic Theatre, Stockholm.

1878	The Falstaff scenes from *1H4* and *2H4* are performed at Copenhagen's Casinotheatret under the title *Falstaffske scener;* the Finnish actress Ida Aalberg travels to Dresden to study with German actress Marie Seebach, beginning work on Juliet; in Iceland, Matthías Jochumsson's translation of *Ham* into Icelandic published; in Norway, Carl Borgaard's Danish translation of *MA* performed at the Christiania Theatre, *MV* performed at the New Theatre in Bergen.
1879	*MND* performed in Copenhagen in HP Holst's acting version; in Finland, first Finnish-language translation of a complete play published, Paavo Cajander's *Ham*; the Italian actress Adelaide Ristori and her company play *Mac* at the Royal Theatre, Stockholm.
1879–1887	The Finnish philosopher and theatre director Wilhelm Bolin publishes a revised version of thirty-three of Hagberg's translations with the latter's publisher Gleerups.
1880	Norwegian church publication declares Shakespeare 'safe reading for Lutheran Christians', *WT* performed at the New Theatre, Bergen; *Mac* at the Nya Teatern (later Svenska Teatern), Stockholm.
1881	In Finland, first Finnish-language production of a Shakespeare play, *RJ* at the Finnish Theatre in Helsinki, starring Ida Aalberg as Juliet, performance hailed as a 'cultural victory' for Finnish culture; in Norway, *Oth* at the New Theatre, Bergen, Hartvig Lassen translates *MV* into modern Norwegian for use in schools, indebted to Hagberg's Swedish, Schlegel's German and possibly also Lembcke's Danish version, Lassen cuts passages deemed inappropriate for students; in Sweden, first performances of *AC* and *JC*, at the Royal Theatre, Stockholm and *Ham* starring Edward Swartz.

1882	In Finland, *MV* at the Finnish Theatre in a translation by Paavo Cajander published the same year, review compares Finnish translation to Hagberg's Swedish, Swedish-language *Cym* at the Swedish Theatre in Helsinki; in Iceland, the first Icelandic *Oth* is published by Matthías Jochumsson, attacked for inaccuracy, causing translator to issue an apology and defend his translation, saying it is indebted to Nicolaus Delius, Hagberg and Edvard Lembcke; in Norway, Lassen translates *JC* into modern Norwegian for use in schools; *RJ* at the Royal Theatre, Stockholm.
1883	In Finland, *TS* performed in Vyborg by the Finnish Theatre company; in Norway, Lassen translates *Mac* for schools, also cut for reasons of propriety, e.g. parts of the porter scene; in Sweden, premiere of Anne Charlotte Leffler's *En räddande engel* [A Saving Angel], contains allusions to Juliet. Swedish literary historian Henrik Schück publishes *William Shakspere: Hans lif och värksamhet* [William Shakespeare: His Life and Work].
1884	In Finland, first Finnish-language performance of *Ham*, in a translation by Paavo Cajander by the Finnish Theatre company, *TN* at the Swedish Theatre in Helsinki; in Stockholm, two premieres: *AYL* at the Svenska Teatern and *MM* at the Royal Dramatic Theatre, the latter not well received; *H4* at the Royal Dramatic Theatre, Stockholm, starring the Norwegian actor Johannes Brun as Falstaff; *Ham* at the Royal Theatre with the famous actor and director August Lindberg in the title role; Swedish writer Anne Charlotte Leffler travels to London, writes about her experiences, e.g. on seeing Ellen Terry play Beatrice (published in 1885).
1885–1886	*Oth* at the Danish Folketheatret starring the Italian actor, Ernesto Rossi.

1885	First complete Danish translation of *Son*, by Adolph Hansen and appearance of an annotated English school edition of *Mac*, ed. Mr A Stewart MacGregor and Mrs S Kinney, for use in Danish schools; Eiríkur Magnússon's Icelandic translation of *Tem* published to mixed reviews, with some asking who wants to read Shakespeare anyway.
1886	The Finnish actress Ida Aalberg invited to perform Ophelia in Finnish in Stockholm and Copenhagen; first Finnish-language performance of *KL* in Finland, translated by Paavo Cajander; in Norway, *Ham* at the New Theatre, Bergen; *Mac* played by Ernesto Rossi at the Royal Theatre opposite Elise Hwasser alternating with Olga Björkegren.
1887–1888	Valdemar Østerberg publishes new Danish translations of *Ham*, *RJ* and *KL*.
1887	In Finland, first Finnish-language performance of *Mac* at the Finnish Theatre, translated by Paavo Cajander, also performances of *Ham* and *MV*; *RJ* published for the first time in Icelandic, translated by Matthías Jochumsson; in Norway, *JC* at the Christiania Theatre.
1888	Norwegian periodical publishes a character study of Ophelia by Just Bing, calling her the 'finest woman' in Shakespeare; the famous German Meiningen Ensemble plays Shakespeare at the Svenska Teatern, Stockholm (previously named Nya teatern).
1889	In Finland, first Finnish-language *JC* and *Oth*, with Ida Aalberg as Desdemona, Aalberg goes to Berlin to train as an actor; in Norway, Knut Hamsun criticizes Shakespeare as outdated, anti-Shakespeare statements continue in the early 1890s.
1890	*Oth* at Copenhagen's Dagmartheatret; Finnish actress Ida Aalberg plays Juliet (in German) at the Ostend theatre in Berlin, with Josef Kainz as Romeo; *Viola*, Sille Beyer's Danish adaptation of *TN*, performed in Norway at the Christiania Theatre; *TS* and *Ham* at the Finnish Theatre.

1891	*TN* performed in Danish using Lembcke's translation, at the Casino theatre; in Finland, first Finnish-language *MND*, with lavish costumes and set decorations, music by Mendelssohn, *MW* at the Swedish Theatre in Helsinki.
1892	In Norway, *TN* at the New Theatre, Bergen, using Lembcke's Danish translation; *MV* at the Finnish Theatre.
1893	*WT* at the Royal Theatre, Copenhagen, this time using Lembcke's Danish translation.
1894	*Mac* at the Royal Theatre, Copenhagen, in Lembcke's translation; Swedish actress Charlotte Raa-Winterhjelm invited to Finnish Theatre to play Lady Macbeth in Finnish, but two decades after early triumphant performances in Finnish, audience react negatively to her accented Finnish, also *TS* at the FT; the Finnish actress Ida Aalberg performs in Stockholm, Gothenburg, Christiania, Copenhagen; Norwegian periodicals publish on the authorship question, outlining Baconian theories.
1895	Theodor Caspari, a Norwegian poet, publishes an essay comparing Ibsen and Shakespeare, to the detriment of Ibsen; guest appearance of *Ham* in Bergen by Swedish troupe led by August Lindberg, who has previously toured with the production in Finland.
1896	In Denmark, Georg Brandes publishes his biography of Shakespeare, read all over the world. The book attacked by Theodor Bierfreund, who publishes his own Shakespeare bio two years later; in Finland, first Finnish-language *AC*, with Ida Aalberg as Cleopatra and *WT*; Finnish translator Cajander celebrated for his contributions to Finnish literature.
1897	In Finland, first Finnish-language *R3*, also *TS* and *KL* at the FT, translations by Cajander; in Norway, *RJ* at the New Theatre, Bergen; *Ham* at the Royal Dramatic Theatre, Stockholm.

1898	The Danish writer Theodor Bierfreund (1855–1906) publishes a book on Shakespeare, in part as a response to Brandes; in Finland, Nikolay Bobrikov is appointed Governor-General, leading to further censorship and restrictions on the Finnish language, *MV* revived by the Finnish Theatre for the third time; *CE* at the Royal Dramatic Theatre, Stockholm.
1899	*MW* performed at the Casinotheatret, Copenhagen, *MND* at the Royal Theatre, Copenhagen, this time using Lembcke's translation; in Finland, *WT* at the Finnish Theatre; in Norway, *TN* at the Nationaltheatret, Christiania.

INDEX

Aalberg, Ida 20
Aasen, Ivar 11
Åbergsson, Gustaf Fredrik 249
Agricola, Mikael 212
Ahlqvist, August 12–13, 119, 236, 241 n.57
Aldridge, Ira 4, 15, 22, 25, 189–209
Almlöf, Nils Wilhelm 249
Andersen, Hans Christian 57 n.19, 183 n.23
Anderson, Mary 259
Andersson, Oskar 19
Anna of Denmark 36
Arfwidsson, Nils 205 n.13

Barfod, Hans Peter 175–6
Baudelaire, Charles 284–5 n.9
Bergbom, Kaarlo 20, 215
Bergman, Ingmar 78
Bernadotte, Jean–Baptiste, *see* Karl XIV Johan
Bernhardt, Sarah 259–61
Beyer, Sille 10, 17, 205 n.12
Birch-Pfeiffer, Charlotte 21
Bjørnson, Bjørnsterne 2, 17–18, 273
Bjurbäck, Olof 24, 90–5, 97–8, 100–10, 112 n.26, 112 n.34, 113 n.36
Bøgh, Nicolai 38
Bonuvier, Karl Gustav 118
Boswell, James 12

Boye, Johannes 10, 34, 56 n.6, 57 n.21, 291
Brandes, Georg 232
Brooke, Arthur 218
Bruun, Thomas 47

Cajander, Paavo 238
Carl, duke of Sweden 70
Caroline Mathilde 6, 26 n.7
Cervantes, Miguel 214
Christian II 47
Christian VII 6, 26 n.7, 32, 46
Christiania 17, 22, 272
Copenhagen 16, 24, 31, 34, 36, 38, 39, 42, 55 n.2, 56 n.4, 57 n.21, n.22, n.23, 160, 291
Cramer, Peter 47
Creutz, Gustaf Philip 111 n.7
Cygnaeus, Fredrik 9, 13, 21, 238

Dahlgren, Carl Fredrik 91–2, 113 n.44
Dahlgren, F. A. 78
Dahlqvist, Georg 192, 205 n.15, 249
Dante Alighieri 119
Diderot, Denis 39, 58 n.23
Dingelstedt, Franz von 19
Ducis, Jean-François 11, 14, 66
Dumas Senior, Alexandre 21
Dyveke (mistress of Christian II) 47

INDEX

Ebbesen, Niels 45, 47
Edelfelt, Albert 118
Elsinore (Helsingør) 31, 36, 57 n.18, 291
England 1, 11, 18, 20, 34, 37, 41, 44, 67, 76, 79, 85 n.48, 101, 232, 258, 266 n.9, 274
Eschenburg, Johann Joachim 42, 72, 148 n.3
Ewald, Johannes 38–9

Foersom, Peter 10–12, 16–17, 24, 32–6, 38–45, 47–53, 55, 57 n.19, 57 n.21, 57 n.22, 58 n.24, 59 n.46, 181 n.10
Formes, Augusta 20
France 7, 20, 37, 41, 42, 44, 66, 251, 255, 258, 286 n.32
Franzén, Frans Michael 20, 68, 85 n.48, 149 n.20
Frederik VI 36, 54
Frederik VII 7
Freytag, Gustav 213, 215, 222
Friebach, Carl Heinrich 33–4, 56 n.4

Galeotti, Vincenzo 46
Ganander, Christfried 124–5
Garborg, Arne 286 n.31
Garrick, David 26 n.7, 32, 34, 59 n.46, 95, 110, 114 n.53
Geijer, Erik Gustaf 11, 24, 63–88, 91, 110 n.5, 118, 145, 148 n.3, 205 n.13
George III 6

Gerhard III 47
Germany 18–19, 20, 34, 37, 41–2, 66, 75, 142, 231–2, 258, 278, 286 n.32
Gleerups (publisher) 9
Godwin, Edward William 266 n.9
Goethe, Johann Wolfgang von 42, 84 n.37, 119, 142–3, 160, 184 n.36, 231–2, 286 n.32
Gossman, Friedrike 20
Gothenburg 6, 11, 14, 78, 80 n.1, 81 n.8, 212
Grabbe, Christian Dietrich 231
Granberg, Per Adolf 24, 81 n.5, 81 n.11, 82 n.15, 83 n.28, 91–2, 95–6, 98–101, 104–5, 106–10, 112 n.26
Gröneqvist, Oskar 211
Gundolf, Friedrich 233
Gustav III 7, 66, 70, 80 n.2, 83 n.26, 251
Gustav IV Adolf 70

Hagberg, Carl August 8–12, 15, 19, 24, 64, 77–8, 80, 83 n.23, 85 n.53, 106–10, 112 n.26, 113 n.44, 113 n.48, 114 n.51, 190–1, 204 n.6, 205 n.13, 213, 221, 232–5, 249, 265 n.4
Hamburg 33, 41–3, 58 n.23, 58 n.33, 202
Hammarsköld, Lorenzo 71, 81 n.5, 83 n.28
Hamsun, Knut 2, 9, 25, 269–89, 293

Hauge, Nils 11
Heiberg, Johan Ludvig 53
Heiberg, Johanne Luise 16–17, 182 n.10, 192, 255–6, 261
Helsinki 19–20, 119, 211–12, 221, 238
Helvig, Amalia von 65, 76
Herder, Johann Gottfried 143
Høedt, Frederik 16, 192
Holst (actor) 50
Holstein 47
Hugo, Victor 13, 21, 241 n.60
Hwasser, Daniel 255
Hwasser, Elise 247, 255, 265 n.8
Hyltén-Cavallius, Gunnar Olof 189

Ibsen, Henrik 19–20, 22, 58 n.36, 248–9, 254–9, 261–2, 264, 269, 273, 282–3, 285 n.20, 286 n.32
Irving, Henry 258, 260, 262

James I 36, 101
James VI of Scotland, *see* James I
Johnson, Samuel 11, 42
Jonson, Ben 79
Juteini, Jaakko 141
Jutland (Jylland) 47, 57 n.18, 167, 172, 177, 183 n.23

Kalmar 7
Karl XIV Johan 7, 70
Karlskrona 14
Keckman, Carl Niclas 150 n.32
Kemble, John Philip 20, 68, 76
Kendal, W. H. 259–60

Kendal, Madge 259–60
Kiel 36
Kielland, Alexander 273
Kierkegaard, Søren 2, 9, 16, 24, 157–87, 293
Kivi, Alexis 2, 9, 19, 21, 23, 25, 211–45, 293
Kuhlau, Friedrich 53

Lagervall, Jacob Fredrik 12, 24, 117–55, 212
La Place, Pierre-Antoine de 66, 81 n.10
Larsen, Bolette 285 n.20
Larsen, Ole Johan 285 n.20
Lassen, Hartvig 11
Leffler, Amanda 249, 251, 264, 265 n.3
Leffler, Anne Charlotte 2, 9, 25, 247–67
Lembcke, Edvard 10–11, 38, 51, 53
Le Tourneur, Pierre 66, 81 n.10
Lessing, Gotthold Ephraim 9, 39, 56 n.7
Lie, Jonas 273
Lind, Jenny 264
Lindberg, August 20, 260
London 19, 26 n.7, 32, 34, 36, 68, 76, 122, 202, 232, 248–9, 258–60, 262–4
Lönnrot, Elias 124, 135, 141, 143, 146, 150 n.32

Macready, William 45, 181 n.9
Malone, Edmond 10–11, 40
Margrethe II 33, 55 n.2
Marie Antoinette 92
Marlowe, Christopher 127
Mendelssohn, Felix 13, 17

INDEX

Millais, John Everett 90
Moberg, Peter 65, 67–8
Molbech, Christian 53
Molière (Jean-Baptiste Poquelin) 14, 274
Mozart, Wolfgang Amadeus 160
Müller, Wilhelm 84 n.37

Napoleon I 4, 6, 7, 32, 36, 47, 55 n.3, 70
Niemann-Seebach, Marie 20
Nielsen, Anna 17
Nielsen, N. P. 195
Nilsson, Kristina 262, 264
Norrköping 14, 65
Novalis 42, 158
Nyblom, Carl Rupert 26 n.10
Nyrop (actor) 50

Odense 33–4, 56 n.4
Oehlenschläger, Adam 16–17, 38, 45
Ortlepp, Ernst 178, 181 n.10
Oulu 14, 118

Paris 20, 32, 37, 46, 58 n.33, 65–6, 122, 253
Poland 37, 43
Potsdam 17

Raa, Frithiof 20
Raa-Winterhjelm, Hedvig Charlotte 19–23, 25, 292
Rachel (Rachel Félix) 255–6
Racine, Jean 14
Rahbek, Kamma 53, 57 n.19
Rahbek, Knud Lyne 40–1, 53, 57 n.19, 57–8 n.23
Randers, Kristofer 286 n.33

Reed, Isaac 11
Ristori, Adelaide 21, 260
Rosenfeldt, Nils 10
Rosenkrantz, Niels 36
Ruda, Elias Wilhelm 106
Rudbeck Senior, Olof 146, 152 n.67
Russia, Russian Empire 7–8, 55 n.3, 122, 124–5, 278

Sallinen, Erkki 124
Salvini, Tommaso 259
Samsøe, Ole Johann 47
Sander, Christian Levin 47
Sargent, John Singer 261
Saxo Grammaticus 31, 38, 57 n.18
Schiller, Friedrich 9, 11–13, 21, 24, 64, 69, 71–2, 75, 77, 83 n.25, 83 n.30, 84 n.37, 85 n.44, 118, 139
Schlegel, August Wilhelm 11–12, 41–3, 64, 66, 75, 159, 181 n.10, 213, 220, 227–8, 231–3
Schlegel, Friedrich 158, 182 n.14, 227–8
Schlegel, Regine 171, 178
Schmidts, Ferdinand 18
Schröder, Friedrich 33, 41–2, 49, 56 n.4, 58 n.33
Schubert, Franz 84 n.37
Schwarz, Frederik 32, 34, 44–6, 48–9, 57 n.22
Scott, Sir Walter 146, 283
Scribe, Eugène 10, 54, 160
Seeman (actor) 50
Seuerling, Carl Gottfried 14, 118
Shakespeare, William

INDEX

All's Well That Ends Well
  17, 205 n.12, n.13
As You Like It 17, 213, 219
Hamlet 4, 10–12, 14–17, 20,
  23–4, 27 n.34, 31–61, 65,
  67–8, 80 n.1, 81 n.11, 82
  n.15, 83 n.28, 89–115,
  118, 171–2, 175, 180,
  181 n.7, 185 n.44, 192,
  205 n.12, n.15, 220,
  240 n.30, 248–50, 260,
  263–4, 272, 279–81, 291
Henry IV 75–6, 205 n.12
Julius Caesar 9–10, 13, 67
King Lear 9, 10, 15–16, 24,
  82 n.11, 157–87, 213,
  220, 223, 226–8, 292–3
Macbeth 10–13, 17, 21–4,
  27 n.26, 63–88, 117–56,
  193, 205 n.12, n.13,
  212–13, 223, 236, 255,
  261, 265 n.8, 291
Merchant of Venice 10–11,
  17, 190, 193, 197, 204
  n.8, 205 n.12, n.13, 211,
  239 n.2
Midsummer Night's Dream
  13, 17, 38, 182 n.10
Much Ado About Nothing
  17, 217, 258, 261, 264
Othello 4, 10, 17, 25, 189–93,
  195–7, 200–1, 203 n.2,
  204 n.6, 205 n.15, 206
  n.26, 213, 221, 239 n.25,
  258–9, 272, 274
Richard II 15, 205 n.12
Richard III 26 n.7, 66, 81
  n.11, 174
Romeo and Juliet 10–11, 14,
  17, 20, 25, 65, 118, 183
  n.22, 205 n.12, 213–16,
  218–26, 229–35, 237–8,
  239 n.25, 247–8, 253,
  256–7, 259
Sonnets 26 n.10
Taming of the Shrew 17,
  205 n.12
Timon of Athens 205 n.12
Twelfth Night 16–17, 213,
  217, 227, 230
Two Gentlemen of Verona
  82 n.11
Winter's Tale 17
Shaw, George Bernard 270,
  282–3, 287 n.35, 293
Sibelius, Jean 118
Siddons, Sarah 68
Silfverstolpe, Malla 76–7
Sjöstrand, Carl Eneas 13
Skjöldebrand, A.F. 46
Slöör, Kaarlo A (Santala) 12, 236
Snellman, J. V. 119, 148 n.5, 214
Stagnelius, Erik Johan 113 n.36
Steevens, George 10–12, 33,
  40, 42
Stjernström, Edvard 20, 193
Stockholm 4, 12, 14, 17, 20,
  22, 25, 64–6, 92, 189–91,
  200, 203, 204 n.2, n.6,
  208 n.40, 212, 247–9
Strindberg, August 8, 192
Sturzen-Becker, O. P. (Orvar
  Odd) 65
Swartz, Edvard 192, 205 n.15,
  248–50, 252–3, 263, 265
  n.1, 265 n.3

Talma, François-Joseph 58 n.33
Tate, Nahum 181 n.9
Tegnér, Esaias 67, 69–70, 83 n.28

Terry, Ellen 258, 260–2, 264, 266 n.9
Thirlwall, Connop 228–9
Thomander, Johan Henrik 64, 78
Tieck, Ludwig 12, 17, 64, 66, 75–6, 159, 181–2 n.10, 213, 231–5
Tolstoy, Leo 270, 279–81, 285 n.16, 293
Topelius, Zacharias 255
Torsslow, Adolf Ulrik 20, 249
Turku 14, 118

United States 200–1, 259, 271, 275, 284 n.3, 292, 294–5

Vienna 20, 181 n.9
Vogler, Georg Joseph 46

Voltaire (Jean-François-Marie Arouet) 14, 111 n.7

Warburton, William 12, 84 n.38
Wecksell, Josef Julius 235
Weissen, Christian Felix 14
Wessel, Johan Herman 39
Wieland, Christoph Martin 42, 72, 148 n.3
Wilde, Oscar 294
Winterhjelm, Kristian 20
Wittenberg 32, 37, 44
Wosemose, Hans Christian 51, 59 n.46
Wulff, Peter Frederik 181 n.10

Zealand (Sjælland) 57 n.18
Zibet, Christoffer Bogislaus 65–6, 68, 80 n.2

www.ingramcontent.com/pod-product-compliance
Lightning Source LLC
Chambersburg PA
CBHW052145300426
44115CB00011B/1523